Schubert's Instrumental Music
and
Poetics of Interpretation

MUSICAL MEANING AND INTERPRETATION
Robert S. Hatten, editor

Schubert's Instrumental Music *and* Poetics *of* Interpretation

René Rusch

INDIANA UNIVERSITY PRESS

This book is a publication of

Indiana University Press
Office of Scholarly Publishing
Herman B Wells Library 350
1320 East 10th Street
Bloomington, Indiana 47405 USA

iupress.org

© 2023 by René Rusch

All rights reserved
No part of this book may be reproduced or utilized in any form or by any means, electronic or mechanical, including photocopying and recording, or by any information storage and retrieval system, without permission in writing from the publisher. The paper used in this publication meets the minimum requirements of the American National Standard for Information Sciences—Permanence of Paper for Printed Library Materials, ANSI Z39.48-1992.

Manufactured in the United States of America

First printing 2023

Library of Congress Cataloging-in-Publication Data

Names: Rusch, René, author.
Title: Schubert's instrumental music and poetics of interpretation / René Rusch.
Other titles: Musical meaning and interpretation.
Description: Bloomington, Indiana : Indiana University Press, 2023. |
Series: Musical meaning and interpretation | Includes bibliographical references and index.
Identifiers: LCCN 2023021592 (print) | LCCN 2023021593 (ebook) | ISBN 9780253067388 (hardback) | ISBN 9780253067395 (paperback) | ISBN 9780253067401 (ebook)
Subjects: LCSH: Schubert, Franz, 1797-1828. Instrumental music. | Schubert, Franz, 1797-1828—Criticism and interpretation. | Beethoven, Ludwig van, 1770-1827—Influence. | Instrumental music—19th century—History and criticism. | BISAC: MUSIC / Instruction & Study / Theory | MUSIC / Genres & Styles / Classical
Classification: LCC ML410.S3 R87 2023 (print) | LCC ML410.S3 (ebook) | DDC 780.92—dc23/eng/20230626
LC record available at https://lccn.loc.gov/2023021592
LC ebook record available at https://lccn.loc.gov/2023021593

Contents

Preface vii

1. Schubert's Musical Reception and Contemporary Schubert Criticism   1
2. Rethinking Conceptions of Unity   25
3. The Value of Diatonic Indeterminacy When Traveling through Tonal Space   53
4. Sonata Forms, Fantasias, and Formal Coherence   91
5. Biography, Music Analysis, and the Narrative Impulse   126
6. Beyond Homage and Critique: Rethinking Musical Influence   159

   Closing Remarks   193

Works Cited   197

Index   215

Preface

Recent scholarship on Schubert's instrumental music not only affirms that after two hundred years, these pieces continue to linger in the consciousness of musical thought; writings on his symphonies and chamber and piano works within the last forty-five years also underscore the extent to which our approaches to understanding his music have evolved. Harmonic progressions that were once perceived as arbitrary or strange can now be rationalized through modified approaches to harmony and voice leading or musical hermeneutic readings. In addition, the composer's sonata forms, which were previously singled out for their excessive lyricism and redundancies, can become more coherent through a new *Formenlehre*. Finally, the same Schubert works that had been previously interpreted as compositional models or homages to Beethoven may now be read as musical critiques, a modification that calls into question how and why our conceptions of the monumental and emplotments of the historical field have changed. For a composer whose "strivings after the highest in art" have been met with reluctance and, at times, disregard both during and after his lifetime, winter appears to have finally ended.[1]

How might we understand this recent shift in the reception history of Schubert's instrumental music? What has motivated us to reinterpret a body of work that has amassed such a mixed reception history, and how might these catalysts influence the ways in which we currently interpret and aesthetically engage with this repertoire? One of the goals of this book is to explore the poetics of contemporary music-theoretical and analytical approaches—to bring to the fore some of the conditions that inform our perspectives of Schubert's music, particularly those that have helped promote a change to the reception of his instrumental works within approximately the last forty-five years. That scholarship's view of this repertoire has radically shifted over the course of the last several decades makes this moment in Schubert's reception history especially ripe for studying the circumstances that have prompted new and revised approaches to interpreting his music (i.e., what compels us to make sense of his music in the ways that currently we do) and the extent to which more recent conclusions about this repertoire may be reflective of certain aesthetic and disciplinary values.

In delving into these questions about Schubert's musical reception, the book explores this shift with regard to four topics that have become central to contemporary discourse on his instrumental works: (1) Schubert's approach to tonality; (2) his approach to sonata form; (3) the relationship between his music and biography; and (4) the relationship between his and Beethoven's instrumental works. Rather than observe a distinction between musical and extramusical topics, I maintain throughout the book that conceptions of Schubert's life and image, along with aesthetic values and narrative constructions of history, often guide conclusions about his instrumental music and cannot be easily disentangled from music-theoretical and analytical observations. Thus, while the subject matter and organization of chapters 2–6 may initially suggest a gradual "rippling" from text to context as we move from matters involving harmony and form (chapters 2–4) to those involving Schubert's biography (chapter 5) and musical influence (chapter 6), each chapter consciously blurs the distinction between this supposed binary by demonstrating their interdependency in an interpretive act.

The point of view that I introduce in chapter 1 and maintain throughout the book is that contemporary Schubert scholarship has sought to rethink prior conceptions of the composer's harmonic and formal practices by demonstrating through new and revised approaches, how musical phenomena that were at one time deemed arbitrary, strange, and irrational can be reconceived as coherent and unified through contextual assimilation. Put succinctly, I propose that the musical aesthetics associated with Schubert's instrumental works throughout the majority of the nineteenth and twentieth centuries become the site of inspection through which contemporary interpretive approaches develop. It is no longer a question of whether Schubert's music is coherent but rather how his music expresses coherence and unity. Chapter 1 attempts to historicize contemporary approaches to theorizing and analyzing Schubert's instrumental works by exploring the circumstances that enabled them to emerge, while chapters 2–6 each explore alternative ways to engage with his music, particularly with respect to the four aforementioned topics. As an alternative to interpreting Schubert's instrumental music as the expression of the always-already given, where strange musical events and contradictions are resolved or absorbed into a larger whole, the book instead introduces an alternative poetics, one that seeks to sustain the tensions among musical moments that our epistemologies may deem unfamiliar or strange. Thus, in addition to exploring the conditions that have motivated this shift in the reception of Schubert's instrumental music and the aesthetic values that appear to underlie this shift, the book also aims to show how an alternative poetics can illuminate our hearing and interpretation of selected works and how our interpretive approaches may reveal just as much insight about Schubert's instrumental music as our sociocultural and aesthetic values.

Most instructive to thinking about the issues that surround interpretive practice are writings on early German Romantic philosophy, poststructuralism (which contains some traces of early German Romantic thought), and historiography. Of central concern among these respective fields is how we re-present reality—how we establish a sense of order among disparate parts. Questions revolving around part-whole relationships not only involve intra- and intertextual relationships but also (1) the very ontology of the pair—what constitutes a part and a whole and, relatedly, a text and a context—and (2) the aesthetic values that may lead us to gravitate toward some forms of coherence more than others. Such points of inquiry are highly relevant to our interpretation of Schubert's music, given both the change in the reception history of his instrumental works and the proliferation of new music theories and analyses since the establishment of the Society for Music Theory in 1977–78. That the status of Schubert's instrumental works has migrated from a marginal position in the classical canon to a more central one, and that the same musical events can be reconceived as coherent under new or revised contexts, can prompt us to ask why we re-present Schubert's approach to composition, his biography, and his contributions within music history accordingly as well as encourage us to explore the aesthetic values that may inform these re-presentations. In bringing these points of inquiry as they relate to contemporary Schubert scholarship into dialogue with writers who have posed similar questions in the fields of philosophy, literary theory, and historiography, it is my hope that this book will offer readers a unique and innovative foray into some of the poetics of our contemporary interpretive practices.

Given the rich and diverse scholarship on Schubert's instrumental music, it seems conceivable that just as there may be multiple readings of a single composition, so, too, may there be multiple ways in which we can approach questions about interpretive practice, some of which will likely overlap. Where readers may find the greatest correspondence between this book's premise and prior scholarship is Suzannah Clark's *Analyzing Schubert* (2011).[2] Clark's monograph has been a tour de force in our music research community for its timely, critical perspective of the complex relationships between Schubert reception history, theory, analysis, and musical meaning—a perspective that I understand to be similarly curious about the poetics that underlie theoretical and analytical readings in music theory discourse (to "use Schubert to analyze music theory" [54]) and about whether there may be other ways to understand Schubert's approach to harmony and form (to "work towards a distinctly Schubertian paradigm, one that analyzes Schubert through Schubertian rather than Beethovenian or Classical or other lenses" [270]). While the point of intersection between our respective projects can be located in our individual efforts to promote a deeper understanding of the poetics of interpretation, our areas of focus and approach differ. Whereas Clark's monograph insightfully shows how our music theories (Schenkerian theory, especially) facilitate certain kinds of conclusions about Schubert's music, this monograph takes as its locus of study the topic of aesthetics—the musical aesthetics that have been tethered to Schubert's instrumental works and the aesthetic values that have informed our judgments about this repertoire. In addition, while *Analyzing Schubert* approaches its questions about interpretive practice by keenly situating our music theories within the arena of the history of music theory, this book primarily draws from the fields of philosophy, literary theory, and historiography in an effort to understand how we re-present Schubert's music in our contemporary discourses. Finally, whereas *Analyzing Schubert* necessarily discusses Schubert's songs and instrumental works in its critique of music theories, the current project intentionally focuses on the latter corpus for two reasons: the marked shift in the reception history of these pieces, and a desire to investigate the poetics of interpreting music without a text. Although the reception history of Schubert's lieder may raise similar questions about interpretive practice, the presence of a poetic text can greatly affect the ways in which we might approach and respond to these questions. Notwithstanding this book's departures from Clark's *Analyzing Schubert* in terms of its focus, procedure, and repertoire, I do not seek to challenge its conclusions but rather approach the question of interpretive practice from an angle that coincides with my secondary interests in our sister disciplines in the humanities. As such, I understand the book's goals, methodology, and impending conclusions as not only complementary but also indebted to Clark's sharp and discerning work.

As briefly mentioned, this book comprises six chapters, including a prefatory chapter that explores the catalysts that have facilitated this new stage of Schubert music criticism (chapter 1) and a concluding section ("Closing Remarks") that reflects on the alternative poetics put forth. In contemplating Schubert's instrumental music and the poetics of our contemporary interpretive practices, my general belief is that it is not possible, or desirable, to discuss the subject matter that occupies the book's central chapters from a single vantage point. In this regard, the incommensurability and multiplicity of approaches that the book employs resonate with the alternative poetics put into practice in each of the respective chapters on unity (chapter 2), tonality (chapter 3), form (chapter 4), biography (chapter 5), and musical influence (chapter 6). From a practical standpoint, the advantages to not applying a single, overarching theory throughout the book is that it opens up the possibility for readers to engage with its contents on a chapter-by-chapter basis, a format that may be especially convenient for upper-level undergraduate special topics courses and graduate seminars, where time is limited and where participants may discuss multiple readings by different authors on a particular research question or topic. Readers who alternatively engage with the book from cover to cover will find both complementary and irreconcilable points of view. It is my hope that if I have even moderately succeeded in this rather ambitious endeavor, readers will have gained a nuanced perspective of the ways in which our aesthetic values, constructions of text and context, and conceptions of a composer's music and life and of the historical field can inform not only our approaches to music theory and analysis but also our understanding of such rich repertoire.

Some of the ideas that I explore in this book began to surface as early as 2006. Undoubtedly, though, my educational experiences in toto have played a role in helping me bring this project to fruition. I am eternally grateful to all of the teachers who have devoted their time and energy to the field of education. I have become a lifelong learner because of you.

I would sincerely like to thank Robert Hatten for his generous support of this project both during and after his tenure as editor of the Musical Meaning and Interpretation series at Indiana University Press. I have been so inspired by his myriad contributions to our field, and to have my work included in a book series that has informed my understanding of musical meaning and interpretation is humbling. I would also like to offer my deepest thanks to the two anonymous readers who reviewed earlier drafts of this manuscript during the pandemic. Your comments and suggestions were immensely helpful, and they played an important role in shaping this book. I owe a debt of gratitude to Eileen Allen, Allison Blair Chaplin, Janice Frisch, Sophia Hebert, David Hulsey, Darja Malcolm-Clarke, and Megan Schindele, all of whom handled my work with such care throughout the book's various stages. Any remaining errors are my own. I am also grateful to the Social Sciences and Humanities Research Council (SSHRC) for funding this research in its early stages.

I am indebted to the amazing colleagues, former professors, and friends at McGill University (Stephen McAdams, Lisa Barg, Tom Beghin, Nicole Biamonte, David Brackett, William Caplin, Isabelle Cossette, Julie Cumming, Ichiro Fujinaga, Robert Hasagawa, Steven Huebner, Richard King, Edward Klorman, Roe-Min Kok, Sara Laimon, Jean Lesage, Lisa Lorenzino, Justin Mariner, Don McLean, Christoph Neidhöfer, Peter Schubert, the late Eleanor Stubley, Joel Wapnick, Lloyd Whitesell, and Jonathan Wild) and the University of Michigan (Christ-Anne Castro, Richard Crawford, Gabriela Cruz, the late James Dapogny, Walter Everett, Karen Fournier, Marion Guck, Patricia Hall, Áine Heneghan, Nadine

Preface xi

Hubbs, John Knoedler, Kevin Korsyn, Nathan Martin, Somangshu Mukherji, Judith Petty, Wayne Petty, Ellen Rowe, Ramon Satyendra, and Alexandra Vojčić); and the incredible librarians, staff, and students whom I have had the utmost privilege of working with. I have learned so much from everyone at these two universities, and to have had the opportunity to work with you on a day-to-day basis has been such a gift.

To Kyle Adams, Brian Alegant, Brian Black, Karen Bottge, Karl Braunschweig, Scott Burnham, L. Poundie Burstein, Evan Campbell, Frank Chiou, Suzannah Clark, Richard Cohn, Alan Gosman, Roger Grant, Jonathan Guez, Dora Hanninen, David Heetderks, Graham Hunt, Brian Hyer, Blair Johnston, Jon Kochavi, Joseph Kraus, David Loeb, Yonatan Malin, Elizabeth Hellmuth Margulis, Gregory Marion, Henry Martin, Caitlin Martinkus, Toru Momii, David Neumeyer, Mitchell Ohriner, Jeffrey Perry, Ian Quinn, Steven Reale, Alexander Rehding, Stephen Rodgers, Lynn Rogers, Frank Samarotto, Keith Salley, Carl Schachter, Janet Schmalfeldt, Hedi Siegel, Gordan Sly, Chris Stover, Timothy Sullivan, Keith Waters, and the many wonderful colleagues in the music theory and musicology communities—thank you so much for your camaraderie, your musicianship and research, your support of me and my work, and your making me feel welcome in academia.

Profound thanks are due to Elaine Bliss, Catherine Kautsky, and Thomas Sauer, all three of whom I was so fortunate to have studied piano with during my most formative years. Your musicianship and instruction have had an enormous impact on how I engage with music in my research and in the classroom. And to Kevin Korsyn and Wayne Petty, who have served as mentors throughout my entire career—thank you for believing in me, for your unfailing support, and for sharing your advice on all matters, from A to Z.

My journey throughout the various stages of life would not have been the same without Rachel, Nola, Stacie, Mandy, Lisa, Phil, Danny, Joyce, Jon, and Amanda. Thank you so much for your precious friendship and for the wonderful memories.

Finally, I would like to thank the Ziino and Rusch families; my late grandparents Anthony, Emanuella, Howard, and Martha; Uncle Brian and Auntie Annette; the late Uncle Wally and Auntie Marianne; Angela, Maria, and Mickey; my parents, John and Vincenette; Derek; Todd; Emanuella (*I love my kid!*); Oona; and God, for your unconditional love, grace, and support.

Notes

1. The quoted passage comes from Schubert's letter to Schott's Sons, dated February 21, 1828, wherein he states: "This is a list of my finished compositions, excepting

three operas, a Mass, and a symphony. These last compositions I mention only in order to make you acquainted with my strivings after the highest in art" (Deutsch 1947, 740). On Schubert's efforts to publish with B. Schott's Sons during his final year, see Gibbs 2000, 144–45. Christopher Gibbs also clarifies that "at first the comment seems curious: Schubert had written some eight operas, five masses, seven (and a half) symphonies and much else; yet he willingly acknowledged only fully mature pieces" (145). See also Gingerich 2014, 268–69.

2. See also Clark 2002.

Schubert's Instrumental Music
and
Poetics *of* Interpretation

1 Schubert's Musical Reception and Contemporary Schubert Criticism

A Recursive Reception History

Writings on the music of Franz Schubert from the nineteenth century to today offer us a unique and complex chronicle of how our understanding of a composer's works can change over time. Reassessments of Schubert's reception history can be attributed to at least two developments. One is the gradual discovery of nearly one thousand of his compositions after his death on November 19, 1828.[1] Before his Symphony in B Minor ("Unfinished") (D. 759), String Quartet in G Major (D. 887), and other such formative works surfaced, Schubert had been primarily recognized in Vienna as a composer of lieder and other domestic music genres;[2] most of his publications were songs, dances, and pianoforte pieces for four hands. Although his String Quartet in A Minor (D. 804), Piano Trio in E-flat Major (D. 929), and three piano sonatas in A minor (D. 845), D major (D. 850), and G major (D. 894), were published during the last four years of his life, full awareness of his efforts to write in the same esteemed instrumental genres cultivated by more renowned composers did not materialize in Vienna and abroad until the posthumous release of his remaining compositions.[3] This trove of newly discovered works, which included seven completed symphonies, twelve more string quartets, and eight additional piano sonatas, as well as a fair number of sketches and incomplete works, naturally called into question prior appraisals of the composer's musical legacy. Posed succinctly by Eduard Hanslick as late as 1862, when Schubert's entire output was still unknown to the world, "If Schubert's contemporaries justly gazed in astonishment at his creative power, what indeed must we, who come after him, say, as we incessantly discover new works of his?"[4]

In light of the discourse that has been published since the posthumous discoveries of Schubert's unknown works, it would be difficult to maintain that our approaches to understanding his music have remained the same, wholly undisturbed by the changes brought forth by a recurring modernity and its interminable revisions to subjectivity. Such differences among interpretive practices enable us to identify a second, more covert development that both complicates and enlivens the history of Schubert's musical reception—namely, that (re)evaluations of his music become intertwined with questions pertaining to the very concept of knowing, especially as they relate to a perceiving subject. The growing skepticism toward theological claims about truth near the end of the eighteenth century, in tandem with the gradual rethinking of hermeneutics—from a system of rules for interpreting select genres to a theory of understanding that was believed to be relevant to all forms of writing[5]—would ultimately draw attention to the nature of the perceiving subject and the extent to which this subject could, as Andrew Bowie (2003, 1) summarizes, "establish its own legitimacy as the ground of truth." That the ways in which we have approached Schubert's music have evolved alongside an increasing awareness of the complexities associated with understanding throughout the nineteenth century and thereafter might thus suggest that reassessments of his works and stature may be attributed not only to posthumous performances and publications but also to changes among our conceptions of what a musical work appears to signify or represent, how we can come to know (or the extent to which we can know) a work, how we define the context(s) for understanding Schubert's music, and whether our epistemologies are uncovered, constructed, or both. As this introductory chapter suggests, scholarship's varying positions toward these and other related matters have affected the ways in which it has not only made sense of Schubert's compositional aesthetic but also aesthetically engaged with his music—a point that can be especially observed when we compare earlier writings on Schubert's music to more contemporary ones. To summarize for now with regards to the history of Schubert's musical reception: if our understanding of his music appears to have changed over the last two hundred years, it may be not only due to the fact that a substantial number of his compositions had at one time been unknown to the world but also because the grounds for determining how the unfamiliar can become intelligible have been in flux. The view suggested here, then, is that the history of Schubert's musical reception conveys a recursive tension between a coming-to-know of his compositions and a coming-to-know of the problems associated with understanding them.

Schubert's Instrumental Music as a Case in Point

This recursive tension especially comes to the fore in writings about Schubert's instrumental works. Whereas Schubert's songs helped him gain visibility as a composer of domestic genres, his symphonies, string quartets, and piano sonatas more often than not hindered his recognition as a composer of high art throughout the latter half of the nineteenth century and well into the twentieth. Criticism of these works tended to primarily revolve around his harmonic and formal practices. As Suzannah Clark (2011a) summarizes of the reception history of Schubert's modulations in relation to perceptions of his approach to musical form: "The suspicion that Schubert's modulations are free and odd has haunted the reception of his music ever since. . . . The nineteenth-century attitude was that this freedom and oddity were signs of Schubert's mismanagement of musical form and lack of technical knowledge" (58). Anne Hyland (2016b) similarly remarks of critics' disdain for the supposed digressions, alarming modulations, extraneous repetitions, and untutored forms—purported compositional missteps that led critics to more generally characterize Schubert's instrumental works, especially those in sonata form, as diffuse and circuitous: "Schubert's instrumental music is too long, it was argued, because of its meandering tendencies, its shocking, underprepared modulations, its propensity towards small- and large-scale repetition and its inexpert employment of form. In particular, the practice of culmination through repetition, from the level of surface detail to whole sections, was seen as contributing to the sense of longwindedness, often creating a feeling of saturation" (54). Felix Salzer's "Die Sonatenform bei Franz Schubert" (Sonata form in Franz Schubert) (1928; Mak 2015), which was published during the Schubert centennial, provides us with one of the most extended and consequential discussions in this regard. As Su Yin Mak confirms, by the time that Salzer's essay appeared in the *Studien zur Musikwissenschaft*, the composer's instrumental music had already become well-known for its "extended lyricism" (2015, 3). Yet despite this recurring criticism, Salzer's study was among the first to attempt to explain more precisely how "Schubert's sonata form movements indulge in a succession of lyrical structures unchecked by improvisation, and are both excessive in length and lacking in organic unity" (2).[6] For many of Schubert's critics, including Guido Adler, whom Salzer studied with at the University of Vienna while completing his thesis *Die Sonatenform bei Schubert* (1926) (an earlier version of the 1928 publication),[7] it was this particular aspect of Schubert's sonata form movements—the "consistent employment of song-forms in the complexities of the sonata-movement"—that "relegates our young master to the second rank in comparison with the classic composers of instrumental music" (Adler and Baker 1928, 480).

Confounding these and other critiques of Schubert's instrumental music is the question of whether his works would have been received differently had his plans for publishing been fully realized. Contrary to family members and friends, who readily offered Schubert's music to publishers after his death, Schubert appears to have been reluctant to promote the large-scale instrumental works that he drafted before 1824—a decision that suggests that they may not have been intended for public circulation (Gingerich 2014, 12; 2016, 22).[8] With this variable hanging in the balance, one can only speculate whether such remarks as "his want of education drives him to the repetition of the subject in various keys, and similar artifices, in place of contrapuntal treatment" (Grove 1883, 361) and "Schubert had always had trouble controlling the rondo" (Cone 1970, 787) would have become as quotidian in his reception history and, conversely, whether such earlier compositions had, in the end, helped solidify his legacy as both an inheritor of the classical style and a progressive who helped initiate a new (or second) practice of tonality and form.

Notwithstanding this schism between indiscrimination and intention with respect to the posthumous releases of Schubert's instrumental music, discouraging responses arose when he tried to promote a curated selection during his last four years. Ignaz Schuppanzigh, one of Vienna's most influential violinists, for instance, expressed reluctance to perform Schubert's works in his chamber music concert series (1823–28), remarking of the String Quartet in D Minor ("Der Tod und das Mädchen") (D. 810), "My dear fellow, this is no good, leave it alone; you stick to your songs!" (Deutsch 1958, 289).[9] The Gesellschaft der Musikfreunde similarly declined performing his Symphony in C Major ("The Great") (D. 944) because of its length and level of difficulty (Gingerich 2014, 200).[10] When Schubert attempted to sell a selection of his works to the Leipzig publishing firm headed by Heinrich Albert Probst in 1826, Probst replied, "I must frankly confess to you that our public does not yet sufficiently and generally understand the peculiar, often ingenious, but perhaps now and then somewhat curious procedures of your mind's creations. Kindly, therefore, bear this in mind on sending me your MSS" (Deutsch 1947, 549–50). Probst eventually published one of the large-scale instrumental works that Schubert had offered, the Piano Trio in E-flat Major in 1828,[11] albeit at a purchase price of 60 florin (fl) Assimilated Coinage (AC) (equivalent to the then value of £6), one-sixth of Schubert's asking price (Deutsch 1947, 774).[12] Altogether, hesitant and unfavorable responses to Schubert's harmonic and formal practices cast a shadow over his instrumental works before and after his death, helping to prevent the decay of the monumental by clarifying what it was not: arbitrary, redundant, and digressive. These attributes tended to be tied to strange modulations, unbridled repetitions, and lyric-epic forms—peculiarities that came to signify Schubert's musical aesthetic.

More charitable perspectives of Schubert's approach to harmony and form, such as those offered by Donald Francis Tovey in his "Franz Schubert" ([1927] 1949) and "Tonality" ([1928] 1949) essays,[13] do appear alongside less favorable critiques as Salzer's (1928; Mak 2015) and others'. Yet it is only within approximately the last forty-five years, from around the time when music theory officially declared itself as a separate research discipline from musicology in North

American academies in 1977–78, that strong objections to Schubert's compositional aesthetic begin to subside. The advent of a Society for Music Theory (SMT) helped solidify two areas of music research, one that aimed to unearth the unique qualities of musical works through close readings and another that sought to theorize musical phenomena that had been either neglected or believed to not have been fully understood. Schubert's instrumental music appears to have served as a suitable candidate for study in both regards, with scholarship after the formation of the SMT arriving at the conclusion that prior adverse reactions to his approach to harmony and form may be a direct consequence of certain privileged contexts for reading—diatonic-based music theories, late eighteenth-century approaches to musical form and rhetoric, and myths about the composer's life, to name a few. Rather than reiterate the same conclusions as its nineteenth- and early twentieth-century predecessors, contemporary Schubert scholarship has instead proposed new ways to interpret musical phenomena in Schubert's instrumental works that were at one time believed to be strange, irrational, or disunified—perspectives that have led to a greater appreciation for his craft. As I outline further, such differences among past and present approaches to comprehending his music appear to primarily pivot on matters related to *aesthetics*—conceived here as pertaining to nonlinguistic, perceptual experiences (e.g., aural, visual, or tactile) that involve assessing the value of something, such as a musical work or painting, or perhaps an aspect of nature. If writings throughout the nineteenth century and during the first three-quarters of the twentieth century tended to view Schubert's instrumental works as aimless and superfluous, discourse thereafter has shown how such works may be perceived as coherent and unified from new perspectives.

Some of these efforts to reconceive Schubert's instrumental works have been prompted by broader attempts to rethink prior understandings of nineteenth-century harmony and form.[14] The potential limitations of diatonic theories, in particular, led some scholars to ask whether nineteenth-century harmonic and key relationships, which often feature common-tone and semitone voice leading and third relations that exploit enharmonic equivalence, operate under a different rubric.[15] The development of neo-Riemannian, pan-triadic, and other related transformational theories may be seen as an outgrowth of these concerns. In proposing new tonal spaces and conceptions of voice leading, the theories have altered the music-analytical enterprise by offering alternatives to Schenkerian theory and other diatonic theories built on the principles of consonance and dissonance, and chord hierarchy. That Schubert's music, along with selected works and passages by Liszt, Wagner, Brahms, and others, frequently served as examples for novel demonstrations of musical coherence and unity led some scholars to conclude that Schubert's approach to chromaticism may not be a mere extension of late eighteenth-century tonal conventions but rather a different kind of harmonic practice altogether. In adopting new lenses to make sense of the pitch relationships in his music, transformational theories have shown how Schubert's modulations and key choices may be reconstrued as rational and calculated.

To briefly explore two consequences that can arise from this change in theoretical purview, let us consider a passage from the finale of Schubert's Piano Sonata in C Minor, D. 958, from a neo-Riemannian perspective.[16] The passage includes a refrain/main theme in C minor (mm. 1–92), a transition in D-flat major (mm. 93–112), and a modulating couplet/subordinate theme group that begins in C-sharp minor (the enharmonic, parallel minor of D-flat major) and concludes in E-flat major (mm. 113–242) (ex. 1.1). From a diatonic perspective, it may seem as though the harmonic regions meander toward the double-flat side of harmonic space, F-double-flat major, rather than E-flat major, the relative major of the home key (ex. 1.2)—an outcome that may lead us to conclude that the harmonic relationships are diatonically indeterminate. A neo-Riemannian perspective can remedy this tonal drift and unveil a new rationale for Schubert's modulations by construing the relationships among regions as a series of transformations (P–S+P–P–LP–RP–RP–P) within an equal-tempered *Tonnetz* (ex. 1.3). The first series of modulations—D-flat major (m. 93), C-sharp minor (m. 113), A major (m. 141), and A minor (m. 145)—might be heard as a motion through the hexatonic PL (parallel + *Leittonwechsel*) cycle, which features root relations by major thirds. The arrival in A minor (m. 145), the hexatonic pole of D-flat major, may serve as a "pivot" region that enables a modulation from the PL cycle to the octatonic PR (parallel + relative) cycle, which features root relations by minor thirds (this modulation from the PL cycle to the PR cycle is marked by the swerve to the diagonal axis on the *Tonnetz* in ex. 1.3). The second series of modulations by minor thirds on the PR cycle leads us from A minor to E-flat minor, the octatonic pole, before swinging back to E-flat major through a final P transformation. Altogether, a neo-Riemannian perspective can offer an alternative rationale for passages that may be diatonically indeterminate, as well as show how a shift from one pattern of transformations to another corresponds to a change of formal design on the musical surface—in this case, motion from the modulating C-sharp minor theme (mm. 113–44) to the model-sequence technique that follows (mm. 145–76).

The theorizing of late eighteenth- and nineteenth-century musical forms have also affected the reception of Schubert's instrumental music in at least four ways: (1) by expanding our conception of sonata form through the inclusion of new formal patterns and concepts, including the "three-key exposition" [*Dreitonartensystem der Exposition*] (Salzer 1928; Mak 2015, 55), "modulating subordinate theme" (Caplin 1998, 119–21), and "trimodular block" (Hepokoski and Darcy 2006, 170–77); (2) by bringing to our attention "the processual character

Example 1.1. Schubert, Piano Sonata in C Minor, D. 958, iv. Excerpts.

of musical form," a principle marker of a burgeoning romantic style (Dahlhaus 1991, 117; Schmalfeldt 1995, 2011), and, relatedly, the ways in which music engages perception, especially our experience of time (Caplin 1998, 2010); (3) by raising an awareness of two different yet concurrent types of rhetorical grammars—hypotaxis and parataxis (Mak 2004, 2006, and 2010); and (4) by questioning whether sonata norms and conventions of the high classical style are constructed as opposed to given (Horton 2005, 2017).[17] Such developments invite us to respond differently to Schubert's approach to form, compared to our predecessors. In contrast to Ludwig Bischoff's 1859 review of Schubert's Symphony in C Major ("Great"), D. 944, wherein he asserts that the "plentiful fantasy

Example 1.1. (Continued)

continually overran the domain limited by proportion and laws of form" (Curtis 1979, 193; quoted in Messing 2007, 247n60), we might instead conclude that the symphony expresses a different balance between part and whole than that of its late eighteenth-century precedents, one that can be illuminated by James Hepokoski and Warren Darcy's (2006) sonata theory or that uses William Caplin's (1998) theory of formal functions as a point of departure. Along similar lines, we might counter Sir George Grove's conclusions about Schubert's formal digressions in his 1882 letter to Mrs. Edmond Wodehouse ("In the construction of each movement, if [Schubert] wanders from the form, it is not from any intention of neglecting it and setting up something fresh, but just because he goes on pouring

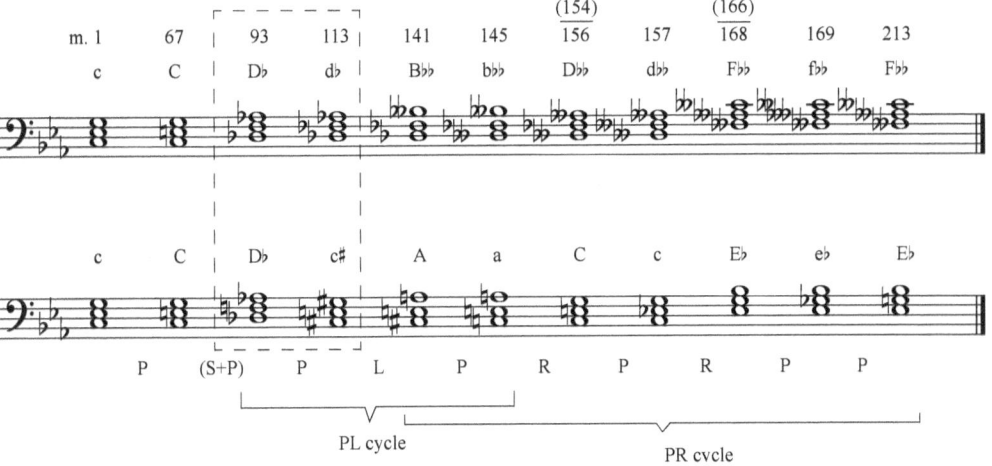

Example 1.2. Piano Sonata in C Minor, D. 958, iv, mm. 1–242. Comparison between a diatonic and a chromatic rendering of the harmonic relationships.

out what he has to say and so gets into all kinds of irregular keys and excrescences" [Graves 1903, 282; quoted in Brown 1958, 344–45]) by suggesting that such wanderings, irregularities, and excrescences may be markers of a parataxis rhetoric that aims to persuade through juxtaposition, rather than a hierarchical syntax.

Alongside modifications to our theories of harmony and form, emendations to Schubert's biography have helped subvert prior myths, including those perpetuated by early twentieth-century Schubertian kitsch.[18] Otto Erich Deutsch's

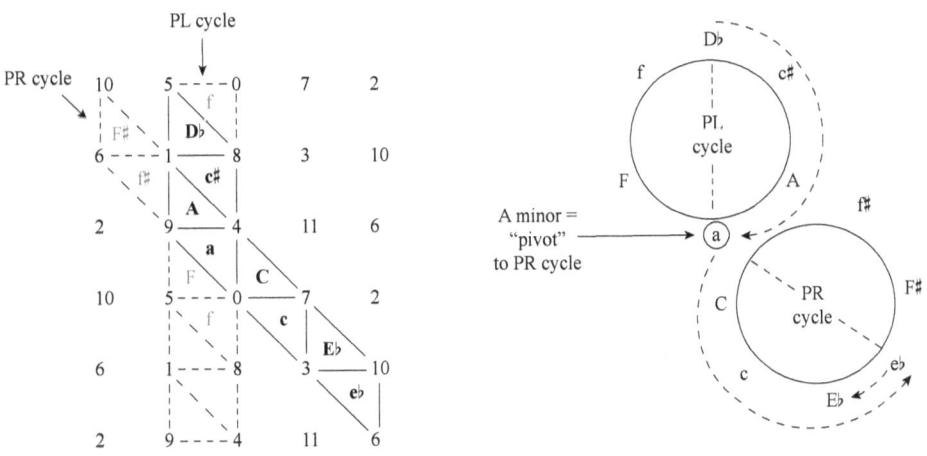

Example 1.3. Piano Sonata in C Minor, D. 958, iv, mm. 93–242. Neo-Riemannian reading of the harmonic regions on the *Tonnetz* and PL and PR cycles.

Schubert's Musical Reception and Criticism 9

three-volume set—*Schubert: A Documentary Biography* (1947); *Schubert: Thematic Catalog of All His Works in Chronological Order* ([1951] 1995); and *Schubert: Memoirs by His Friends* (1958)—has especially lain the groundwork for rethinking the composer's life and music, altering the landscape for future Schubert scholarship.[19] Through meticulous archival research, Deutsch has helped clarify the chronology of Schubert's entire musical output and uncover a plethora of unknown documents while offering informative commentaries on the composer's social, cultural, and political milieus. The residual effects of Deutsch's efforts can be observed in all corners of Schubert research, more so after his contributions were published in English around the second half of the twentieth century. Contemporary biographies on the composer, including those by Elizabeth Norman McKay (1996), Brian Newbould (1997), and Christopher Gibbs (2000), adeptly synthesize the documentary material collected by Deutsch and expand on his work. Other branches of Schubert scholarship have regularly turned to Deutsch's research to help verify or substantiate conclusions that can only otherwise be surmised in the composer's music. These matters have tended to involve Schubert's exposure to and attitude toward other composers' music, especially Beethoven's, where questions about musical influence abound; Schubert's musical education and working habits; and personal events that may have directly informed his compositional choices and output.

Revisions to Schubert's biography have become especially relevant to making sense of his instrumental works and musical aesthetic after the formation of a new musicology in North American universities in the 1980s. Both the unveiling of the politics implicit in a classical canon and the criticism surrounding pre- and postwar persuasions of instrumental music's nonreferential purity opened up space for a new kind of musical hermeneutics, one that combined sociocultural and biographical aspects of a composer's life with contemporary approaches to music analysis. With the advent of Eric Sams's (1980) reexamination of Schubert's illness and Maynard Solomon's (1981, 1989a) reassessment of Schubert's sexual orientation, such developments in toto appeared to call for renewed understandings not only of the composer's life and character but also of his instrumental works, especially those that seem more perplexing or strange. Edward T. Cone's "Schubert's Promissory Note: An Exercise in Musical Hermeneutics" (1982) offers us a primary case in point with respect to this significant turn of events both in Schubert studies and the field writ large. Published shortly after Sams's article, which concluded that the cause of Schubert's death may have been tertiary syphilis rather than typhus, Cone's analysis of the last *Moment musical* in A-flat Major, D. 780, no. 6, draws a parallel between a pestilent E-natural near the opening of the piece and the venereal disease that slowly wreaked havoc on the composer's health. In sum, revisions to Schubert's biography, in conjunction with the establishment of a new musicology, invited music scholarship to reexamine the potential connections between the composer's instrumental works and his sociocultural milieu, gender, and sexuality. Such efforts have helped foster new conclusions about musical meaning with respect to his instrumental works.

These collective changes to our contexts for reading—revisions to conceptions of nineteenth-century harmony and form and the development of a new kind of musical hermeneutics that conjoins music analysis with substantial amendments to Schubert's biography—amid the formation and preservation of new research areas in North American universities have invited us to come to know Schubert's instrumental works in unprecedented ways. This recursive moment in Schubert's musical reception history appears to revolve around scholarship's reexamination of the contexts within which the composer's works were formerly read. Through revision of such contexts, the same instrumental works and musical moments that were at one time chided for their digressions, redundancies, and idiosyncrasies can obtain a new kind of intelligibility. The strange and aberrant may be transformed into the familiar and the conventional or assimilated into a larger whole that rationalizes their existence. If Schubert had been relegated "to the second rank in comparison with the classic composers of instrumental music," to return once more to Adler and Baker's (1928, 480) assessment of Schubert's legacy during the centennial year of the composer's death, his instrumental works, as William Kinderman (2016) writes, "have begun to assume their rightful place beside those of Beethoven as works of an almost unsurpassed wealth of expression" (41).

Exploring the Poetics of Contemporary Approaches to Schubert's Instrumental Music

These positive changes to Schubert's musical reception notwithstanding, the stark contrast between past and present conclusions about the same instrumental works can introduce new questions about why we currently interpret Schubert's instrumental music as we do.[20] That reassessments of his instrumental works within the last forty-five years appear to revolve less around the question of whether prior scholars could interpret his harmonic progressions and musical forms and more around how they went about doing so suggests that what may be of most concern and potentially at stake among different conclusions "is not merely different readings of cultural objects but the frameworks in which interpretation becomes possible" (Korsyn 2003, 40). In an effort to further understand the motivations for the recent revisions to these frameworks and, more broadly, Schubert scholarship's current discursive practice—which encompasses an interplay of perspectives that seem complementary and, at times, contradictory—then, we might ask: What principles, or *poetics*, underlie the ways in which we currently interpret Schubert's instrumental works? Furthermore, how might these precepts encourage us to aesthetically engage with his music?

As the previous section suggested, the most recent shift in the reception of Schubert's instrumental music appears to have been largely motivated by efforts to rethink prior negative aesthetic judgments of these works: it is not Schubert's instrumental music that is questionable but rather certain perspectives that have been used to make sense of his harmonic and formal practices and determine its historical significance. This change in focus—from Schubert's music to the very lenses through which we view this repertoire—may suggest that contemporary approaches to interpreting his instrumental works have been propelled by the premise that his music is, by nature, coherent and that one can unearth meaningful unities and relationships among phenomena as well as uncover the rationale for why the music's harmonic and formal processes are the way they are by adopting the proper theoretical, historical, or biographical context. As I discuss further in this chapter and those that follow, this position may be entwined with certain ideas about closure (whether this be in relation to the musical work in question, a group of works, or a historical period), which lends stability to an interpretive act by demarcating the boundaries between inside and outside and by enabling the possibility for unity to emerge among part-whole relationships. With the rise of transformational theories alongside reassessments of the value of diatonic theories, as well as a new *Formenlehre* and a new musicology, such unities may be uncovered through more than one approach, raising additional questions about the musical "codes" that persuade us to adopt one particular perspective over another.[21] Differences among contemporary views of Schubert's approach to harmony and form notwithstanding, the search for new kinds of intelligibility primarily in the form of newly discovered unities among phenomena—guided by the underlying premise that his instrumental music is coherent—may be seen as one of the driving forces of contemporary discursive practice. Rather than continuously question or, in some cases, refute the intelligibility of Schubert's instrumental music and its associated compositional aesthetic, contemporary practice has instead aimed to revise some of the prior contexts and theories for reading in order to make intelligibility possible.

The claim that contemporary approaches to theorizing and analyzing Schubert's instrumental music have been propelled by a desire to show how it is inherently cohesive may seem archaic in light of the pivotal work that has transpired since Joseph Kerman's (1980) formative article "How We Got into Analysis, and How to Get Out." Yet it can be difficult to ignore the conditions that have helped facilitate change in the reception history of Schubert's instrumental works. It seems less by chance that Schubert's harmonic progressions and musical forms begin to obtain a new kind of intelligibility after music theory became an established research program in North America; our modern music theory research discipline, which has been largely predicated on uncovering hidden relationships and deep structures in Western art works (McCreless 1997, 21), appears to have provided the ideal climate for rethinking prior charges of compositional waywardness in Schubert's instrumental music, even more so after the inauguration of the Society for Music Theory in the late 1970s. As Kerman (1980) had posited of the goals of analysis shortly after this inauguration: "Analysis sets out to discern and demonstrate the functional coherence of individual works of art, their 'organic unity,' as is often said, and that is one of the things—one of the main things—that people outside of music mean by criticism. If in a typical musical analysis the work of art is studied in its own self-defined terms, that too is a characteristic strategy of some major strains of twentieth-century criticism" (312).[22] Although the new musicology has helped transform music analysis into a form of criticism that is more inclusive of sociocultural and historical contexts, such as biography, gender, and sexuality—matters that at one time appeared to have been peripheral to the work itself—writings published after Kerman's critique suggest that engagements with certain kinds of functional coherence, including the assimilation of the strange into a large unified whole, still prevail. In "Superior Myths, Dogmatic Allegories," for instance, Alan Street (1989) remarks on "the championship of unity over diversity" (80), concluding that "theory and aesthetics alike are troubled by the prospect of musical equivocality and indeterminacy" (79). Adam Krims (1998b), in his essay "Introduction: Postmodernism and Musical Poetics to the Problem of 'Close Reading'" in the edited volume *Music/Ideology: Resisting the Aesthetic*, which appeared twenty years after the formation of the SMT, offers a related diagnosis, noting that "whether in the form of Schenker analysis, set or serial post-tonal theory, or even adoptions of Harold Bloom's literary theories, the internal coherence of artworks remains even today an enabling assumption of most work in the field" (1). And in her article "Music's Vibratory Enchantments and Epistemic Injustices: Reflecting on Thirty Years of Feminist Thought in Music Theory," Judith Lochhead (2020) comments on the discipline's long-standing commitment to empirical and objective orientations, and its reluctancy to more fully embrace postmodern and post-structuralist perspectives, which have helped diversify content, methodology, and demographics in the field of musicology:[23]

> North American music theory has done little to address music's enchantments, preferring to frame its discourse around empiricism and objectivity. Since the 1990s various postmodern and post-structuralist perspectives have brought about changes of content—what music is considered—and methodology, including a consideration of music's "magical" powers. These new perspectives have, in part, resulted in an increased diversity in the demographics of musicology, but there

have not been changes of sufficient significance in either content or methodology in North American music theory.... While there are clear signs of change in music-theoretical circles since the turn of the millennium, the originating impetus in the mid-twentieth century for a disciplinary focus on "structure" and how it should be formulated by music theories has a legacy. (15, 17)

These writings, along with the responses to Robert Morgan's "The Concept of Unity and Musical Analysis" (2003) in the July–October 2004 issue of *Music Analysis*, the collection of essays in *Beyond Structural Listening* (2004), edited by Andrew Dell'Antonio, and other publications underscore the extent to which the art of making sense of music has been largely defined as the task of uncovering musical unities and structures. The ways in which we currently theorize and analyze Schubert's instrumental works might thus be seen as carrying a historical index that is interlaced with some of the goals of the discipline, which invite broader questions about aesthetic engagement and "what kind of music theory one wishes to engage" (Krims 1998b, 3).

If the recent shift in the reception of Schubert's instrumental music has been partly driven by efforts to unveil new unities and structures among a determined whole, how might this goal affect our aesthetic engagements with this repertoire? One potential consequence is that it can encourage us to interact with an instrumental work or group of works as though they were musical puzzles that have a determinate solution; harmonic and formal relationships that seem perplexing or strange may transform into musical problems that can be puzzled out within the boundaries of a determined, closed structure. Or put differently, an analysis may aim to show how unusual musical phenomena relate a larger whole that is taken to be complete. The impression that there is some kind of structure in the first place may be one of the primary factors that encourages us to engage with Schubert's music as a puzzle. In *Why Are Our Pictures Puzzles? On the Modern Origins of Pictorial Complexity*, James Elkins (1999), who uses the jigsaw puzzle as a metaphor to describe one of the dominant discursive practices in contemporary approaches to understanding artworks that are complex or ambiguous, similarly remarks that "any such intuition of structure is enough to set the picture-puzzle model into motion" (59):

> It is a common experience in research: first comes the intuition that there is a puzzle, together with some hint of what the solution might be; and then the details build one by one until they reach a critical mass. It does not matter for this model how the pieces correspond to passages in the paintings. In iconographic research it may happen that a painting seems to come apart along the lines of its painted figures and symbols; but I intend this as a very general model, since it applies to any reading that understands a picture as a

structure, something with internal differences that demand separate acts of attention. (59)[24]

In music theory scholarship, structures such as *Ursätze*, equal-tempered *Tonnetze*, and formal archetypes may function as silhouettes by which to comprehend part-to-part relationships in Schubert's instrumental works. Once one has an impression of how the parts may constitute the whole and how the whole may be constituted by its parts, relationships among the strange and familiar may either begin to materialize according to what seems permissible within the parameters of a music theory or reimagined altogether in such a way that alters the structure envisaged. Making sense of Schubert's instrumental music along these lines can thus entail contemplating within the parameters of a determined whole the boundaries of a musical part, how the parts relate to one another, and how the parts in relation to the whole communicate the work's aesthetic significance. As Elkins (1999) further remarks, such an approach can indeed be enjoyable for the analyst and the reader who engages with the analyst's point of view: "The pleasure in completing a puzzle is to see every piece in its proper place, and to see how they form a single continuous unity. . . . The reader's pleasure in following the solution re-enacts the writer's pleasure in finding it" (59, 61).

Notwithstanding this aesthetic appeal, the search for unity within a closed structure may also limit the ways in which we engage with Schubert's instrumental music. As Hyunree Cho (2015) observes of structuralist approaches to music in general in "Music as Poetry": "Within a structuralist perspective, change is difficult to conceive. When a model structure or an ideal type is given with a pregiven set of elements (and their relations and functions) . . . one could only rearrange, omit, or modify those elements" (174). With respect to Schubert's music, such a sense of restriction might arise, for instance, when attempting to make sense of unfamiliar or peculiar musical moments in his sonata form expositions. One might "rearrange, omit, or modify" the pregiven set of elements within a sonata form archetype or group of archetypes, as long as the general formal and tonal outline of the archetype remains intact. A similar case may obtain when connecting aspects of Schubert's biography or sociocultural milieu with his music through a narrative reading. The events and piece(s) selected may differ from analysis to analysis, yet when taken together, the analyses may employ one of the four archetypal narrative modes (romance, tragedy, comedy, satire) to not only explain the significance of one or more biographical or musical events but also assign a moral outcome and offer closure to the selected sequence of events. Were our discipline to succeed in theorizing every aspect related to Schubert's instrumental works in ways that ward off equivocality or indeterminacy, such an achievement could help further allay prior negative critiques of his music. Yet the act of transforming the foreign into something more familiar and perhaps conventional may also run the risk of neutralizing an aesthetic experience.

To some extent, then, demonstrations of unity and coherence within a closed structure might be construed as a kind of exercise, wherein both the problems and solutions arise not only as a potential product of the very lens constructed or chosen, but also as a consequence of attempting to unearth new unities, structures, and continuities—to uncover an order among a work's particularities from a particular theoretical lens within the boundaries of a determined whole. While the results that fall out from this exercise can offer one an omnipresent view of how all of the parts convey a single continuous unity—one that may resemble a completed puzzle—as well as facilitate closure with respect to an interpretive process, the exercise may run the risk of excluding or rendering marginal, observations about Schubert's music that may have emerged through other kinds of aesthetic engagements. If the act of establishing a determinate order for the unfamiliar or unusual through a music-theoretical or analytical approach may thus be regarded as a play with form—"form" in this context referring to one of several "paradigms of organization" that help us make sense of an aesthetic art object[25]—we might therefore ask, What other forms of play might we engage with when we come across musical phenomena that seem strange or foreign? How might these forms of play modify some of the goals for theory and analysis and, most importantly, our hearing of Schubert's instrumental music?

From Playing with Forms to Potential Forms of Play

The remaining chapters aim to explore this very line of inquiry by contemplating the unfamiliar and purportedly strange in Schubert's instrumental music via an alternative poetics. In particular, the chapters invite readers to engage with other kinds of subjectivities, or subject positions, all of which seek to reconstitute his music and the concentric circles that seem to surround it as open, divided entities—to, in other words, embrace indeterminacies and multiplicities in lieu of textual or historical unities that establish a determinate order for music phenomenon, especially those that seem unusual or inchoate. In seeking to introduce new forms of play, the chapters will aim to show, for instance (1) how we might embrace a single event's plurality of meanings or significations in ways that invite us to rethink notions of structure; (2) how the potential relationships among musical codes and music-theoretical perspectives may intersect within the same musical work; and (3) how we might conceive a Schubert work as an intertextual product of musical forms and harmonic patterns that cut across one another in ways that transform the familiar into something foreign. Rather than show how the seemingly irrational or unusual can be either normalized or absorbed into a closed structure, the remaining chapters will instead attempt to contemplate from multiple and sometimes incommensurable perspectives the value of conceiving of Schubert's music as an indeterminate object whose intelligibility is unfixed—to explore the interplay between that which we may provisionally appear to know and that which may appear to resist knowing.

In light of these objectives, chapters 2–6 present a fantasia of alternative subject positions that engage with four research topics that have become central to contemporary Schubert scholarship: (1) Schubert's approach to tonality; (2) his approach to musical form; (3) the relationship between his music and his biography; (4) and musical influence, especially with regard to Beethoven's instrumental works. In an attempt to mirror the kinds of indeterminacies and multiplicities that we might experience in Schubert's instrumental music and thus decenter the notion of a unified subject (whether this subject is taken to be the composition in question or a perceiver who aims to synthesize the particularities of a determined whole), the chapters deliberately avoid employing an overarching music theory for engaging with Schubert's music.

This being said, three strands of thought—each of which contain their own internal divisions—are instructive to the book's aims: early German Romanticism, post-structuralism, and historiography. All three areas of discourse convey a preoccupation with the ways in which reality may be re-presented by a perceiving subject and explore this and related issues, including the role that language plays in helping one communicate and understand various aspects of the world, through different means and arrive at different conclusions. Whereas writings by the early German Romantics tend to contemplate these issues primarily in relation to subjectivity, post-structuralist writings explore them in relation to their critiques of the purported structures or systems believed to underlie cultural phenomena. In addition, while both philosophical domains question the extent to which meaning is fixed, they part ways on whether the "absolute" or truth exists. As Andrew Bowie (2003) notes of this intersection between early nineteenth-century German philosophy and post-structuralism: "The Romantics' arguments have distinct echoes in aspects of post-structuralism: a philosophy of inherent incompleteness can be construed as a philosophy of deferral. It should be remembered, however—and this is what separates Romanticism from deconstruction—that if there were not some, perhaps inarticulable sense of a lacking completion, the notion of deferral would be meaningless. Deferral means putting off for later, not abolishing. At the same time, the question remains . . . whether the Romantic regulative idea of truth as the goal of our spiritual life might not be better abandoned" (52). In essence, early German Romantic philosophy primarily conceives the subject as infinite and forever seeking to grasp itself and that which appears to lie beyond articulation (a view that enables the literary fragment, allegory, and irony to play a central role in their writings), whereas post-structuralist writings tend to suggest that there are no absolute truths to be found, only differences and deferrals. As Jonathan Culler (1997) remarks on this tenet of post-structuralist thought, "[Post-structuralists] recognized the impossibility of describing a complete or coherent signifying system, since systems are always changing. In fact, post-structuralism does not demonstrate the inadequacies or errors of structuralism so much as turn away from the project of working out what makes cultural phenomena intelligible and emphasize instead a critique of knowledge, totality, and the subject. It treats each of these as a problematic effect. The structures of the systems of signification do not exist independently of the subject, as objects of knowledge, but are structures for subjects, who are entangled with the forces that produce them"[26] (125). Rather than aiming to master or unveil the underlying structures that appear to govern cultural phenomena, writings on post-structuralism instead turn their attention to the conditions that enable such structures to emerge as well as to the subject, the "site" where such structures are produced. The third general strand of thought, historiography, similarly explores the role that subjects may play in re-presenting reality—in this case, the historical field and the events or aging texts that comprise this field. One central point of inquiry is how subjects organize or emplot the historical field—how they determine the relationships among a selected sequence of events and convey through their arrangements an understanding of the moral meaning(s) of this sequence. With respect to Schubert's music, such matters become especially relevant to questions pertaining to causation, origin, originality, and repetition.

The remaining five chapters engage with these three strands of thought to varying degrees of emphasis. In chapter 2, "Rethinking Conceptions of Unity," I suggest that the notion of Romantic irony can transform our understanding of Schubert's music by providing an alternative to an aesthetic of unity. Using his *Moment musical* in A-flat Major, D. 780, no. 2, as a test case, the chapter offers a view that resists the pressure to explain idiosyncratic musical events as contributing to a greater whole. I also show how Schubert's use of tonality and large-scale organization may coexist with notions of conventional diatonicism and form and need not be conceived either as derivative of these customary procedures or as independent of them. The discussion invites us to reflect on larger issues of historical continuity with regard to Schubert's tonal and formal practices as well as further contemplate the epistemological frameworks that come into play in our efforts to come to know that which seems foreign or unusual.

In chapter 3, "The Value of Diatonic Indeterminacy When Traveling through Tonal Space," I take up a question raised in recent studies of chromaticism in Schubert's music, namely whether harmonic passages that cross an enharmonic seam are diatonically indeterminate when tonal coherence is sought on deeper levels of harmonic organization. The chapter explores what consequences may arise if we were to embrace diatonic indeterminacy in our engagement with Schubert's music, especially with respect to our listening experiences and conceptions of structure. Using Donald Francis Tovey's ([1928] 1949) discussion of an excerpt from Schubert's Piano Sonata in G Major, D. 894, iv, in his article "Tonality" as a point of departure, I explore how the peculiarities that arise from indeterminate, harmonic relationships in two passages from Schubert's Piano Sonata in B-flat Major, D. 960, i, can invite us to engage with a different kind of coherence and, hence, a different kind of aesthetic experience with respect to structure. In taking into account the role that musical form and cadential closure can play in our hearing of passages that cross an enharmonic seam, I suggest that both form and closure can affect our perception of the relationships among harmonic regions in ways that can transform the familiar into the foreign and vice versa. The chapter concludes by rethinking the value of indeterminacy and its consequences for music analysis.

In chapter 4, "Sonata Forms, Fantasias, and Formal Coherence," I revisit recent proposals of a *four-key* exposition in select Schubert sonata forms as a means to further probe his earlier formal practices and to consider what we might gain by bringing other contextual frames of listening into dialogue with that of sonata form. Here I explore the intersection between sonata and fantasia—the latter of which resurfaced in late eighteenth- and nineteenth-century compositional thought as a genre and as a musical aesthetic—in an effort to further consider the ways in which formal coherence in Schubert's expositions has been constructed and problematized. I suggest that the tension between both contextual frames points toward the ways in which the fantasia can function as a loosening device, lending a sense of unpredictability with respect to each exposition's tonal trajectory and thematic unfolding. I discuss how the fantasia (1) invites development in the form of thematic variations, unraveling the tight-knit design characteristic of sonata form expositions in relation to their development sections; (2) motivates modulations to several key areas, enabling key relations to obtain multiple significations; and (3) encourages us to self-reflexively examine the heuristic devices we may use to make sense of a work's structure. The second half of the chapter considers how these points can enrich our understanding and hearing of select three-key expositions.

Chapter 5, "Biography, Music Analysis, and the Narrative Impulse," asks how the shifts in our understanding of Schubert's life and of our own cultural condition have affected the ways in which we narrativize musical events in his instrumental works. Drawing from selected writings by Wilhelm Dilthey ([1883] 1989, [1910] 2002, 1959) on works of art, which he construes as expressions of lived experiences, I suggest that, just as an instrumental work may be conceived as an expression of a composer's lived experience, so, too, may a music analysis be seen as an expression of an analyst's lived experience of an instrumental work. I then explore how narrative can function as a way to synthesize the events in a musical work and our respective experiences of this work into a unified, self-contained expression. As such, I propose that music analysts may take on the role of narrators who define the agents and actions in instrumental works and explain how these phenomena are related through cause and effect, so as to communicate their possible significance. I then explore some of the narrative strategies used in hermeneutic analyses of Schubert's instrumental works as a means to (1) further contemplate how narrative can enable us to move between music and biography and to (2) suggest that explanations of the significance of a sequence of musical events through narrative structures may be partly motivated by an impulse to moralize certain events in the composer's life. What I deduce from our music analyses is that the proposed revisions to the composer's biography amid a burgeoning cultural pluralism have modified the ways in which we both emplot and ascribe an outcome to the musical events in these works. I conclude the chapter by considering the value of narrativity in our analyses of Schubert's music while, concomitantly, highlighting the creative acts embedded in our emplotments of musical events against the background of a shifting biographical and cultural context.

Chapter 6, "Beyond Homage and Critique: Rethinking Musical Influence," reconsiders the topic of influence in Schubert's music from a post-structuralist position, drawing from Jacques Derrida's writings on grafting—the act of placing separate texts side by side to produce a new structure. Using the opening measures from Schubert's Sonata in C Minor, D. 958, i; the theme from Beethoven's Thirty-Two Variations in C Minor, WoO 80; and the opening measures from Mozart's Piano Concerto in C Minor, K. 491, i, as examples, the discussion aims to rethink the categories of homage and critique by proposing that (1) each composition contains a heterogeneity of texts, which calls into question the notion of an original text, and (2) matters related to musical appropriation do not lie solely within any of these musical texts but rather between them, inviting us to further contemplate how emplotments of the historical field can affect our understanding of appropriation and repetition, and our music analyses of Schubert's works.

Closing this exploration of an alternative poetics are concluding remarks that readdress the monograph's central topics—musical unity and coherence, aesthetics and aesthetic values, and subjectivity or subject positions—in relation to contemporary Schubert scholarship's writings on tonality, form, biography, and musical influence. In addition to discussing the provisional conclusions that arise from the book's five chapters, I briefly reflect on how the ideas offered here may be similarly conditioned by a historical situatedness and may thus be seen to carry their own historical index.

Notes

1. For a summary of the 478 works published during Schubert's lifetime, see Deutsch 1947, 938–46. Here Otto Erich Deutsch clarifies: "In order to appreciate this amount properly it should be borne in mind that, although it appears to represent about one-third of Schubert's complete works, a single dance or variation (the Diabelli variation) or a song is counted as a unit and thus appears as weighty as a mass, an opera, or a symphony" (946). Breitkopf and Härtel's release of the Schubert *Gesamtausgabe*, edited by Eusebius Mandyczewski et al. (1884–1897) around the time of the composer's birth centennial served as a capstone to multiple efforts to disseminate his music. As Deutsch (1951b), Peter Clive (1997, 20–21), and others confirm, though, not all of Schubert's music was published in this critical edition, which had already comprised thirty-nine folio volumes.

2. On Schubert's stature as a composer before and after his death, see especially Deutsch 1951a; Gibbs 1997a, 1997b, 2000; Reed 1997; Hascher 1997; Gingerich 2014, 2016.

3. The slow turnout of Schubert's instrumental works may partly be attributed to Schubert's publishers, including Diabelli (headed by C. A. Spina) and the Paris firm C. S. Richault, who were more inclined to release his songs, as opposed to his instrumental works. For more on the dissemination of Schubert's works after his death, see Grove 1883, 355–59; Deutsch 1947, 1951a; Brown 1958, 312–53; Brown, Sams, and Winter 2001. On the prestige of the symphony and string quartet genres, in comparison to that of the piano sonata during the first quarter of the nineteenth century, see especially Gingerich 2014, 240–46. During this timeframe, the piano sonata had been primarily played by women and "remained a resolutely cloistered genre until well after the deaths of both Beethoven and Schubert" (243).

4. Hanslick's statement appears in a concert review for *Die Presse*, March 11, 1862. The original German reads, "Wenn Schubert's Zeitgenossen seine Schöpferkraft mit Recht angestaunt, was müssen erst wir Nachkommen sagen, die noch unaufhörlich Neues von ihm erleben!" (Strauss 2008, 1/6:60). Quoted and translated in Deutsch 1951a, 202–3; 1958, 383.

5. As Peter Szondi (1978) clarifies, hermeneutics is not exclusively one or the other:

> That hermeneutics was once only a system of rules, while it is today only a theory of understanding, does not mean that an unarticulated concept of understanding did not underlie the rules once practiced, nor does it mean that a theory of understanding today must renounce the reformulation of rules or can impute that the former rules have preserved their validity. . . . Rather the concept of understanding itself changes in history, just as the conception of the literary work changes, and this double change can also have as its consequence a modification of the rules and criteria of interpretation, or can at least make their reconsideration necessary. (18–19)

6. For further discussion of Salzer (1928) 2015, see Mak 2004, 2006, 2010.

7. On this version of Salzer's study, see Koslovsky 2009.

8. For more on Schubert's late style, see especially Byrne Bodley and Horton 2016b.

9. Schuppanzigh's reaction to the quartet is recounted by Franz Lachner, composer and conductor, and friend of Schubert's. John Gingerich (2014, 74 and 77) clarifies that Schuppanzigh's concert series only performed once, three of seven chamber works that Schubert composed between 1824 and 1828: the String Quartet in A Minor (D. 804), the Octet in F Major (D. 803), and the Piano Trio in B-flat Major (D. 898). With exception to the Piano Trio in E-flat Major (D. 929), the String Quartets in D Minor (D. 810) and G Major (D. 887), and the String Quintet in C Major (D. 956) premiered after Schubert's death (74). Gingerich (2016, 27–28) further adds that Schubert's mingling of high and low genres—the string quartet and the lied—may have discouraged Schuppanzigh from further promoting the composer's works; whereas the string quartet was linked to the aristocracy and the proficient, the lied was deemed a folk genre and associated with amateurs.

10. See also Griffel 1997, 203; Gingerich 2016, 29–31. On the "heavenly length" of Schubert's instrumental music, see Schumann (1840) 1965; Burnham 1999; Daverio 2000, 2002; Wollenberg 2011; Médicis 2015.

11. In his letter to Probst, Schubert indicates that the final movement has been trimmed. Deutsch (1947) remarks that the cuts were made because "the work had proved too long in performance" (774).

12. Schubert received a similar tepid response when he offered the same works to Breitkopf & Härtel as Probst in 1826. Breitkopf & Härtel asked the composer to send only "one or two pieces for the pianoforte, solo or duet," because they were "wholly unacquainted with the mercantile success of [his] compositions" (Deutsch 1947, 551). For more on Schubert's relationships with Viennese and Leipzig publishers, see Gingerich 2014, 253–70.

13. Although Donald Francis Tovey ([1927] 1949) also condemns the digressions in Schubert's sonata forms, he proposes that "Schubert, like other great classics, is pressing his way towards new forms. . . . The fruition of Schubert's new instrumental forms is to be found in Brahms" (122–23). In his article "Tonality" ([1928] 1949), Tovey reiterates this conclusion: "This is not to say that the first movement [of the Quintet in C Major] had not its diffuseness and redundancies, like every large instrumental work of Schubert. . . . But defects may coexist with qualities; and Schubert's defects are often half-way towards the qualities of new art-forms. Upon Brahms the influence of Schubert is far greater than the combined influences of Bach and Beethoven" (151). Sir George Grove's (1883) entry on "Schubert" in *A Dictionary of Music and Musicians* similarly combines criticism with praise.

14. See also the introduction to Byrne Bodley and Horton 2016a, which also offers a summary these innovations.

15. See, for instance, Proctor 1978; Bailey 1985; Cohn 1996, 1999, 2012; Satyendra 1998; Kopp 2002; Kinderman and Krebs 1996; Clark 2011a; Rings 2011b.

16. My discussion of this finale is drawn from the analysis presented in Rusch 2013b. Whereas the earlier article suggested that the musical form of this tarantella is a rondo, this discussion adopts a more agnostic perspective with respect to identifying

the movement's formal procedure. Although the formal plan appears to share attributes with a sonata, rondo, and sonata-rondo, its fantasia-like characteristics (e.g., modulations, sudden shifts in rhetorical tone, pauses), prevent it from strictly adhering to a single archetype. The potential admixture between form and fantasia in Schubert's instrumental works, especially with respect to his sonata form practices, is further addressed in chapter 4.

17. Julian Horton (2005, 2017) poses this question in relation to the theorizing of nineteenth-century sonata form practices. For further remarks on this topic, see Vande Moortele 2013.

18. Heinrich Berté, Alfred Maria Willner, and Heinz Reichert's operetta *Das Dreimäderlhaus*, for example, was "performed more than 80,000 times since its debut in 1916" (L. Kramer 1993, 3). See also Lindmayr-Brandl 2016, which explores the myths surrounding Schubert's Symphony in B Minor ("Unfinished"), some of which were further propelled by the 1958 film version of *Das Dreimäderlhaus*.

19. As Deutsch 1947 (xiv) and 1958 (v) clarify, a four-volume set was initially planned: Grove's Schubert Biography, vol. 1 (German translation with revisions); Documents, vol. 2, part 1 (initially published in Germany in 1914 and then in English in 1946–47; German expanded edition in 1964); Memoirs, vol. 2, part 2 (1958); *Sein Leben in Bildern*, vol. 3 (1913); and Thematic Catalog, vol. 4 ([1951] 1995; German edition expanded in 1978). The translated and revised version of Grove's Schubert Biography was never completed. For more on this four-volume set, see Brown 1965.

20. The latter clause is adapted from Jonathan Culler (1981). In aiming to clarify the distinction between hermeneutics and poetics, Culler proposes that the former "serve[s] as a method of interpretation" whereas the latter "explain[s] why we interpret literary works as we do" (8–9).

21. This reference to codes invokes Roland Barthes's *S/Z* ([1970] 1974), which presents a structural analysis of the lexias in Honoré de Balzac's "Sarrasine." As Culler (1983) summarizes, "each code [proairetic, hermeneutic, semic, symbolic, and referential] is the accumulated cultural knowledge that enables a reader to recognize details as contributions to a particular function or sequence" (84). See also Culler 1975, 202–4, 242–43. While the current monograph does not directly engage with Barthes's five codes, it explores the effect of certain perceived musical codes and why they might lead us to interpret Schubert's instrumental music in certain ways.

22. The notion that a musical work may be "studied in its own self-defined terms" may recall M. H. Abrams's (1953) "objective orientation" in his theory of criticism. As Abrams suggests, writings that engage works of art typically identify four coordinates in their discourses, each of which may be flexibly defined: the work (which he positions in the center of this constellation), the universe, the artist, and the audience. One can begin to distinguish among different approaches to criticism by observing how writings situate a work in relation to these coordinates and to the work itself. As Abrams proposes, although writings may conceptualize the significance of an object in relation to all four coordinates, explanations may gravitate toward one coordinate, a decision that tends to be reflective of a hermeneutic outlook on the nature of

art at a certain point in time. From this constellation emerges four approaches to art criticism—a *mimetic*, a *pragmatic*, an *expressive*, and an *objective* orientation—the first three of which explain the significance of the work in relation to one of the external coordinates. A *mimetic orientation* primarily views an art object as an imitation of the universe, which may be broadly conceived as nature, ideas, feelings, or events (for Abrams, Plato's dialogues on the relationship between works of art and ideas offer one example) (8). A *pragmatic orientation*, which emerged from theories of rhetoric and the art of persuasion, conceives the aesthetic significance of an object in terms of "an instrument for getting something done, and tends to judge its value according to its success in achieving that aim" (15). And an *expressive orientation*, which came into focus around 1800, views a work's aesthetic significance in terms of "the internal made external, resulting from a creative process operating under the impulse of feeling, and embodying the combined product of the poet's perceptions, thoughts, and feelings" (22). Positioning a work in relation to itself generates a fourth approach to criticism, an *objective orientation*. This orientation, which Abrams views as one of the dominant modes of criticism emerging in the mid-twentieth century, seeks to explain a work without a direct reference to the universe, artist, or audience, conceiving it instead as an autonomous entity made up of distinct components (7, 27).

23. See also Lochhead 2016, 17–45.

24. Although Elkins's (1999) monograph primarily concerns the field of art history, there are significant parallelisms that can be drawn between his observations about the modern state of the discipline and our modern music theory discipline, not least "the sheer volume of writing" that separates both contemporary discourses from their respective pasts (1999, 20) as well as an analogous attraction to the "analytically complex [and] conceptually challenging" (54).

25. The quoted material, "paradigms of organization," appears in Culler 1981, 12–13.

26. See also Culler 2007, which suggests that the general distinction between structuralism and post-structuralism is tenuous, at best, as writings on structuralism already show a keen awareness of the problems involved with attempts to both uncover and master, or fully realize, the underlying structures that are presumed to govern social, cultural, and literary phenomena.

2 Rethinking Conceptions of Unity

Rationalizing the Irrational

To begin exploring in more depth an alternative poetics for engaging with Schubert's instrumental music, the current discussion offers a different way to understand the sudden harmonic shifts, remote tonal regions, and discontinuities of gesture that we often find in this repertoire, an approach that resists the pressure to explain idiosyncratic musical events by subsuming them within a larger whole.[1] My attempt to engage with Schubert's music along these lines is motivated by previous concerns that have been raised about musical unity, and by the negative reception history of the composer's approach to harmony, which has led to concerted efforts within Schubert scholarship to rationalize, by precepts of unity, modulations that were once considered strange or illogical.[2]

Such efforts to make sense of Schubert's music through demonstrations of unity can seem especially warranted when we situate these aims alongside critics' earliest reviews of his harmonic practices. Consider, for instance, an excerpt from one of the first extensive reviews of the composer's instrumental works—the Piano Sonata in A Minor, D. 845—which appeared in the Leipzig *Allgemeine musikalische Zeitung* on March 1, 1826: "It is easy to see that these inventions are often somewhat odd, and that their exposition is even more curious.... Also, that the composer now and again hardly knew the ins and outs of the sometimes strange harmonies that visited him (even as regards grammatical writing); and there are other things of the sort over which one can hardly refrain from shaking one's head a little" (Deutsch 1947, 513). A similar stance is expressed in a review of Schubert's "8 Variations on a Theme from Herold's 'Marie'" for pianoforte four-hands, D. 908, which was published in the same periodical on February 6, 1828: "Of course it may yet fail here and there. For that reason, however, it will seem only the more delightful to the vast majority of amateurs, since that which befogs this crystal clarity is precisely what is most characteristic of our time; that is to say, frequent surprise attacks with strange chords, or rather transitions and modulations which mostly show our tonal beauties in confusion, which here too are to be occasionally found again" (Deutsch 1947, 733). Although both reservations are situated within more positive assessments of the two compositions under review,[3] such critiques of Schubert's harmonic practices have nonetheless helped set the tone of his musical reception history and reverberate in later reviews of his instrumental works.[4]

Positioning these and similar critiques of Schubert's harmonic practices alongside more recent readings of his music highlights the extent to which contemporary Schubert scholarship has shown through different theoretical and analytical approaches how such perceived oddities may be assimilated into a greater whole. As examples, let us revisit two discussions of Schubert's *Moment musical* in A-flat Major, D. 780, no. 2 (a complete score appears as Example 2.8 near the end of this chapter). The first is Allen Cadwallader and David Gagné's (1998, 272–89) Schenkerian analysis of the piece in *Analysis of Tonal Music*. The authors rationalize the abrupt modulation from A-flat major to F-sharp minor (mm. 55–56) using the concepts of motivic enlargement, voice leading, and prolongation (288–89). Initially, D-flat major served as a pivot between these two harmonic regions (mm. 15–17), functioning as both the subdominant of A-flat major and the dominant of G-flat minor—here spelled as F-sharp minor—and yielding, in turn, a harmonic sequence of ascending fourths: A-flat major, D-flat major and G-flat/F-sharp minor. When preparing for the return of the F-sharp minor section (mm. 55–56), however, Schubert eliminates the pivot harmony, directly juxtaposing A-flat major with F-sharp minor. The authors view these two harmonic regions as an enharmonic major second (I–♭VII♭) and explain that the modulation to G-flat minor and subsequent return to A-flat major (mm. 74–75) permits a composing-out of the neighboring motion C–D-flat–C (^3–^4–^3) introduced in the opening bars.[5] With regard to the large-scale A-B-A'-B'-A" form of the *Moment musical*, "a three-part form that expands to five parts through the varied restatements of the B and A sections" (273), the authors propose that the repetition of the B and A sections provides balance and harmonic closure to the first half of the piece. Although the first coda gesture (mm. 48–55) "gives a surprising effect to the resumption of B . . . [where] Schubert clearly intends us to believe that, at bar 55, the piece is over," (273) the return to F-sharp minor (m. 56) necessitates a return to the home key, A-flat major, the harmonic region of the final A section. This last A section resolves the D-flat major cadence that concluded the first A section (mm. 16–17) by closing with a cadence in the home key (mm. 81–82) (281).[6]

Compared with Cadwallader and Gagné's reading of the *Moment musical* in A-flat Major, which suggests that musical unity can be found among the tonal processes on the foreground and middleground levels of a Schenkerian analysis, Charles Fisk's (2000a) interpretation of the same work suggests that meaning for unusual events in the piece, such as the return of F-sharp minor (m. 56), can arise when narrative functions as a vehicle for connecting Schubert's music to his biography.[7] Both the music and biography are seen to complement each other, forming a whole that realizes the possibility of reading the composer's life in his works of art. In turning to Schubert's biography, Fisk relates the *Moment musical* to the composer's allegorical tale "Mein Traum," which some scholars believe to be an autobiographical confession (Dahms 1912; Hitschmann 1915; Solomon 1981). Centering on themes of exile and redemption, the story tells of a protagonist who wanders for many years in foreign lands, singing songs of pain and love after being banished from home twice for rejecting his father's beloved garden. When the protagonist returns home a third time to mourn the death of a virgin, he is tearfully accepted by his father. Fisk traces this Romantic narrative of exile, homecoming, and redemption through the contrasting sections, where the musical form, A-B-A'-B'-A", resembles the narrative structure of the poem: "home—exile—return home—return to exile—transfigured homecoming" (Fisk 2000a, 7). In an earlier article on the *Moment musical*, Fisk (1990), like Cadwallader and Gagné, explores the motivation for the striking return to the B section (m. 56). According to Fisk, the B' section revisits past events in the music, whereby the "re-enactment of the memory as a present *experience* leads to a catharsis" (1990, 11, italics in the original). The "epiphanic" change of mode from F-sharp minor to F-sharp major (mm. 67–69) enables "an inner reconciliation between past and present experiences" (11). Weaving biography and analysis, and past and present, into a rich, variegated tapestry, Fisk provides a reading of the *Moment musical* that enables us to experience a "unity of consciousness" (11) and "new kinds of continuity" (12).

These two discussions of the *Moment musical* illustrate not only how the irrational in Schubert's music can be transformed into the rational but also how interpretations of his approach to composition, particularly with respect to the unity of a particular work, often diverge. Whereas Cadwallader and Gagné's analysis suggests that coherence between seemingly disparate musical events may be found through motivic unity within a Schenkerian framework, where motives that occur as foreground events reappear as motivic enlargements on deeper structural levels, Fisk's reading demonstrates how narrative can allow us to conjoin such events, and how a musical work and a potential, biographical anecdote can function as complementary halves in the exploration of musical meaning. In the process of illustrating new and enlightening ways of understanding the peculiar gestures in Schubert's music, these two approaches, taken together, help demonstrate that varying conceptions of unity coexist.

What such perspectives can conversely call into question is whether such musical peculiarities need to be resolved or subsumed under a larger complete structure. That is, what if we were to entertain the possibility that these musical gestures do not coalesce into a greater whole? More fundamentally, what if we were to reevaluate the criteria by which the merit of Schubert's musical works have been judged? What other options are available to us for understanding part-whole relationships, and how might these options affect the meaning of musical phenomena that seem strange or bizarre? In the discussion that follows, I suggest that the notion of Romantic irony might transform our understanding of the *Moment musical* by providing an alternative to an aesthetic of unity.

Romantic irony was an issue that preoccupied many of Schubert's late eighteenth- and early nineteenth-century German contemporaries, such as Johann Gottlieb Fichte (1762–1814), Friedrich von Hardenberg (1772–1801) (who published under the pen name Novalis), Ludwig Tieck (1773–1853), Friedrich Schlegel (1772–1829), and Heinrich Heine (1797–1856). For these writers, irony served as a catalyst for exploring the rapport between nature and subjectivity, and the grounds for what constitutes knowledge and understanding. In addition to embracing self-reflexivity and refusing a fixed identity, they recognized that language was a system of arbitrary signs and thus an inadequate vehicle for communicating thought. This linguistic turn—acknowledging the gap between one's own thoughts and a language formed prior to oneself—freed the creative mind from fixed forms of syntax and grammar; irony enabled one to interrupt or undo a discourse at any point in time, resulting in an irrational play of signifiers. Rather than resolving the internal divisions experienced between the self and one's language by reducing identity to a fixed meaning, the early Romantics accepted these divisions, which allowed them to engage with multiple and often contradictory meanings. They thus reacted against the idea of a unified, monologic consciousness, turning instead toward an ironic consciousness that continually questioned and confronted in a self-reflexive manner the epistemological foundations that informed one's ability to know. The advantage of an ironic consciousness—one that repeatedly objectifies itself in "attempts to grasp itself" through an infinite process of self-reflection, yielding irreducible, multiple meanings—was that it afforded one freedom and the possibility of transcending the absolute (Wellbery 2000, 194).

Here we must keep in mind that the early German Romantics viewed irony quite differently from those who came before them: they transformed what was once understood as a rhetorical device into a philosophical stance. This distinction is a crucial one, but it can be hard to maintain. As Paul de Man (1996, 166) suggests, the potential to control meaning by stabilizing the definition of irony is, to some extent, unattainable because of what Søren Kierkegaard (1989) refers to as irony's "absolute infinite negativity." Once one begins to question whether a text or statement is ironic, de Man sees "no inherent reason for discontinuing the process of doubt at any point short of infinity" (1996, 166). Nonetheless, one can see among Schubert's contemporaries a concern with irony not as a figure of speech or as a mere tool for the art of persuasion but, rather, as an aesthetic and philosophical demeanor that could permeate an entire work.[8]

Inquiries into the rapport between Romantic irony and Schubert's music are not new to music research: several scholars have commented on the ways in which irony is suggested in the composer's settings of poetry, especially of texts by Heine (*Der Doppelgänger* is a well-known example).[9] Using the second *Moment musical* as a test case, the following analysis will demonstrate how certain instrumental pieces by Schubert can also be understood in terms of irony because they seem to interrupt or undo received notions of tonality and form, engaging in a dialectical relationship with harmonic and formal structures from the past. My motivation to view this work through the lens of early German Romantic philosophy stems in part from the notion that the composer was familiar with Schlegel's writings and, perhaps more importantly, that his approach to tonality and musical form seems to resonate with the early German Romantics' concern with unity as it relates to both subjectivity and the work of art.[10] Drawing from the philosophical writings from Fichte's *Wissenschaftslehre* (1982) and Schlegel's *Athenaeum* (1968, 1991; Schulte-Sasse et al. 1997), this analysis offers one alternative to perceiving Schubert's music as having been modeled on a monologic, unified consciousness— a view that refrains from domesticating discontinuities by showing how they serve a larger whole that is complete. The perspective provided here also invites us to reflect on broader issues related to historical continuity and compositional practice by suggesting that Schubert's approach to tonality and form need not be conceived either as a derivative of more conventional approaches or as independent of them.

In presenting an analysis that not only embraces Romantic irony but also exemplifies it, I shift between two positions: music as object, with myself as the perceiving subject, and music as a kind of subject, with myself as the reflected object. As the following discussion outlines, self-reflexivity is crucial to the exploration of irony, since, as Peter Szondi (1986) summarizes, "in the romantic conception of irony the subject is the isolated man who has become his own object" (68). Rather than providing a final answer to the oddities we may encounter in the *Moment musical*, my analysis will thus adopt an ironic perspective, representing one of the many possible linguistic descriptions that may be used for Schubert's piece.

Schubert's *Moment musical* in A-flat Major, D. 780, no. 2, from a Romantic-Ironic Perspective

Measures 1–17

Brian Newbould's (1997, 341) assertion that the juxtaposition between A-flat major and F-sharp minor in measures 55–56 is "one of the most astonishing tonal junctions in all Schubert" highlights perhaps the most striking event we encounter when we engage with the *Moment musical*. If we are to understand this passage, as well as the work's five-part form, in ironic terms that do not depend on a monologic, unified consciousness, how might we interpret this striking harmonic turn away from the home key? To address this question, we first need to consider how the notion of interrupting or breaking the musical "tone" can manifest itself in earlier events in the piece.

The piece, reproduced as Example 2.8, begins conventionally with an eight-bar phrase that moves toward a weak cadence on the dominant. Coupled with the next subphrase (mm. 9–12), these opening measures may begin to suggest an antecedent phrase, one that belongs to a sixteen-bar compound period.[11] Here we might recall other pieces in A-flat major with triple meter that begin with a sixteen-bar compound period, such as the first-movement theme of Beethoven's Piano Sonata in A-flat Major, op. 26 (ex. 2.1), and Schubert's Impromptu in A-flat Major, D. 935, no. 2 (ex. 2.2). In the Beethoven theme, the compound period begins with an eight-bar antecedent phrase that cadences on the dominant harmony; in the impromptu, the compound period's antecedent phrase approaches a tonic harmony without cadential motion in the bass. In both pieces, an eight-bar consequent phrase concludes with a perfect authentic cadence in the home key. Returning to the *Moment musical*, Schubert appears to disrupt the symmetrical balance between the antecedent and consequent phrases, which these pieces might have led us to expect, by extending the consequent to nine measures and by modulating to the subdominant, an unusual goal for a modulating consequent phrase. Example 2.3 presents a voice-leading graph of the piece. As previous analyses of this work have emphasized, the chromatic descent from C-flat to A-flat in measures 14–16 that propels the surprising modulation to the subdominant region—highlighted by the *pianissimo* dynamic—is divided between two registers: the chromatic descent first sounds in the alto and is then repeated three octaves lower, in the bass.[12] In the reading presented here, this chromatic descent is interpreted initially as a minor third, from C-flat to A-flat, and then as a perfect fourth, from D-flat to A-flat, which overlaps with the first chromatic descent. As we shall see, this perfect fourth, which contains the minor third, takes part in all of the modulations that move away from the tonic harmony, accumulating multiple meanings as it is constantly fragmented and reworked.

The turn away from convention in measures 1–17 of the first large A section appears to break the narrative: what seemed to be the beginning of a sixteen-bar compound period has evolved into a seventeen-bar modulating compound period. Comparing the opening theme of Schubert's *Moment musical* to what we may define as a sixteen-bar compound period can suggest that music has a dual nature: the potential for anticipation and surprise emanates from its capacity to appear to either conform to or diverge from our expectations.[13] From the listening perspective suggested here, the ability to know or assign an identity to a

Example 2.1. Beethoven, Sonata in A-flat Major, op. 26, no. 1, mm. 1–20.

particular passage—based on formal functions and theme types (Caplin 1998)—comports with Fichte's (1982) view of one's knowledge of a particular object, whereby the identity of an object is intrinsically rooted in language.[14] Fichte suggested that language has just such a dual nature in that it can identify the self and the nonself simultaneously; that is, the nonself is present as the self is posited (de Man 1996, 173). The idea that language can posit the self and the nonself at the same time suggests an alternative to perceiving Schubert's music as a monologic entity. From our listening perspective, informed by Fichte, we can hear Schubert's *Moment musical* as identifying or describing itself in the actual sounds that unfold through a temporal process, representing a positive self, while music that we do not really hear but may imagine or expect connotes a negative self whose presence is asserted by its absence. In other words, by saying y rather than x, the music can suggest the presence of x through its absence. Speaking y therefore also speaks of its negation, x, thus yielding the presence of a double consciousness.

Most important to note here is that in this dialectical system, the negative self emerges from our own epistemologies, which can include expectations arising

Rethinking Conceptions of Unity 31

Example 2.2. Schubert, Impromptu in A-flat Major, D. 935, no. 2, mm. 1–32 and 47–50.

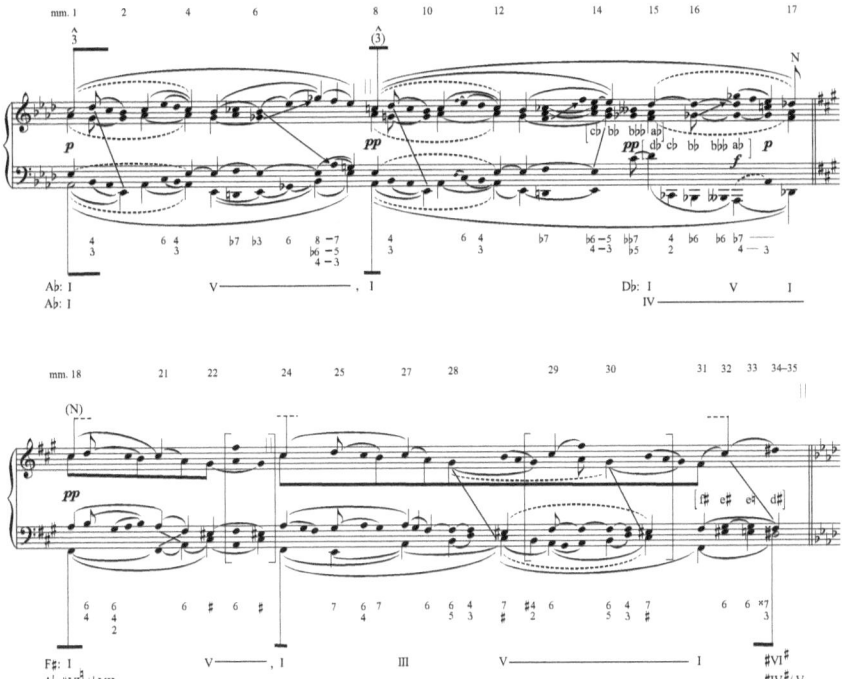

Example 2.3. Schubert, *Moment musical* in A-flat Major, D. 780, no. 2. Voice-leading graph.

Example 2.3. (Continued)

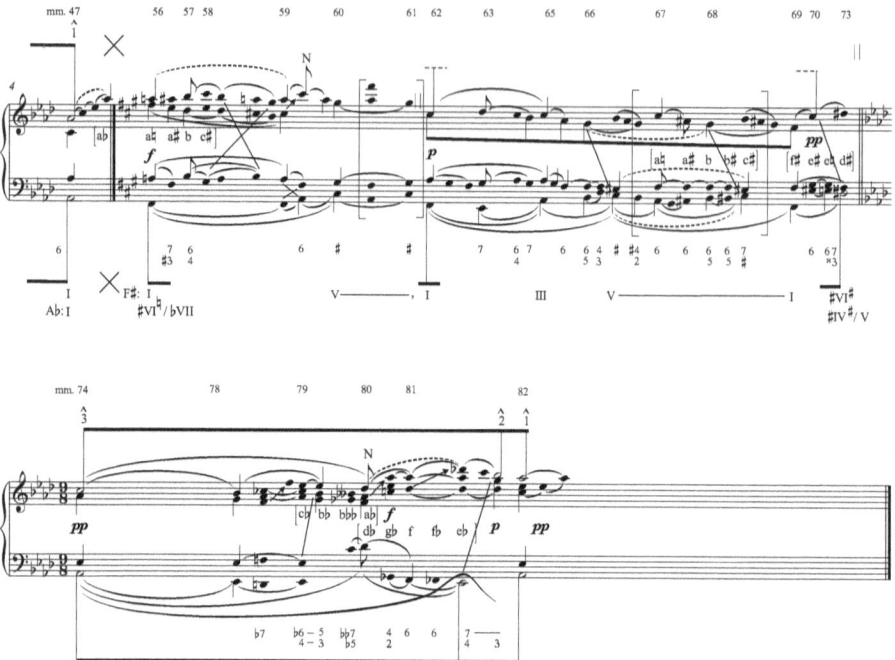

Example 2.3. (Continued)

from genre, form, or instrumentation. The possibilities for what we define as the negative self, *x*, are thus limited by the epistemological frameworks that enabled us to recognize the existence of this negative self in the first place. From a Romantic-ironist view of the *Moment musical*, this point regarding epistemology relates strongly to early German Romanticism's philosophical stance toward the rapport between subjectivity and objectivity. During this period, philosophers regarded the work of art as a model for investigating a much larger issue: the rapport between nature and subjectivity. Given the increasing, skeptical attitude toward theology around the end of the eighteenth century, the challenge to philosophers lay in explaining human reason as a legitimate form of knowledge without theological support. This shift in the rapport between nature and subjectivity radically transformed philosophers' conception of the subject, from a passive receptor of a preformed body of knowledge to an active agent who determined meaning through interaction with the environment. No longer was it the subject's task to uncover and understand a world in which knowledge and truth were guaranteed by a deity; instead, late eighteenth-century philosophers claimed that the basis of knowledge and meaning in the world was constructed by a perceiving subject.[15] Thus, they tended to shift their focus from the metaphysical to the epistemological—one's capacity to know oneself and the world as an object—where the act of knowing is susceptible to alterations and revisions through infinite processes of self-reflection.

Returning to Fichte's self and nonself and its relevance to our reading of Schubert's *Moment musical*, the meeting of the two selves—the positive (what we hear) and the negative (what is paradoxically heard through "not hearing")—can give rise to three types of judgments, which Fichte (1982, 111–15) calls synthetic, antithetic, and thetic judgments.[16] According to Fichte, both synthetic and antithetic judgments compare properties of two entities. Synthetic judgments reveal similarities between these entities where they are distinguishable by at least one property; antithetic judgments reveal differences between two entities that share at least one property.[17] As Fichte (1982) explains, each judgment is contained within the other: "There can be no antithesis without a synthesis; for antithesis consists merely in seeking out the point of opposition between things that are alike. . . . And conversely, too, there can be no synthesis without an antithesis. Things in opposition are to be united . . . so that reflection may bring to consciousness only the ground of connection between them" (112).[18] The third judgment, thetic judgement, which is also synthetic and antithetic, is a reflexive judgment. The entity does not relate to another entity but only to itself. It is this thetic judgment that allows the entity's individual existence to be asserted (Fichte 1982, 113–15). When we listen to the opening of the *Moment musical*, it seems plausible to shift among these three different judgments, where we constantly compare and contrast not only previous musical events within the same work but also musical events outside of the work as they relate to the piece, with the intent of knowing it. The catch in Fichte's system is that the ability to know an entity's identity in a thetic judgment is not absolute.[19] Because reflexivity is an inherent aspect of thetic judgments, where the assertion of the self, "I am," is empty—in other words, not comparable to another self—the possibility of knowing an entity becomes boundless.[20] As we move further in our analysis of the *Moment musical*, it is this notion of the infinite that presents us with a double-edged sword, being both problematic and advantageous. It is problematic in that it becomes difficult to comprehend certain musical aspects of the piece; the work swerves away from what we know toward the infinite and, thus, toward the indeterminate and sublime. Yet accompanying this quandary is a perception of originality: the delimitation of what is possible can reveal the potential for new avenues of exploration and creative insight on both fronts, from composer to analyst. It is this potential that the *Moment musical* seems to unveil to us.

Drawing on Fichte's tripartite scheme, we can experience the opening section of the *Moment musical* according to his dialectical system. The positive self, represented by the compound period that we actually hear, encounters its negative self, the compound period derived from our generic understanding of a sixteen-bar compound period, which we do not hear. When the positive and negative selves meet, they are able to define and comment on one another, such that what is said is also not said; the two selves enter a dialectical relationship, comparing and contrasting the self with its nonself. Focusing on the opening bars—from the antecedent phrase to the middle of the consequent phrase (mm. 1–14)—we might explain this passage in terms of the three judgments: (1) synthetic—the opening measures suggest a balanced sixteen-bar compound period (eight-bar antecedent plus eight-bar consequent) yet sound an original harmonized melody; (2) antithetic—the opening measures sound an original harmonized melody yet seem to resemble a balanced sixteen-bar compound period; and (3) thetic—the opening measures present original harmonized melodic material that is unique to itself in that there are no other pieces in the classical literature that contain these exact measures. As we can observe in this example of Fichte's system, all judgments implicitly refer to one another: one judgment assumes the other two.

Fichte's system of comparing two entities by means of similitude and difference, as we have done here, has been explained usefully by de Man (1996, 176) as both a performative system, which he defines as the act of positing, and a theory of metaphor. The initial act of positing (comparing Schubert's opening theme to a conventional sixteen-bar compound period) throws a system of tropes into play, wherein the final stage yields a turn back toward the identity of the original object, projecting an infinite self. This entire process forms a tropological narrative that de Man describes as "the story of the comparison and the distinction, the story of the exchange of the properties, the turn where the relation is to the self, and then the project of the infinite self" (176). For de Man, a tropological narrative is a theory of metaphor created through the act of comparing two entities as a means of enabling us to pursue the identity of a given object.

A useful term to describe the moment when our tropological narrative of a sixteen-bar compound period is interrupted by the phrase expansion and modulation to the subdominant in the consequent phrase would be *parabasis* (translated literally from ancient Greek as "going aside" or "stepping forward"), a term favored by Schlegel (1963, 18:85, fragment 668).[21] For Schlegel, parabasis describes moments of interruption in a narrative line or an undoing of a discourse by means of a shift in syntax or rhetorical register (de Man 1996, 179). Originating as a strategy used in Greek plays, parabasis enables a work to comment on itself, question its subjectivity, and remind the audience that the work inhabits a certain perspective.[22] It is thus closely allied to irony. That Schlegel defines irony as a "permanent parabasis" seems paradoxical, yet it is this flexibility to interrupt the discourse at any point that frees the mind from syntactical or fixed forms of language. Irony depends on an historical consciousness, which can exist either within the work itself or outside of it. Our capacity to detect an interruption of a tropological narrative depends on our knowledge of past structures, whether those structures concern categories of genre or of grammar and syntax. Both the negative self and the idea of presence through absence depend on a consciousness of the past, wherein our expectations—defined by our epistemologies—are thwarted by the appearance of the unexpected. A single work can thus appear to create a tropological system based on itself, as well as on structures of its predecessors, and interrupt or undo its own narrative or metanarrative (whether this be based on form or genre, for instance) through parabasis. Listening to a musical work thus involves the act of comparing and contrasting the work to itself and other musical works in order to create a framework for understanding the piece. When it diverges from that part of the framework that is established by what we know—either by turning away from our conventions or by reworking the same musical event—the piece can appear to interrupt or comment on what it has just musically stated. Parabasis seems to occur in the *Moment musical* when the piece interrupts the tropological narrative of a conventional sixteen-bar compound period that it had set up in the antecedent phrase, thus breaking the fictional illusion and freeing itself from fixed forms of syntax.

Measures 18–35

After the opening A section cadences in the subdominant, the D-flat sustained in the melody is enigmatically juxtaposed with C-sharp at the opening of the B section. If we trace the function of D-flat in the opening A section (mm. 1–17), we find that it provides no hint of foreshadowing of its nemesis, C-sharp, which is tonally stable in its new environment. In the piece's opening measures (mm. 1–3), D-flat had previously functioned as an upper-neighbor to C, as a passing note within the falling third-progression E-flat–D-flat–C in a prolongation of the tonic harmony (m. 3), and as the root of the subdominant harmony (mm. 15–17) (see again ex. 2.3). In the B section, C-sharp's identity is revealed to us as D-flat's negative self. As the section unfolds, we might sense the presence of D-flat through its absence as its negative self, C-sharp, sounds repeatedly throughout. That is, presence through absence is inverted; the D-flat, the positive self that was so prominent in the opening A section, now becomes the negative image, C-sharp, in the B section.

Schubert's decision to modulate to F-sharp minor in the B section seems simultaneously to adhere to and interrupt the tropological narrative of form and design. The appearance of a contrasting B section seems expected. That the B section begins not in G-flat major but in G-flat minor—spelled as F-sharp minor—is quite striking and much more unusual. Just as D-flat's presence is suggested through its absence in the B section, G-flat major also becomes the negative self in the B section. The striking change of texture at the beginning of the B section—a melody with triplet accompaniment, as opposed to the pastorale-influenced chorale in the A section—also suggests another parabasis in the piece, here with regard to formal process. Let us consider, by contrast, Schubert's Impromptu in A-flat Major, D. 935, no. 2 (see again, ex. 2.2), where, in addition to opening with a compound period, Schubert explores the same harmonic areas—D-flat major and G-flat minor—as in the *Moment musical*. In the impromptu, Schubert begins the small b section with the same texture as the small a section and does not change the texture until the trio. Comparatively, in the *Moment musical*, Schubert does not continue with a small b section after the opening compound period, which would yield the possibility of a small binary or small ternary theme. Rather, the change in texture suggests that Schubert moves immediately into the large B section of a *large* ternary form. This omission of the b section in the opening A section might be heard as another parabasis, or another break in the fictional illusion: the potential for the realization of the A section as a small binary or small ternary is thwarted by the appearance of the large B section, resulting in a hybrid form.[23] With regard to harmonic procedure, both the impromptu and the *Moment musical* move to G-flat minor and F-sharp minor, respectively, through the subdominant harmony, D-flat major. Whereas in the impromptu, however, G-flat minor functions as the minor subdominant of D-flat major, tonicized by means of a chromatic voice exchange (mm. 21–27) (ex. 2.4) and explored as a key area in the trio section, in the *Moment musical*, G-flat minor—spelled as F-sharp minor—functions as the local tonic harmony of the B section, introduced by its own dominant, D-flat major (see again ex. 2.3).[24] In essence, the tonal hierarchy between G-flat minor and D-flat major in the impromptu is reversed in the *Moment musical* (ex. 2.5).

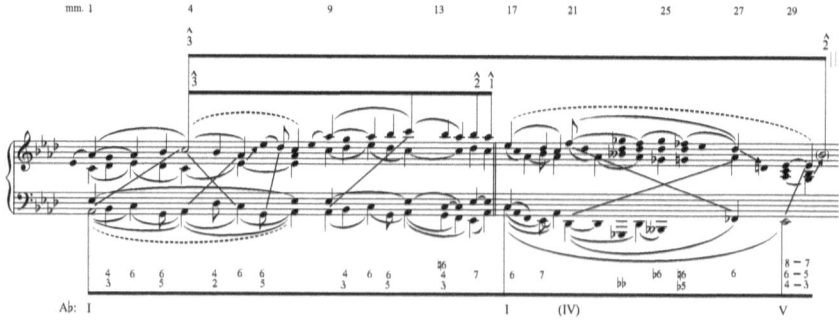

Example 2.4. Impromptu in A-flat Major, D. 935, no. 2, mm. 1–30. Voice-leading graph.

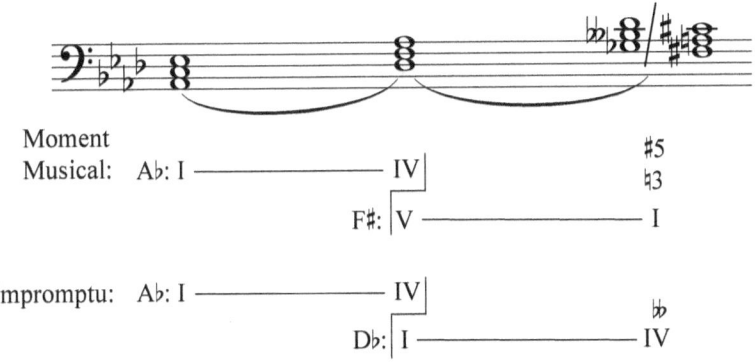

Example 2.5. *Moment musical* in A-flat Major, D. 780, no. 2, and Impromptu in A-flat Major, D. 935, no. 2. Hierarchy of tonal regions.

As the B section of the *Moment musical* comes to a close, Schubert signals the return of the A section by means of a brief transition (mm. 32–33). In these measures, the melody insists on C-sharp—covertly reminding us of D-flat's absence and presence—and ascends to D-sharp (mm. 34–35), while the bass leaps up a major seventh to E-sharp in the tenor register in order to complete the chromatic descent of a minor third (see again ex. 2.3). Like the chromatic descent of the minor third and perfect fourth that assisted in the modulation away from the tonic harmony in the A section, the chromatic minor third descent from F-sharp to D-sharp (mm. 31–35) facilitates the move back to the tonic harmony. We may hear a move toward the dominant harmony, E-flat, yet the notation reveals a D-sharp seventh chord; Schubert's notation does not revert to the flat side until the opening theme returns. Here, the music literally states a D-sharp seventh chord, suggesting a G-sharp tonic resolution, but acquires a different meaning—an E-flat seventh chord. This moment might convey the notion of a split consciousness, an awareness of the surface meaning and its inverted meaning at the same time, enabling this play with notation. Perhaps even more striking is the possibility that the theme from the A section will return in the minor mode, as opposed to the major mode.[25] That ^4 in F-sharp minor (the tonal region of the B section) is B-natural, as opposed to B-sharp, strongly suggests that this B-natural will be reinterpreted as C-flat, the third of an A-flat minor triad. At the last possible moment (m. 35), the tenor voice ascends to B-sharp in an attempt to swerve away from a thematic return in A-flat minor. Although we do not actually hear a thematic return in A-flat minor, its presence seems especially pronounced when the theme returns in A-flat major. Yet even though this reference to A-flat minor seems unexpected and particular to the *Moment musical*, Schubert invokes a similar harmonic illusion in the impromptu just before the return of the small a section (mm. 21–30) (see again, exs. 2.2 and 2.4). Here, his use of modal mixture during a tonicization of the subdominant harmony and move toward the augmented sixth chord, which contains a C-flat, suggests that the opening theme will return in A-flat minor. As in the *Moment musical*, Schubert suddenly veers away from A-flat minor through a cadential 6/4 harmony in the major mode (m. 29).

Measures 36–55

When we return to A-flat major in the second large A section, the thematic material that was first presented in the opening large A section is fragmented. The first subphrase in this thematic repetition begins with the first two measures from the antecedent phrase (mm. 36–37, mirroring mm. 1–2) but is then completed in measures 37–39 with measures 10–12 from the consequent phrase rather than measures 3–5. The phrase continues (mm. 39–41) with the beginning of the second subphrase of the antecedent phrase (mm. 4–6). Rather than concluding the entire phrase in the minor dominant or the subdominant, which were the two possible phrase endings presented to us in the first A section, the piece explores a new harmonic path, moving instead to G-flat major (mm. 43–44). This is reminiscent of the intended goal of the D-flat major harmony at the end of the opening large A section; however, the G-flat major harmonies (mm. 43–44) function not as local tonics, but as dominants, hinting at C-flat major. It is as though the "promissory" resolution of the D-flat major harmony from the initial A section were broken: G-flat major finally appears but not as a tonic resolution.[26] Its appearance as a dominant and its nonliteral statement as a tonic (m. 18) contribute to the *Moment musical*'s fractured identity.

As Cadwallader and Gagné (1998, 280–81) note, this middle A section revisits the chromatic descent, F-sharp–E-sharp–E–D-sharp, which concluded the previous B section (mm. 31–35). This descending minor third, F-sharp–D-sharp, becomes an ascending minor third, E-flat–G-flat, in the second A section (mm. 39–44) (see again, ex. 2.3). Yet also accompanying this minor third is the perfect fourth initially heard in the modulation to the subdominant in the opening large A section; the descending perfect fourth, D-flat–A-flat, has been modified to an ascending fourth, A-flat–D-flat. Like the transformed minor third, this perfect fourth is situated within a new context, assisting in the ascending 5–6 motion that leads us away from the tonic harmony. From our Romantic-ironic perspective, the context in which these pitch collections first appeared has changed, revealing different meanings for these collections. These particular connections are highlighted by the change in register. In both presentations of the minor third, the bass leaps upward to the tenor inner voice and then returns to its previous register when the tonal center is regained. Similarly, in the first presentation of the perfect fourth, the bass also leaps to a new register, completing the chromatic descent three octaves below its initial starting point (as noted previously). Moreover, like the previous occurrences of the minor third and perfect fourth, the permutations of these pitch collections assist in moving away from or toward the home key. After this surprising departure from A-flat major (mm. 41–44), it appears as though the resolution of the dominant 6/5 harmony (m. 44) will resolve to A-flat minor in m. 45, since A-flat minor is ♭VI in relation to C-flat major. As in the passage before the return of the large A section (mm. 31–35), the music seems to swerve away from A-flat minor at the last possible moment, resolving instead to A-flat major.

The final two phrases of this section (mm. 48–51 and 52–55) may create the impression of a coda. The home key is reaffirmed by a tonic prolongation and a dominant pedal on ^5, first in the tenor voice and then in the soprano. Both phrases conclude on ^1, a-flat^1 in the first phrase (m. 51) and a-flat^2 in the second phrase (m. 55), closing both registers addressed thus far. With these coda-like rhetorical gestures, the music appears to have reached its conclusion. Nothing could prepare us for what follows.

Measures 56–90

The intrusion of F-sharp minor (m. 56), marked with the only *forte* dynamic in the piece, can interrupt our expectations from the previous coda-like section, fracturing the tentative feeling of closure just achieved.[27] From the Romantic-ironic perspective, this particular moment, where the F-sharp minor triad sounds with force and vigor, may appear to create another parabasis in the piece, or another interruption in the tropological narrative. Because the preceding two phrases strongly resembled a coda, the tropological narrative suggested a large three-part ternary form—albeit a hybrid one owing to the unexpected entrance of the large B section—reminiscent of the more familiar A-B-A structure: A (mm. 1–17)–B (mm. 18–35)–A' (mm. 36–47)–coda (mm. 48–55). With the juxtaposition of A-flat major and F-sharp minor after the apparent coda, the completed narrative appears to have been suddenly interrupted or undone. This reading is further supported by the voice-leading events that take place at this particular moment. In the previous two A sections, the chromatic voice leading that directs us away from the tonic harmony (mm. 14–16 and mm. 39–44) is expressed as a descending or ascending perfect fourth, respectively, from D-flat to A-flat or from A-flat to D-flat (see again, ex. 2.3). At this climactic point in the piece (mm. 55–58), the upper voice ascends in the motion A-flat–A–A-sharp–B–C-sharp, "undoing" the perfect fourth that had been so prominent in the previous sections to reveal instead an augmented third.

As the music continues in F-sharp minor, the theme from the preceding B section resurfaces (m. 62). Instead of cadencing in F-sharp minor, however, the phrase moves toward F-sharp major (mm. 67–69). As the voice-leading graph illustrates, a fragment of the recomposed "perfect fourth"/augmented third—slightly altered to A–A-sharp–B–B-sharp–C-sharp—may be heard but now in the context of F-sharp major.[28] Here presence through absence is inverted in this move toward the parallel major mode of F-sharp minor. Throughout the piece, the presence of G-flat major was consistently suggested by its absence, first in the intended resolution of the subdominant at the opening of the large B section and then in the middle A section, when the music swerved away from A-flat major. When the second large B section moves from F-sharp minor to F-sharp major, the intended meaning suggests G-flat major, but again the notation reveals something else: F-sharp major. As this section moves toward a close, the same chromatic descending minor third—F-sharp–E-sharp–E–D-sharp—that occurred near the end of the first B section leads us back to the tonic region. Here we may be reminded of the music's split consciousness: although the music indicates a D-sharp major seventh chord, its unspoken meaning signifies E-flat major, the dominant of A-flat. Once again, it appears as though the theme from the A section will return in A-flat minor. Instead, the music seems to swerve away from this goal toward A-flat major.

The final large A section restates the beginning of the consequent phrase from the first large A section (mm. 9–14, correlating with mm. 74–79). Rather than modulating to the subdominant at the end of this final section, Schubert cadences in the home key. As Cadwallader and Gagné (1998, 282) and Fisk (1990, 9 and 18) point out, the bass descent that diverts the modulation to the subdominant—G-flat–F–F-flat–E-flat—resembles that found at the half cadence at the end of the B sections, F-sharp–E-sharp–E–D-sharp (see again, ex. 2.3). Rather than hearing these pitches as a reconciliation of "the 'conflict' that has been so essential to the drama of this work" (Cadwallader and Gagné 1998, 282) or as signifying an "integration of those contrasting episodes into their present A-flat major environment" (Fisk 1990, 9), it seems plausible from the reading laid out here that these moments could also reveal to us multiple perspectives of these pitch collections, which refuse a stable, unified identity. What was once a descending perfect fourth—D-flat to A-flat—(mm. 15–16) is now interrupted, juxtaposed with another version of the minor third that sounded during the transitional passages at the end of the B sections and in the bass of the ascending 5–6 sequence in the middle A section. Yet although the literal notation of this minor third—presented here as G-flat–F–F-flat–E-flat—resembles the one that occurs during the ascending 5–6 sequence, its particular function correlates with its F-sharp–D-sharp counterpart in the transitional passages because it facilitates a move back to the tonic harmony.

The final two phrases (from m. 83 to the end) recall the coda-like section (mm. 48–55), verbatim. Once again, they reaffirm the tonic key by means of the dominant harmony and E-flat pedals, signaling the close of the section and of the piece. Yet given the previous dramatic interruption (m. 56), perhaps the sense of closure is only an illusion: Will our narrative be interrupted once more?

Conclusion

The listening perspective that we have adopted for the *Moment musical* suggests that several layers of irony coexist throughout the piece. With regard to formal process, these include:

1. the unbalanced consequent phrase and modulation to the subdominant harmony, and the omission of the small b section in the opening large A section; and
2. the undoing of closure of the large hybrid three-part ternary form (A-B-A) and coda via a return of the F-sharp minor passage.

In terms of notes or chords, they consist of:

3. the two nonoverlapping pitch collections, D-flat–A-flat and F-sharp–D-sharp, which gain multiple meanings throughout the piece as they are transformed within new contextual frameworks (exs. 2.6 and 2.7);
4. the double meaning that is produced as a result of the variance between a passage's notation and its implied significance (for example, the D-sharp major dominant seventh chord in mm. 35 and 73);
5. the harmonic and syntactical treatment of G-flat major/F-sharp minor/F-sharp major; and
6. the suggestion, on several occasions, of A-flat minor (mm. 31–35, 42–45, and 69–73), which does not explicitly surface.

These moments of parabasis can suggest that meaning is not fixed but open to multiple significations. Put differently, we can engage with contradictory meanings and not have to settle on a fixed identity for a work. This last point is especially apparent when we consider the *Moment musical* in light of the impromptu: the musical features shared by the two pieces—in particular, the compound period opening and the reference to D-flat major and G-flat/F-sharp minor—are construed differently. Yet here we reach an interruption in our own narrative. Are we to accept the notions of convention laid out thus far by our own epistemologies? If so, then we may be able to recognize moments of parabasis, moments

Example 2.6. *Moment musical* in A-flat Major, D. 780, no. 2. Perfect fourth/augmented third pitch collection D♭/C♯–A♭ and permutations.

Example 2.7. *Moment musical* in A-flat Major, D. 780, no. 2. Minor third pitch collection F♯/G♭–D♯/E♭ and permutations.

where a larger discourse or multiple frames of reference impinge on the music's individual statements (Handwerk 2000, 204). Yet even to define these narratives, as I have attempted to do here, has been a difficult task, particularly because irony prevents narratives from being completely and conclusively defined. As de Man (1996) comments, "It is ironic, as we say, that irony always comes up in relation to theories of narrative, when irony is precisely what makes it impossible ever to achieve a theory of narrative that would be consistent" (179). Defining prior narratives and conventions in order to detect irony can therefore seem ironic in itself, as irony prevents these narratives from being consistent or harmonious.

In offering this alternative interpretation of the *Moment musical*, my intentions here are not to favor some form of disunity over forms of unity. As several authors have noted, questions concerning unity in music analysis only reveal the complexity of the matter, precluding the possibility of reducing the conflict to a mere binary opposition.[29] Rather, what I hope to have shown in this discussion is that the notion of Romantic irony can offer us another perspective from which to consider the disjunct musical gestures we may perceive in this and other works by Schubert, a perspective that provides an alternative to those guided by an aesthetic of unity and, to some extent, challenges our own subject positions. As noted previously, late eighteenth-century philosophers also began to view the work of art as an autonomous entity that could reflect on human experience (Bowie 2003). The artist's capacity to create a work whose individual parts coalesce into a greater whole mirrors the subject's potential to synthesize the world's infinite particularities as they are presented to this subject. Studies in aesthetics and subjectivity have further suggested that, in the late eighteenth century, the work of art was anthropomorphized into a kind of subject, modeled on the human subject (Eagleton 1990). This led to a reversal between subject and object, raising the reflexive question: What kind of objects are we who choose to view the work of art as a unified subject? Terry Eagleton (1990) has claimed that the search for unity in a work of art reflects our own desire for unity. As Kevin Korsyn (2004) thus explains regarding music analysis: "it is now *our own unity* that is at stake in discussions of artistic unity, and this may explain our frequently intense investment in the idea of musical unity" (338–89; see also Eagleton 1990). In this light, we can observe a parallel between the fear of meaningless randomness when there is no deity or center to organize the endless particularities of the world, and the fear that music analysis metaphorically dies, or at least becomes meaningless, when unity is found to be lacking in a work. To some extent, it is both this fear of indeterminacy and the fear of that which presents itself as chaos, resisting synthesis on some higher level, that gives unity its value as a privileged aesthetic. Unity affords us the possibility of understanding and assigning meaning to a work's parts and of revealing how these parts function within a greater whole. Additionally, as Korsyn and Eagleton suggest, it allows us to confirm our own unity as a subject. With the notion of a center around which to organize the parts, order is restored.

In closing my discussion, yet concomitantly opening it for further reflection and critique, I hope to have introduced an alternative way to interpret the musical gestures that we find curious and unusual in Schubert's music. The German Romantics' view of language as an open semiotic entity, because of the arbitrariness of the sign, led Schlegel (1968, 1971) to posit that *reelle Sprache*, or authentic language, was the language of error and madness (see also de Man 1996, 181). The turn away from one's inherited language was also understood as a necessary component in the search for an identity. With regard to a musical work, it seems plausible that multiple contextual frames can bring meaning to a single musical statement, especially when these frames presuppose constructed norms or conventions of tonality and musical form. This can enable us to hear Schubert's music as interrupting or undoing these frames of reference and, on some level, allow us to

Example 2.8. *Moment musical* in A-flat Major, D. 780, no. 2.

contemplate the reelle Sprache of music. In thus positioning Schubert's harmonic procedures within a dialectical space, the disjunct progressions and musical gestures, along with the alterations made between the proportions of a work's part and whole, may be heard as the result of an ironic swerve away from perceived conventions, the outcome of an effort to find a unique voice in music such that the destruction of that which can seem limiting—the absolute—is a necessary path toward revealing that which is infinitely possible.[30] From an early Romantic point of view, it is these moments of negativity that enable a new period to develop. As Szondi has posited, Schlegel's pre-Hegelian, dialectical view of history—antiquity,

Example 2.8. (Continued)

modernity, eschatology—was manifested in the idea that the present period was a "chemical one" of amalgamations and disjunctions, whereby the future "will neither repeat the first nor be entirely new . . . [but] develop, through a dialectical reversal, out of the very heart of the modern age, out of the latter's negative traits themselves" (Szondi 1986, 58, 65). Schubert's approach to harmony and form in the *Moment musical*—the juxtaposition of remote key areas, hybrid presentation, and disruption of closure—appears to strongly resonate with this dialectical view of history. The *Moment musical* seems to blend and separate, to engage with and

Example 2.8. (Continued)

turn away from the musical attributes of a nonrecoverable past, whose negative aspects may or may not viewed in terms of progress.[31] Romantic irony thus enables us to think about Schubert's music as inhabiting a historical position, where, as de Man has suggested, the writer can become "both the historian and the agent of his own language" (de Man 1983, 152; quoted in Korsyn 1993a, 90).[32] By establishing a dialectical relationship with itself and with works outside of itself, pieces such as the second *Moment musical* can be perceived, like Schubert himself, as neither passive followers of convention nor entirely independent of it.

Notes

1. An earlier version of this chapter was published as "Rethinking Conceptions of Unity: Schubert's *Moment musical* in A♭ major, D. 780 (Op. 94), No. 2" in *Music Analysis* 30, no. 1 (2011): 58–88.

2. See especially Morgan 2003 and the commentaries on this article published as "The Concept of Unity: Responses to Robert P. Morgan" in *Music Analysis* 23, nos. 2–3 (2004), by Chua, Dubiel, Korsyn, and J. Kramer. See also Cook and Everist 2001, Street 1989, and Korsyn 2003.

3. Otto Erich Deutsch (1947) lists "[? G. W. Fink]" as the signatory for both reviews.

4. The review from February 6, 1828, also suggests that Schubert's approach to harmony resonates with the general practices of the time. A review of Schubert's lieder, opuses 21–24 (D. 553, 536, 525; 771, 772; 751, 743, 744, 761; and 583, 527) in the same periodical, dated June 24, 1824, offers a similar appraisal: "But the reviewer deems himself entitled to speak in greater detail about the unwarrantably strong inclination to modulate again and again, with neither rest nor respite, which is a veritable disease of our time and threatens to grow into a modulation-mania to which unfortunately even famous composers succumb, either willingly or for the sake of following the fashion" (Deutsch 1947, 355).

5. On this point, Allen Cadwallader and David Gagné (1998) note that "the key of G-flat (F-sharp) is the only key that will permit the upper-neighbor D-flat (= C-sharp) to function as a local scale degree" (287).

6. The authors further contend that "the reestablishment of a-flat^2 in the second A section subtly prepares for a further extension in the upper register," which commences in measure 55 (Cadwallader and Gagné 1998, 281).

7. On this use of narrative, see, for instance, Korsyn 1993b, 2003; McClary 1993a. Chapter 5 in this monograph further explores this hermeneutic approach.

8. Lilian Furst (1984) traces the metamorphic transition from rhetorical irony to Romantic irony, which began roughly around the mid-eighteenth century. See also Wellbery 2000.

9. See, for instance, Brauner 1981; Agmon 1987; Kurth 1997; R. Kramer 1994. Unlike Eytan Agmon (1987), Richard Kurth (1997), and Richard Kramer (1994), Charles Brauner (1981) appears to interpret Schubert's songs according to rhetorical irony. More generally, Romantic irony within the context of nineteenth-century philosophy has been explored in other composers' music, most notably works by Robert Schumann. See Daverio 1993; Rosen 1995; Perrey 2002. Kevin Korsyn (1991) observes the potential for irony to operate in our critical apparatuses, namely, Schenker's theory of structural levels and Weber's *Mehrdeutigkeit*. See also Korsyn's November 1994 letter to Jairo Moreno, cited in Moreno 2003.

10. See Bowie 2002, 32; Feurzeig 1997, 2014. Lisa Feurzeig (1997) discusses the rapport between the Schubert and Schnorr-Schlegel circles in Vienna during the 1820s. Deutsch (1947), in his editorial commentary on a letter from Schlegel to Ludwig Schnorr, also confirms this connection between the Schubert and Schnorr-Schlegel

circles, though he notes that "nothing is known of a more intimate relationship of Schubert and Schober with Schnorr" (254).

11. For further discussion on compound themes, see Caplin 1998, 64–70.

12. See Fisk 1990, 8, 15; Cadwallader and Gagné 1998, 277–78. Charles Fisk (1990) highlights this repetition of the chromatic descent from C-flat to A-flat.

13. This notion of expectation recalls Leonard Meyer's (1956) and Eugene Narmour's (1992) work on musical experience. Whereas Meyer and Narmour approach the topic of musical expectation from a music-cognitive viewpoint, the analysis offered here draws from philosophy and literary theory.

14. Taking their departure from Kant, the early German Romantics' concern lie with the notion of subjectivity, bringing about a reversal between subject and object positions: for these philosophers, the subject became an object of study, to determine how, if possible, this subject as an object comes to know and synthesize the world around them.

15. For further discussion on the rise of subjectivity and modern aesthetics, see Bowie 2003.

16. See also Paul de Man's (1996, 174) discussion of Fichte. With regard to antithetic judgments, de Man uses Kant's term *analytic* instead of *antithetic*.

17. Drawing from Fichte's example in the *Science of Knowledge* (1982), de Man provides examples of synthetic and analytical judgments. Of synthetic judgements, he says: "If I say that A is like B, it supposes an X in which A and B are distinct or different. If I say that a bird is an animal, this supposes a distinction between animals, that there are differences between animals which allow me to make this comparison statement, between animals in general and birds in particular" (1996, 174). Of analytic (or antithetic) judgments, however, he observes: "If I say that A is not B, then it supposes a property X in which A and B are alike. If I say, for example, that a plant is not an animal, it supposes a property that plants and animals have in common, which in this case would be the principle of organization itself, which plant and animal have to have in common for me to be able to say, to make the analytic judgment, that something is not like something else" (174). See also Fichte 1982, 114.

18. De Man (1996, 174) also highlights this point.

19. Contrary to de Man (1996), who appears to interpret this last judgment in Fichte's dialectic as infinite, Walter Benjamin (1996) stresses the opposite. According to Benjamin, Fichte attempted "to make reflection into a philosophical organon by destroying its infinitude" (Benjamin 1996, 125), whereas Schlegel, adopting Fichte's philosophical stance on subjectivity while at the same time rejecting certain elements, alters this philosophy by embracing the infinite.

20. On self-positing as it relates to "I am" and the absolute, see Fichte 1982, 96–99.

21. For the Greek etymology of the term *parabasis*, see Cuddon 1991, 676.

22. See Handwerk 2000, 216. For the early German Romantics, Shakespeare's and Tieck's plays are also exemplarily models of works that break the fictional illusion. For further discussion on this point, see Szondi 1986.

23. My thanks go to Kevin Korsyn, personal communication, for suggesting this notion of a hybrid form and the impromptu example. William Caplin has alternatively

suggested, in a personal communication, that measures 1–8 could also be heard as the first A section of a small ternary form that modulates to the dominant, where measures 1–4 resemble a compound basic idea and measures 5–8 a consequent phrase. He proposes that measures 9–17 appear to convey a written-out repeated A section "gone awry," on account of the modulation to the subdominant harmony (a whole step lower than the dominant of A-flat major), which in turn prepares for the move to G-flat/F-sharp at the beginning of the B section. That the form of the piece can also be read in this compelling way seems to support a romantic-ironic perspective, whereby the piece's departure from perceived norms can open itself up to multiple readings.

24. David Beach's (1998, 80) analysis of the Impromptu in A-flat major similarly reads measures 21–27 as prolonging the subdominant harmony through a voice exchange.

25. I would like to thank William Caplin, personal communication, for proposing to me in a private conversation the piece's continuous reference to A-flat minor.

26. On promissory notes and chords, see Cone 1982.

27. Although it might appear that my analysis of the *Moment musical* overemphasizes the modulation by step from A-flat major to F-sharp minor, the situation here seems radically different from that found in works by other composers, particularly Beethoven. Both diatonic and chromatic modulations by a whole step below the tonic occur in Beethoven's music. The slow movement of the Cello Sonata in D Major, op. 102, no. 2, and the scherzo movement of the Ninth Symphony are examples of the former, where, in both instances, he modulates from D minor to C major. An example of the latter can be found in the recapitulation of the first movement of the *Eroica* Symphony, where he moves from E-flat major to D-flat major, or from I to ♭VII). I am not, however, aware of an example in Beethoven's oeuvre where a chromatic modulation occurs between a major tonic and a minor key a whole step below this tonic—and at such a marked place in the form—that is comparable to the *Moment musical*.

28. Fisk (1990, 9 and 17) also highlights this connection. Whereas he views this change of mode to an enharmonic G-flat major as bringing us closer to A-flat major and negating the previous "jarring [cadence] encountered in the forte beginning of this second B section" (9), my intent here is to suggest that these varied chromatic ascents and descents between A-flat/A and D-flat, and A-flat/A and C-sharp, are constantly reinterpreted throughout the piece, contributing to our Romantic-ironic reading.

29. See note 2 of this chapter.

30. On this point regarding the destruction of the form, see Szondi 1986; Benjamin 1996.

31. John Daverio (1993) makes this salient point with regard to Schumann's music: "If Schumann's 'new forms' are so difficult to evaluate according to the standards of traditional *Formenlehre*, it is largely because they set forward a critique of the very structural principles that *Formenlehre* tends to idealize" (15). Although not adopting an ironic perspective himself, Donald Francis Tovey's ([1927] 1949, [1928] 1949)

progressive view of compositional procedure seems to resonate here, where Schubert's experiments with form were understood to be realized in Brahms's music.

32. See also Korsyn 1991. Adopting a Bloomian approach in his comparison between Chopin's Berceuse, op. 57, and Brahms's Romanze, op. 118, no. 5, Korsyn suggests that Brahms "ironizes [the Berceuse], by framing his D major variation set between two F major sections . . . thus embedding it within a larger narrative" (34–35). Wayne Petty (1999) relatedly shows how Chopin alludes to Beethoven in his Sonata in B-flat Minor, op. 35, yet also "sets himself apart . . . by situating his own voice antithetically to Beethoven's" (298).

3 The Value of Diatonic Indeterminacy When Traveling through Tonal Space

Diatonic In/determinacy and Aesthetic Experience

Among contemporary music theory's contributions to our understanding of Schubert's approach to harmony, none has been as groundbreaking as those offered by neo-Riemannian theory.[1] In proposing a different rationale for triadic proximity—defined not by the relationship to a governing tonic or approximate membership to a diatonic collection but rather by voice-leading efficiency among (037) trichords—scholars have shown how chromatic passages that are "triadic but not altogether tonally unified" (Cohn 1998, 167) may operate under a different logic, one that departs from the principles of classical tonality. Chromatic phenomena that appear to call into question such principles may thus obtain a new kind of coherence when situated within an equal-tempered *Tonnetz* where semi- and common-tone voice leading prevail.[2]

A recent demonstration appears in Richard Cohn's *Audacious Euphony* (2012),[3] which opens with a discussion of the recapitulation from the first movement of Schubert's Piano Sonata in B-flat Major, D. 960 (ex. 3.1). The first forty measures of the recapitulation wend through the harmonic regions B-flat major (m. 216), G-flat major (m. 235), F-sharp minor (m. 239), and A major (m. 241/242) before returning to B-flat major (m. 255). Citing Cohn at length:

> We have yet to consider how the local keys (or, from a different perspective, the triads prolonged by the local spans) relate to one another and how they work together to express the global tonic of B-flat major. If we are unable to do so, we just have a bunch of tubs floating around on their own bottoms. Each vessel is internally coherent and occupies a space bounded by the B-flat shores. But in relation to one another, their relation is random, for all we know. And there is no way to express a tonality. We can't just go <B-flat major, Cough, Wheeze, Honk, B-flat major> and pretend that we have made coherent music in B-flat major (Straus 1987). If a tonal theory is to meet its claims of explanatory adequacy, it needs to be able to specify the role, with respect to tonic, of the harmonies that separate the bounding tonics. (2–3)

Example 3.1. Schubert, Piano Sonata in B-flat Major, D. 960, i, mm. 216–59, excerpt from the recapitulation.

Example 3.1. (Continued)

Of this passage, Cohn concludes that the local keys are diatonically indeterminate in relation to the sonata movement's global tonic, B-flat major. Attempts to preserve the diatonic function of the global tonic causes the entire passage to stray either too far toward the flat side (C-double-flat major) when the tonic returns in measure 255 or too far toward the sharp side (A-sharp major) if working backward from measure 255 to the perfect authentic cadence in B-flat major in measure 233 (ex. 3.2). Cohn suggests that the relationships among harmonic regions may be rationalized instead as a series of semitone displacements among major and minor harmonies within a *Tonnetz* composed of four hexatonic cycles that are linked by perfect fifths (ic5).[4] F-sharp minor—a harmonic region that would otherwise be construed as remote to B-flat major from a diatonic perspective[5]—can be rationalized as B-flat major's hexatonic pole through three semitone shifts, in this case the parsimonious transformations P (parallel)–L (*Leittonwechsel*)–P (ex. 3.3).[6] By placing "at least some of Schubertian passages that provoke attributions of absoluteness, arbitrariness, or aimlessness into an

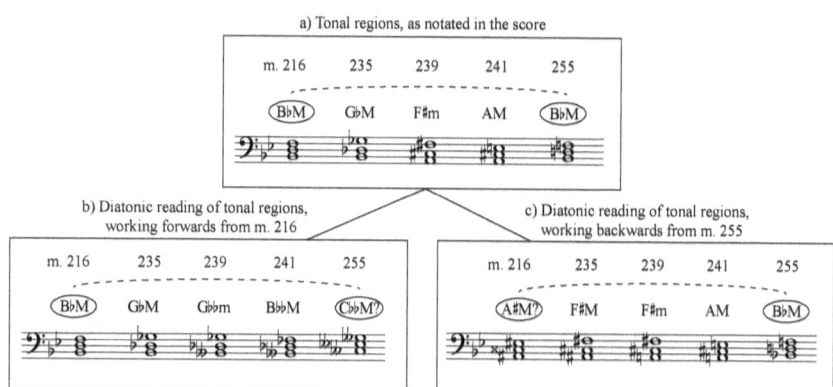

Example 3.2. Piano Sonata in B-flat Major, i, mm. 216–55, excerpt from the recapitulation, summary (after Cohn 2012, 2–8; see also Cohn 1999).

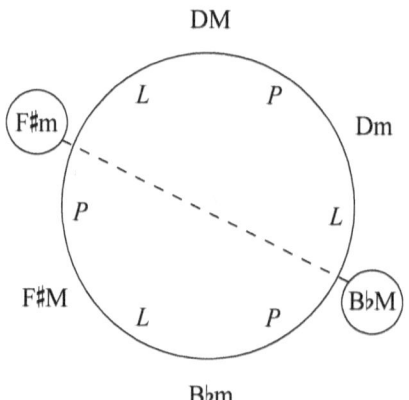

Example 3.3. Southern (tonic) hexatonic cycle, where F-sharp minor = B-flat major's hexatonic pole (after Cohn 1999; see also, Cohn 2012, 125–27).

alternative syntactic framework" (Cohn 1999, 214; 2012), the once diatonically indeterminate can become internally consistent.

As can be gleaned from Cohn's and other pan-triadic and neo-Riemannian perspectives, the alternative syntactic framework(s) within which Schubertian passages are reconceived entails a fundamental revision to tonal space.[7] Whereas under the rubric of diatonic theories, chromatic phenomena tend to be viewed either as altered versions of their diatonic counterparts or as tones derived from other diatonic scales, neo-Riemannian theory regards the twelve pitch classes of the chromatic scale as foundational to an equal-tempered *Tonnetz*. Pitch-based phenomena that seem diatonic or diatonic-like constitute a subset of this chromatic space.[8]

Neo-Riemannian perspectives also bring to the fore a critical distinction between two different types of enharmonicism. Following Gregory Proctor's "Technical Bases of Nineteenth-Century Chromatic Tonality: A Study in Chromaticism" (1978), these two types may be referred to as "enharmonic notational equivalence" (or "enharmonic equality") and "enharmonic tonal equivalence" (or "enharmonic equivalence") (131–39). In the case of enharmonic notational equivalence, the diatonic function of a note or chord can be preserved regardless of its enharmonic respelling. An example of this type of equivalence can be observed in Schubert's Impromptu in E-flat Major, D. 899, no. 2, where the notated key area of the large B section (mm. 83–154), B minor, serves as an enharmonic substitute for C-flat minor and can be construed as ♭VI♭ in relation to E-flat major, the initial home key (or mode) of the outer A sections. When enharmonic tonal equivalence is operative, respelled pitches are indeterminate to the prevailing diatonicism. Cohn's rendering of the harmonic relationships in the recapitulation from the first movement of Schubert's Piano Sonata in B-flat Major offers us one such example (see again, ex. 3.2). The ubiquity of this latter type of enharmonicism in musical works throughout the long nineteenth-century has especially called into question the utility of diatonic theories, lending further support to the idea that nineteenth-century music, including works by Schubert, warrant new music theories.

Rather than position diatonic and neo-Riemannian theories as rivals, some scholars have instead regarded them as complementary, demonstrating how one analytical perspective can illuminate another. Matthew Bribitzer-Stull (2006, 179–81), for example, has shown how a Schenkerian reading can help clarify the directionality of a progression within a hexatonic cycle—whether, for instance, motion to a hexatonic pole may be better conceived as PLP or LPL—and how a neo-Riemannian perspective can sharpen our understanding of chromatic-third progressions in a Schenkerian analysis. Steven Rings (2007) has similarly suggested viewing Schenkerian and neo-Riemannian theory, as well as related transformational perspectives, not "through competition but through *dialogue*," because the latter "explores a *different set of relationships*" (43–45, italics in original).

Notwithstanding these and other discussions that aim to clarify the distinctions between each theoretical purview and respective strengths,[9] music theory scholarship as a whole has only begun to explore how neo-Riemannian theory, in comparison to diatonic theories, can affect our aesthetic experience of a musical work. Two writings that have helped launch this introspection are the exchange between Charles Fisk and Cohn (2000) in *19th-Century Music*'s "Comment and Chronicle" (prompted by Cohn's [1999] earlier analysis of the first movement from Schubert's Piano Sonata in B-flat Major, which was published in the same journal) and Rings's essay, "Riemannian Analytical Values, Paleo- and Neo-" in *The Oxford Handbook of Neo-Riemannian Music Theories* (2011). Both writings ask whether neo-Riemannian theory, in its efforts to outline a new kind of musical coherence, normalizes harmonic progressions that would otherwise be perceived as marked under some form of diatonicism.[10] Fisk, for instance writes: "For some readers, his [Cohn's] model may have the effect of making even the most extraordinary progressions in Schubert seem ordinary—or at least, in some respects, normative" (Fisk and Cohn 2000, 301). Rings (2011a), in his comparison of neo-Riemannian theory to Riemann's tonal theories, appears to adopt a similar position as Fisk when he suggests that neo-Riemannian analyses "dwell on the most remarkable sounding passages in a chromatic work" yet primarily remain invested in unearthing certain forms of coherence in these passages: "Despite some obvious differences in philosophical underpinnings, both projects are underwritten by a drive toward systemization and local rigor; a penchant for elegant, symmetrical theoretical structures; and a desire above all to detect *order* in complex music, containing harmonic extravagances in controlled, rational spaces. These values, it would appear, are pan-Riemannian" (499). As Suzannah Clark relatedly points out in *Analyzing Schubert* (2011a), one issue at stake in the exchange between Fisk and Cohn are the hermeneutic windows or "openings" that emerge as a consequence of the principles that govern each system.[11] When Fisk expresses some misgivings about "the phenomenological salience of [Cohn's] analytic observations," his concerns appear to extend not only to the erasure of the semantic distinction between the two enharmonically related triads, G-flat major and F-sharp minor, that contribute to the movement's "tonal tension or drama" in Schubert's Piano Sonata in B-flat Major but also to the revision of what counts as a close key relation—criteria that make possible a hermeneutic narrative about inclusion and banishment (Fisk and Cohn 2000, 302).[12] Acknowledging that "Fisk's criticism is hard to dismiss," Rings (2011a) demonstrates how one might recover the "sonic effect" of Schubert's extraordinary progressions through Riemann's functions, here conceived as "actions that listeners perform as they interpret sounding harmonies with respect to the tonal center" (500). These efforts to devise a halfway point between neo-Riemannian and Riemann's theories notwithstanding, Rings ultimately concludes that such representations of musical experience may be restrictive, if not overdetermined. As he additionally posits, "No formal model can capture all aspects of our musical experience, even when we limit ourselves to one parameter, such as harmony" (506).

If after having examined scholarship's collective approaches to understanding Schubert's harmonic practices we conclude that the relationships among pitch phenomena can be rearranged but never fully determined or resolved, we might turn our attention instead toward exploring how indeterminacy can affect our aesthetic musical experience of chromatic passages.[13] Such a change in focus would not entail disavowing the myriad insights that neo-Riemannian and other transformational theories bring to our understanding of chromatic progressions that employ enharmonic tonal equivalence or refuting the forms of coherence that these theories promote. Indeed, transformational perspectives have played an imperative role in reassessing Schubert's musical reception history; neo-Riemannian and pan-triadic theories not only encourage us to reconsider how our syntactic frameworks can affect aesthetic judgments of Schubert's harmonic practices but also invite us, by way of extension, to further contemplate how such judgments may be influenced by a preference for certain kinds of musical coherence. A change in focus would instead involve reappraising the value of indeterminacy within the realm of a guided diatonicism, in an attempt to directly engage with the unwieldy aspects of Schubert's harmonic progressions that neo-Riemannian perspectives can astutely order—to, as Rings (2011a) puts it, "relish that unruly part of musical experience that resists formal containment" (506). Put succinctly, then: If among neo-Riemannian perspectives, determinacy has functioned as a catalyst for rethinking chord proximity when enharmonic tonal equivalence is present, what consequences would arise if we embraced indeterminacy in our odysseys through Schubert's harmonic fields? What listening acts would such a perspective invite us to perform, and how might this perspective affect our conception of a work's tonal structure?

In contemplating these questions in this chapter, the following discussion attempts to show how the peculiarities that arise from diatonic indeterminacy can facilitate a different kind of aesthetic experience—one that invites a play between synchronic and diatonic perceptions of musical structure. To begin exploring this alternative perspective, I first revisit Donald Francis Tovey's ([1928] 1949) "Tonality" article, which reflects on the role that musical form can play in our hearing of musical passages (in this case, an excerpt from the finale of Schubert's Piano Sonata in G Major, D. 894) that cross an enharmonic seam. I then return to the opening movement of Schubert's Piano Sonata in B-flat Major, a work that has received much attention in a number of writings that similarly contemplate the music's pull between the diatonic and chromatic.[14] The discussion will focus on two passages: the exposition's first eighty measures and the excerpt from the recapitulation discussed at the beginning of this chapter. Both passages sound a similar group of harmonic regions amid the same enharmonic juncture, G-flat major and F-sharp minor, but within a different formal context. As I suggest, the formal context can affect our perception of the relationships between harmonic regions, first by encouraging us to hear adjacent harmonic regions as either more closely related or remote, regardless of their proximity to the global tonic, and second, by correcting the tonal drift to the apparent double-flat side of the harmonic spectrum. The chapter concludes by reexamining the value of diatonic indeterminacy when it comes to engaging with harmonic phenomena that seem perplexing or strange, and by discussing the implications that this alternative perspective, or subject position, may have for music analysis.

Case Study 1: Schubert's Piano Sonata in G Major, D. 894, mm. 124–70

The notion that diatonic indeterminacy can impinge on the tonal unity of a musical work that crosses an enharmonic seam raises the following two questions: If an enharmonic shift causes a musical passage to seemingly drift to the double sharp or flat side of the harmonic spectrum within a diatonic universe, how might we be able to aurally recognize when the home key, or global tonic, returns? Furthermore, how might we hear the relationships among harmonic regions during longer stretches of music, particularly in cases where the home key recedes from our aural memory? To begin to respond to these two questions, let us turn to Tovey's ([1928] 1949) "Tonality" article, which, in addition to proposing a rationale for Schubert's key relations,[15] explores the extent to which the musical form of a work can affect our hearing and comprehension of passages that cross an enharmonic seam. His comments will prove to be in instructive when it comes to contemplating (1) when neo-Riemannian and diatonic listening perspectives may converge and when they might depart, (2) the indeterminate harmonic relationships in the two passages from Schubert's Piano Sonata in B-flat Major, and (3) the value that diatonic indeterminacy can bring to our hearing of these passages.

Example 3.4. Tovey, "Ex. 21." From "Tonality," *Music and Letters* 9:341–63. Reprinted as "On Tonality in Schubert," in *Essays and Lectures on Music*, 134–59. London: Oxford University Press.

Toward the end of his article, Tovey ([1928] 1949) discusses one of several hypothetical divisions of harmonic space, the circle of fifths. As he notes, the two halves of the circle marked by the axis (or "date-line") that cuts across the tritone pairs C–G-flat and F-sharp–C are conjoined by "temperaments, equal or unequal ... [that] distribute their defective intonations to the best of their ability" (ex. 3.4). Yet within the context of a tonal work, the ability to aurally recognize that one has orbited an enharmonic space that is divided into equal parts depends on the way in which the harmonic return is positioned within the musical form: "But the actual curvature of harmonic space is local, and depends on musical forms as the curvature of Einstein's time-space depends on the presence of gravitating matter. Editorial time-space and the occasion compel me to hurl this dogmatically at the reader. I will only point out that there are several other enharmonic circles between the short-circuit of Ex. 21 [ex. 3.4] and the whole circle of 5ths; and will again remind the reader that no master of tonality expects a key to be recognized merely by pitch when it returns after intervening modulations" (154–55). To illustrate his point, Tovey refers to a passage from the last movement of Schubert's Piano Sonata in G Major, D. 894. The excerpt, shown in example 3.5, occurs during the second refrain of the rondo form and features a sequence of tonicizations related by major thirds (expressed as ascending minor sixths) that begins and ends in the home key, G major. Tovey explains that we have remained in the home key since the return of the refrain (m. 124), and that the return of the G major theme within this refrain (m. 168) enables us to aurally conclude that the preceding sequence ended in G major, as opposed to A-double-flat major:

> If Schubert (or Brahms) goes round an enharmonic circle of thirds in this fashion, the reason why we know that Schubert has returned to G and not arrived at A double flat is not because the pianoforte expresses no difference, but because this passage did originally remain in G with no modulations at all, and because it here also returns to the opening theme as usual. If it could be heard in just intonation, the most delicate ear would hardly detect the minute difference in pitch between the G major of the original theme and the A double flat of its return here; and if the ear did note the difference, the inference would not be, "we are now in the vastly remote key of A♭♭," but "the pitch is beginning to shift." (155)

Here Tovey's imagined retuning of the passage from tempered thirds to the pure thirds of just intonation aims to emphasize the codependency between musical form and the identity of the harmonic regions. Were we to hear the passage in just intonation, the division of harmonic space by three major thirds (where each major third is equivalent to the ratio 5/4) that begins on the G major 6/4 chord (m. 154) would be approximately forty-one cents shy of an octave (i.e., ~1159 cents vs. 1200 cents, if an octave = 2/1), or about a quarter tone away

Example 3.5. Schubert, Piano Sonata in G Major, D. 894, iv, mm. 123–70 (after Tovey [1928] 1949, 155).

from its orbital "return" when the progression reaches the G major 6/4 chord an octave higher (m. 160). The return of the opening rondo theme, which had initially sounded in the key of G major, would rectify the tonal drift to the apparent double-flat side of harmonic space (A-double-flat major), informing the ear that the progression leads us back to G major despite the G/A-double-flat gap (ex. 3.6). For Tovey, then, the perceptual rendering of the identity of the harmonic regions within an enharmonic space is dependent on musical form.

Tovey employs roman numerals to describe the harmonic relationships in this sequence, though we could also construe these relationships as three consecutive

Example 3.5. (Continued)

PL transformations (ex. 3.7). Both perspectives aurally promote a return to G major, as opposed to A-double-flat major, yet arrive at this conclusion differently. Tovey's proposed hearing relies on the way in which the progression is situated within the form; the specific location of the chromatic sequence within the formal process confirms the orbital departure and return to the tonic, regardless of the implied enharmonic shift. Comparatively, in the neo-Riemannian hearing, the return to G major can solely arise as a consequence of conceiving the passage as a

The Value of Diatonic Indeterminacy

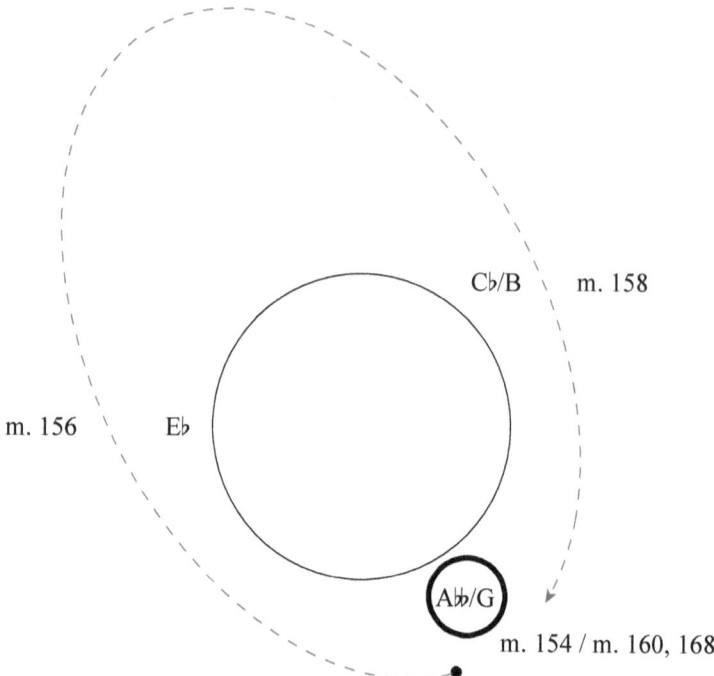

Example 3.6. Piano Sonata in G Major, D. 894, iv, mm. 154–68. "Modulations" mapped onto an enharmonic circle of thirds.

series of PL transformations within an equal-tempered *Tonnetz*, a view that offers an eloquent solution to the enharmonic exchange required between A-double-flat and G in the diatonic perspective.[16] Although we may aurally observe a connection between the PL transformations and the formal grouping structure of these measures in the refrain, the identity of the harmonic regions (or modulations, as per Tovey) can be perceived independently of their location in the musical form.

Certainly we could question the extent to which the integrity of the harmonic function of the G major triad in this brief passage from Schubert's Piano Sonata in G Major is imperiled by the sequence of chromatic thirds, given the brevity of the progression and the possibility of aurally retaining the home key throughout the refrain. Furthermore, from an alternative diatonic perspective, the harmonies within the sequential passage may be construed as nonfunctional within a prolongation of the dominant harmony, D major. Yet if we were to consider Tovey's position within the context of a larger musical work, where both the establishment of the home key and subsequent double return of the main theme and home key can be temporally separated by intervening modulations, we might conclude that such double returns would be imperative to aurally "resetting" the home key, especially if the harmonic progressions between the home key and double

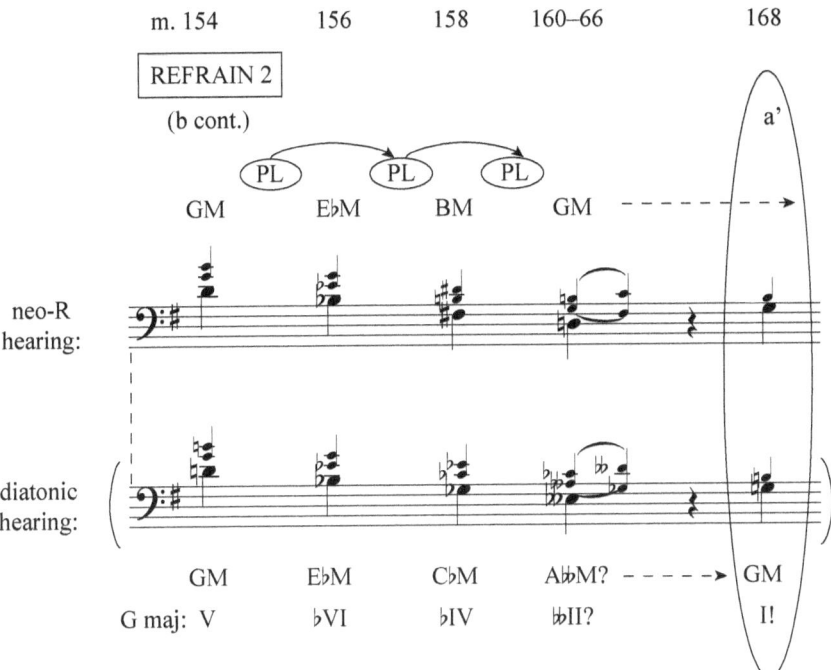

Example 3.7. Piano Sonata in G Major, D. 894, iv, mm. 154–68. Comparison between a neo-Riemannian and diatonic hearing.

return lead us across one or more enharmonic seams. With regard to Tovey's perspective, we could relatedly ask how we might aurally make sense of a series of harmonic regions that involve an enharmonic juncture amid longer stretches of music, where the expectation of a double return seems far off in the distance, such as when we approach the beginning of a subordinate theme group or development section. If Tovey's argument can be shown to be relevant to both scenarios, his position could offer an additional response to the diatonic indeterminacy that Cohn identifies in the recapitulation from Schubert's Piano Sonata in B-flat Major, as well as provide a springboard for contemplating how we might perceive the harmonic relationships in the exposition.

Complicating this picture, however, is the notion that Schubert's musical forms in his longer instrumental works may be read differently, a point that can readily be observed in contemporary readings of the first movement from his Piano Sonata in B-flat Major.[17] Opening sonata form movements such as this one not only invite multiple interpretations; they also call into question the very criteria used to identify key markers of sonata form archetypes, a point that will be explored in more depth in chapter 4. Such form-defining criteria include the identification of and boundary points between interthematic (e.g., transition and subordinate

The Value of Diatonic Indeterminacy 65

theme) and intrathematic functions (e.g., basic idea and continuation), for which Schubert's instrumental music can appear to resist. If harmonic function and form are codependent, as Tovey suggests, we might take into account in our current exploration of diatonic indeterminacy, then, the impact that formal ambiguities and retrospective hearings can have on our perception of harmonic function and the relationships among harmonic regions. Since the exposition from Schubert's Sonata in B-flat Major precedes the excerpt from the recapitulation previously discussed, let us revisit this passage first. Doing so not only helps illuminate Schubert's resetting of the tonal plan in the recapitulation's first forty measures—and consequently offers a complementary view to both Cohn's and Tovey's points—but also elucidates Tovey's position within the context of a much more complex musical setting.

Case Study 2: Piano Sonata in B-flat Major, D. 960, i, mm. 1–80

The exposition from Schubert's Sonata in B-flat Major traverses a similar group of harmonic regions amid the same G-flat major/F-sharp minor enharmonic juncture as the first forty measures of the recapitulation, concluding in F major instead of B-flat major (ex. 3.8). With Tovey's view of harmonic space in mind, how

i) harmonic regions in the exposition

m. 1	20	48	58	80
B♭M	G♭M	F♯m	AM	FM

ii) harmonic regions in the recapitulation

m. 216	235	239	241	255
B♭M	G♭M	F♯m	AM	B♭M

Example 3.8. Piano Sonata in B-flat Major, i, mm. 1–80 and 216–55. Comparison of harmonic regions.

might our perceptions of the formal context affect the way we hear the relationships among harmonic regions as they unfold in the exposition, and how might repeating the exposition alter our interpretation of these relationships?

To begin, the exposition appears to open with an expanded compound period that establishes the home key, B-flat major, with two cadences: a half cadence at the end of the compound antecedent (m. 7) and a perfect authentic cadence (PAC) at the end of the compound consequent (m. 18) (ex. 3.9).[18] The formal and cadential closure of this compound period in tandem with the departure from the home key toward the lowered major submediant, G-flat major (m. 20), may at first suggest that a transition is underway. The common-tone transformation of the initial tonic, from ^1 during the anacrusis (m. 19) to ^3 on the downbeat arrival of G-flat major (m. 20), gently leads the ear toward the harmonic region of the lowered major flat submediant, where a variant of the melody from the main theme begins to unfold; the parallel sixths between the melody and "tenor" voice from the main theme (mm. 1–2) invert to parallel tenths in G-flat major (mm. 20–21), bringing the initial tenor melody into focus while relegating the initial melody to an accompanying role. Especially remarkable of the latter passage is that the transposition of the invertible counterpoint at the octave a major third lower (from B-flat major to G-flat major) facilitates an aural connection between the main theme and its varied repetition. Throughout most of this G-flat major passage (mm. 20–35), the melodic motion amid the rustling of sixteenth notes creates the illusion of a harmonic progression in G-flat major, yet the persistent bass pedal on G-flat hampers cadential confirmation in this subordinate harmonic region; the gradual rhythmic augmentation of the G-flat bass pedal tone (from quarter notes to a tied whole note; mm. 26–33) against the rhythmic augmentation of the upper voice (from quarter notes to sixteenth notes) only further intensifies the pedal point. In a startling move, the leading tone (F) descends a semitone just as the low G-flat bass reenters (mm. 33–34), upending the stability of the G-flat major harmony that has dominated the entire transition thus far and narrowing the possible places where the progression might proceed— either further away from the home key to the Neapolitan (C-flat major; ♭II in relation to B-flat major), if the descending semitone motion connotes a move from F to F-flat, or a return to the home key by way of an augmented sixth chord, if the semitone motion leads us from F to E-natural. Heightening the suspense of this harmonic uncertainty are the repeated G-flats in the bass and gradual thickening of the musical texture amid a crescendo that permits the music to sound its loudest volume thus far. The dissonant chord resolves as an augmented sixth (m. 35.4), ushering in a surprising return of both the home key and the opening theme's compound consequent phrase, now at a *forte* dynamic. This striking double return may suggest a retrospective hearing of the exposition's

Example 3.9. Piano Sonata in B-flat Major, i, mm. 1–83.

interthematic functions, whose regrouping will affect the proportions of the movement's remaining interthematic functions. The main theme, which initially suggested an eighteen-bar compound period, appears to transform into a small ternary theme a-b-a', whereby the preceding transition (m. 20ff) becomes the b section. In an effort to revive the exposition's dramatic motion away from

Example 3.9. (Continued)

the home key, closure in B-flat major is averted near the end of the a' section by a startling deflected cadence that plunges us into F-sharp minor (mm. 45–48), which may sound like the lowered minor submediant, G-flat minor.[19] This surprising harmonic swerve can invite a second retrospective hearing of the form, where the a' section of the small ternary theme (mm. 36–48) becomes the transition that steers us toward the subordinate theme group.[20]

In light of the exposition's apparent move away from both the main theme and home key (m. 20), why might the compound consequent phrase return (m.

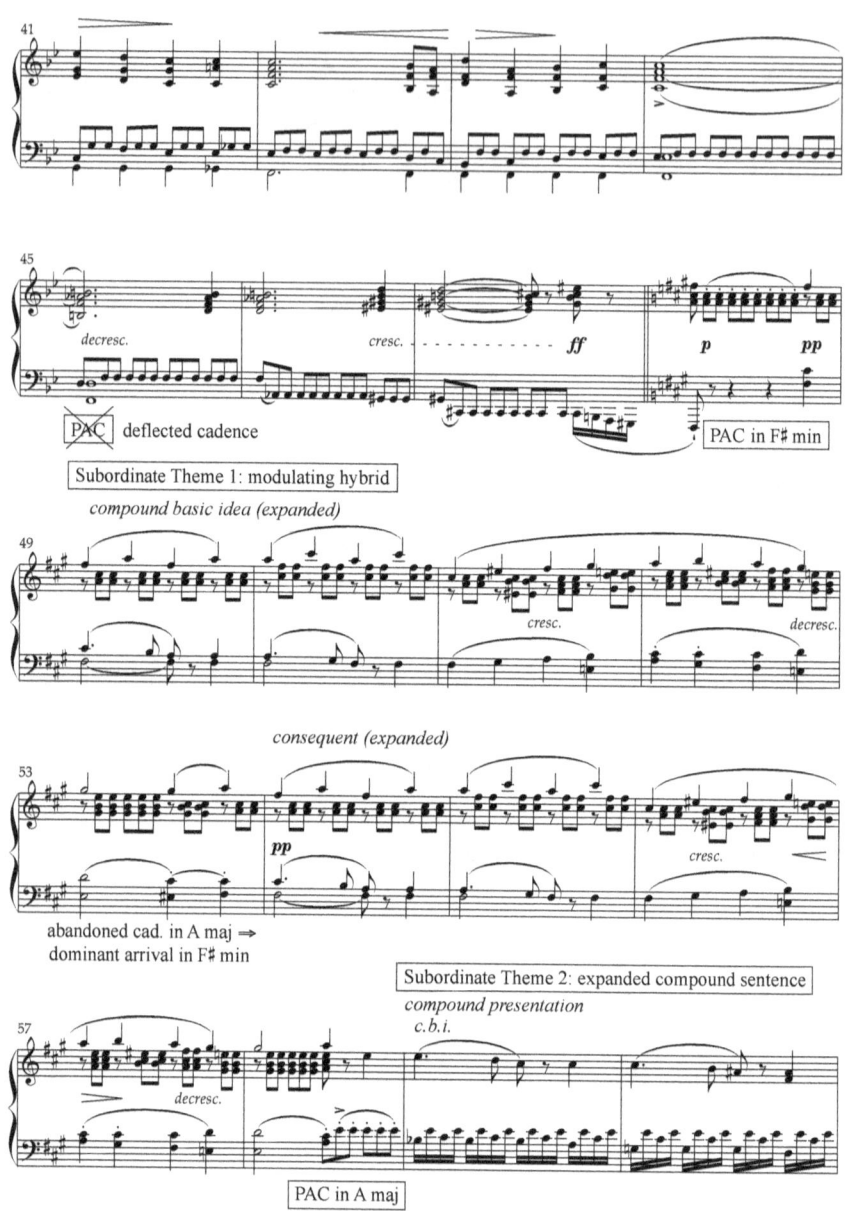

Example 3.9. (Continued)

36)? Had both lowered submediants, G-flat major and F-sharp minor, sounded contiguously, F-sharp minor may have been perceived as a mere modal shift (ex. 3.10). The double return can conceal this modal connection by encouraging the ear to calibrate the distance to F-sharp minor from the home key instead, which is aurally verified by the thematic return of the compound consequent

Example 3.9. (Continued)

phrase. Approaching each lowered submediant from the home key therefore makes it possible to promote the second of the two submediants, F-sharp minor—which initiates the shift toward the apparent double-flat side of the harmonic spectrum—as more distant than G-flat major.[21] The contrast between these two versions of the lowered submediant appears to be further emphasized by modulatory technique and by a retrospective hearing of the formal grouping structure. Both the common-tone modulation that eases us into G-flat major (see again, ex. 3.9, mm. 19–20) and the related thematic design between the small ternary's

The Value of Diatonic Indeterminacy 71

Example 3.9. (Continued)

b and outer a sections aurally emphasize the close relationship between B-flat major and G-flat major. Comparatively, the deflected cadence that dramatically casts us into F-sharp minor before the onset of the first subordinate theme (mm. 45–48), which lies on the edge of the ternary theme group, can persuade us to hear F-sharp minor as more distant from B-flat major.

So far in our journey from the main theme to the beginning of the first subordinate theme, we have oscillated between the home key, B-flat major, and each version of the lowered submediant, G-flat major and F-sharp minor. How might the formal context within which the remaining harmonic regions unfold affect our hearing of F major, the exposition's harmonic goal? The first subordinate theme (mm. 49–58) seems to open with an expanded five-bar compound basic idea (c.b.i.) (mm. 49–53) that begins to lean toward A major near the end of the phrase. At first, it may seem as though the harmonic progression will conclude with a PAC in A major, a cadence that would cause the entire theme to close too early. As the bass surprisingly ascends from E to E-sharp before returning to the F-sharp pickup that begins the next phrase (m. 53), closure in A major is abandoned. That this opening phrase ends on beat three of the measure with

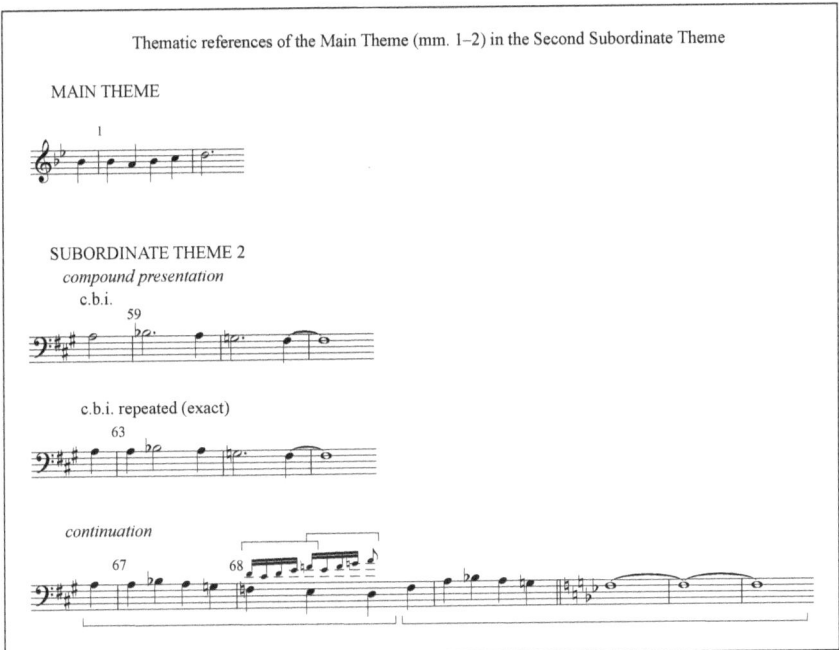

Example 3.9. (Continued)

the arrival on E-sharp in the bass may invite an alternative hearing to the abandoned cadence reading, one where the five-bar phrase ends with a dominant arrival (V6/5) in F-sharp minor. Complicating this latter hearing is the slur between G-sharp and A in the upper voice countermelody, which bridges the phrase boundary.[22] Following this opening five-bar compound basic idea is a five-bar consequent phrase (mm. 54–58), which reaches the A major cadential goal (m. 58). Altogether, the first subordinate theme may appear to unfold as a ten-bar modulating hybrid theme that leads us from F-sharp minor to A major.

A recomposition of the passage as an eight-bar modulating hybrid theme (c.b.i. + consequent) can further emphasize the theme's loose-knit construction and, more importantly, the significance of the gravitational pull toward A major near the end of the first phrase boundary (ex. 3.11). Although the pull toward A major was introduced earlier in the phrase (ex. 3.9, mm. 51.4–52.1), the second pull near the phrase's conclusion (mm. 52.4–53.2) lends greater emphasis to the PAC in this subordinate key at end of the consequent phrase. In this first subordinate theme, then, the anticipated closure in A major helps distribute the tonal "weight" between F-sharp minor and A major more evenly, offering the ear a chance to gradually acclimate to A major.

The second subordinate theme (mm. 59–80) presents a variant of the thematic material from the first subordinate theme in the upper voice and modulates

The Value of Diatonic Indeterminacy 73

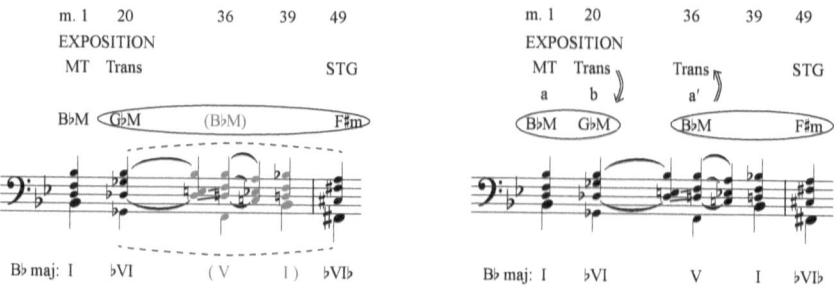

Example 3.10. Piano Sonata in B-flat Major, i, mm. 1–49. F-sharp minor calibrated from G-flat major (m. 20) versus F-sharp minor calibrated from B-flat major (m. 36).

Example 3.11. Piano Sonata in B-flat Major, i. Recomposition of the first subordinate theme, mm. 49–58.

from A major to F major. Form-wise, this theme might be heard as an expanded compound sentence that begins with a compound presentation (c.b.i. + c.b.i.; mm. 59–66), proceeds to a continuation (mm. 67–73), and ends with a cadential function (mm. 74–80). Within the compound presentation, both compound basic ideas augment the counterpoint between the tenor melody and bass in the first subordinate theme's two phrases by raising the last tone in the second of the two third descents (here, from A-natural to A-sharp) and by decorating the initial bass pitch (A) with an upper-neighbor note before descending to F-sharp—small but consequential changes that facilitate two B minor tonicizations (mm. 60–62 and 64–66). As the appendage to example 3.9 shows ("Thematic references of the Main Theme [mm. 1–2] in the Second Subordinate Theme"), the bass appears to initiate the first of four melodic inversions of the main theme. The last two melodic inversions (A–A–B-flat–A–G-natural–F) restore the diatonic intervals of the main theme.[23] The melody in the first fragmentation of the continuation (mm. 67–68) repeats the second subordinate theme's opening descending third (E–D–C-sharp), though stops short of completing the second descending third (C-sharp–B–A-sharp) by pivoting on C-sharp, which becomes the leading tone of a D minor tonicization. During the second fragmentation (now extended; mm. 69–72), the melody and bass begin to repeat the same counterpoint as the first fragmentation, landing on the harmonic sixth, D–F, albeit now with a more open voicing (cf. m. 68.1 to m. 70.1). Schubert alters the melodic design once more, extending the melody one half step beyond the threshold of the previous high A to the high B-flat. The high B-flat confirms that the harmonic sixth has been "reset" (m. 70), sounding now within the context of a B-flat major tonicization as opposed to the previous D minor tonicization. To mark this unexpected turn to the B-flat major region, Schubert sets the melodic line in octaves, pushing the boundary of the exposition's ambitus to a more extreme range (recalling, perhaps, the low register introduced by the opening trill, mm. 8–9). Similar to the melodic design of the two compound basic ideas that opened the second subordinate theme, the last tone in the melodic descent in this second fragmentation passage is raised (from B-flat to B-natural; m. 72). The tone's resolution to C (m. 74) helps initiate the cadential progression that will lead us from the B-flat major tonicization to a PAC arrival in F major (m. 80).

Unlike the first return of the B-flat major harmonic region (mm. 36–44), the second return (mm. 70–71) is not accompanied by a full or partial restatement of the main theme. Although the pitch-class identity of the B-flat major region resembles that of the home key, and the two preceding melodic turns (D–C-sharp–D–E–F and F–E–F–G–A, m. 68) may recall the main theme (B-flat–A–B-flat–C–D), both the tonal and formal environment that this B-flat major region is situated might render the region as a *Fremdling*, or a "strange tonic illusion" (Burstein 2002) instead. Moreover, if after crossing the G-flat major/F-sharp minor enharmonic seam we preserve the diatonic function of the remaining harmonic regions, the B-flat major tonicization at this moment in the exposition would appear to connote C-double-flat, a point that will be further unpacked with respect to the tonal drift among the exposition's harmonic regions.

Within the subordinate theme's expanded compound sentence, then, are three tonicizations that gradually transport us from an A major tonality to an F major one, with A minor serving as a portal between the two harmonic regions: (1) a B minor tonicization during each compound basic idea (mm. 61 and 65); (2) a D minor tonicization during the continuation's first fragmentation (m. 68); and (3) a B-flat major tonicization during the continuation's second fragmentation (mm. 70–71). As example 3.12 illustrates, the PAC in A major at the end of the first subordinate theme (m. 58), which was rhetorically emphasized by the preceding abandoned cadence/dominant arrival at the end of the compound basic idea (m. 53), can function as a magnetic field for which the three subsequent tonicizations in the second subordinate theme gravitate. Along the lines suggested by Clark (2011a, 2011b), in this passage we might hear the harmonies "turn" on two notes, C-sharp and D, where in a modally mixed A major/minor tonality, B minor could be heard as the minor II-chord, D minor as the minor IV-chord, and B-flat major as the major ♭II-chord. The last of these two tonicizations, D minor and B-flat major, help prepare the ear for the forthcoming modulation to F major, as both are diatonic to F major. The order in which Schubert introduces the three tonicizations after the PAC in A major seems imperative to tilting the tonal hierarchy from A major/minor to F major—the crucial swap occurring between B minor (the first tonicization) and B-flat major (the third tonicization). D minor (the second tonicization) straddles the two outer tonicizations, belonging to both A minor (or A major via mixture, to refer to Tovey's discussion of Schubert's key relations in the "Tonality" article) and F major.

Example 3.13 offers a synchronic perspective of the exposition's central harmonic regions, summarizing how they might be aurally construed as lowered submediant relations that are connected by one relative-major motion. B-flat major to G-flat major may be heard as a motion from I to ♭VI, B-flat major to F-sharp minor as I to ♭VI♭, F-sharp minor to A major as I to III (or motion to the relative major), and A major to F major as I to ♭VI. Although not previously discussed, the move from F major to C-sharp minor near the beginning of the development section (mm. 116–17) may similarly be heard as a motion from I to ♭VI♭. With respect to the choice of mode for the lowered submediant relationships, motion to a lowered minor submediant (B-flat major–F-sharp minor and F major–C-sharp minor) helps emphasize the formal division between the main

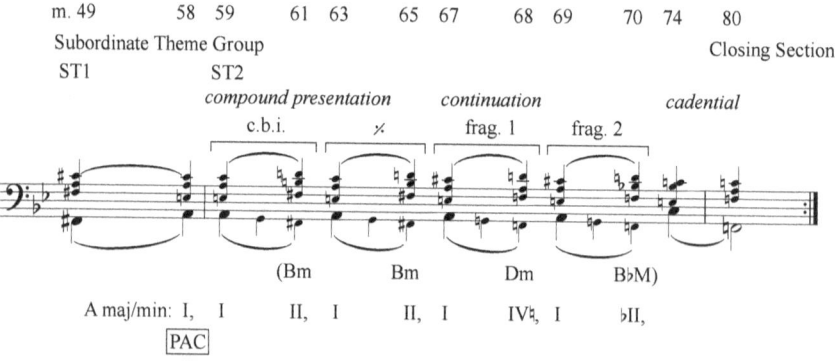

Example 3.12. Piano Sonata in B-flat Major, i, mm. 49–80, subordinate theme group.

theme and subordinate theme group and, later, the exposition and development sections. In comparison, motion to a lowered major submediant (B-flat major–G-flat major and A major–F major) helps articulate the sections within these larger divisions—between the a and b sections of the main theme's small ternary design and between the second subordinate theme and the closing section. In terms of each lowered submediant's signifying potential, motion from a major tonic to its lowered minor submediant has been linked to passages that astonish or invoke uneasiness—expressions that may be associated with the uncanny.[24] As both motions to the lowered minor submediant in the B-flat major sonata also involve a move toward the sharp, or dominant, side of an enharmonic tonal space, such motions, as Scott Burnham (2013) summarizes, "involve an increase of tension and a sense of moving out of that key" (103). Comparatively, motion from a major tonic to its lowered major submediant might be associated with Tovey's "purple patches," which, to return to Burnham's (2013) observations, "are deeply colored, richly expressive passages ... [that] almost always involve a move into tonal regions on the flat side of the prevailing key center, the subdominant side" (103). Cohn's observations about the number of common tones between each pair of consonant triads seem especially relevant here; a motion to the lowered minor submediant may sound discordant, because the progression does not retain any common tones.[25]

To summarize our discussion up to this point, the proposed hearing of the first eighty measures of the exposition has focused on exploring the ways in which the unfolding of formal and tonal processes amid an unbound musical context can both shape and reshape our perception of the passage's grouping structures and harmonic relationships. The analysis has also attempted to make a case for how the PACs in B-flat major (m. 18), F-sharp minor (m. 48), A major (m. 58), and F major (m. 80) can each function as a base or "shore" for which to aurally perceive the distance between

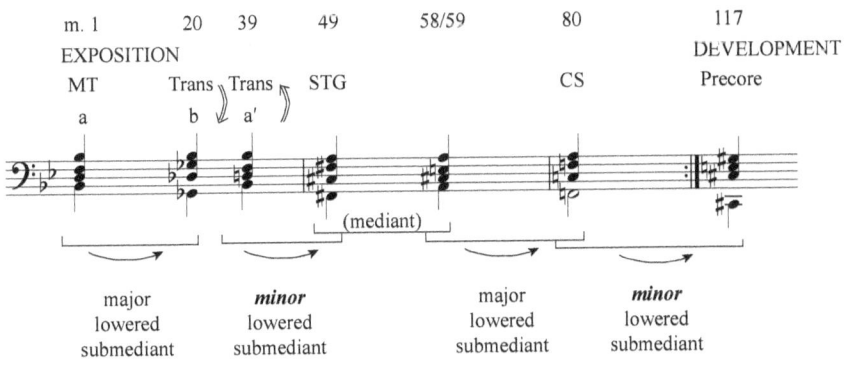

Example 3.13. Piano Sonata in B-flat Major, i. mm. 1–117. Synopsis of lowered submediant relationships.

The Value of Diatonic Indeterminacy 77

adjacent key areas and local tonicizations. Such a perspective resonates with Tovey's ([1928] 1949) primary thesis, that "the most fundamental rule for operations in large-scale tonality is that key-relation is a function of form" (145).

That the exposition's harmonic regions resemble those traversed in the excerpt from the recapitulation discussed at the opening of this chapter may raise a similar question regarding diatonic indeterminacy. Similar to Cohn's reading of the harmonic regions in the first forty measures of the recapitulation, a diatonic reading of the harmonic regions in the exposition would hypothetically lead us far astray from the home key to the unruly and inhospitable terrain of G-double-flat major, as shown in the lower staff of example 3.14 (a suggested neo-Riemannian hearing appears in the upper staff). If we imagine traversing the four harmonic regions that achieve cadential closure (B-flat major, F-sharp [G-flat] minor, A major, and F major) within a circle-of-fifths harmonic space (ex. 3.15), it would appear as though Schubert has taken us around the *longer* path to our final destination, G-double-flat (F) major, as opposed to moving counterclockwise by one fifth. That Schubert's exposition traverses this longer path may help explain why the proportions within the exposition are much greater compared to late eighteenth-century sonata form expositions: such an arduous path across an enharmonic seam would

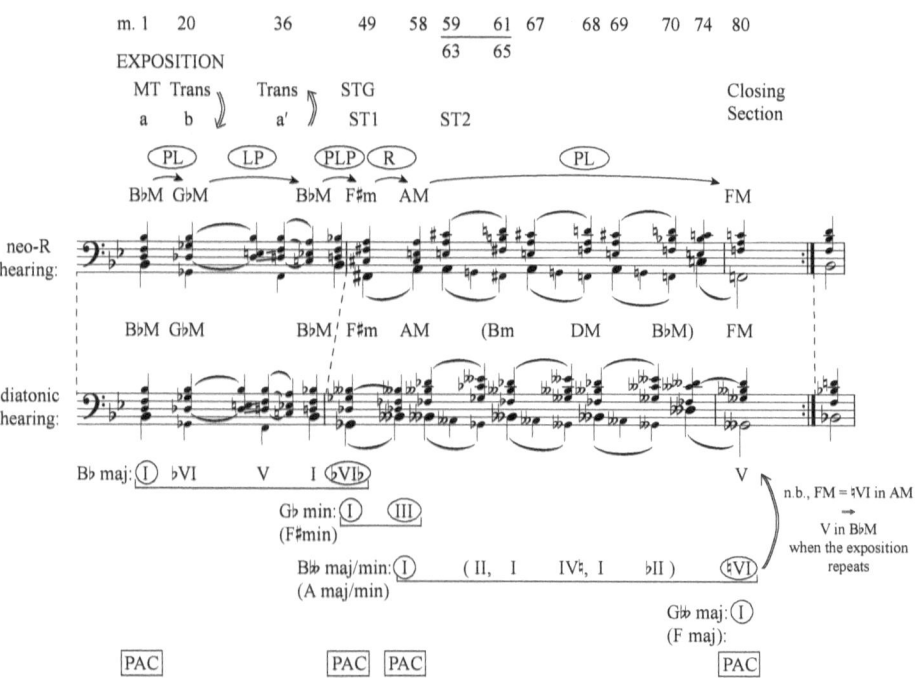

Example 3.14. Piano Sonata in B-flat Major, i. mm. 1–80. Summary.

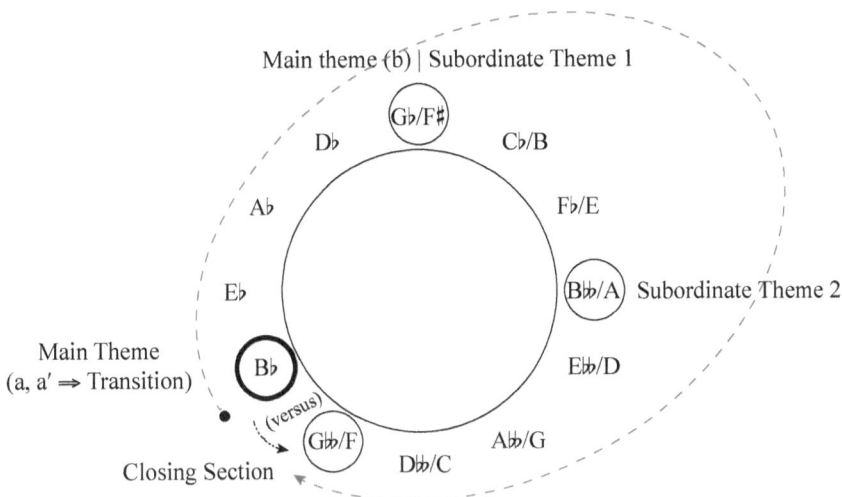

Example 3.15. Piano Sonata in B-flat Major, i. mm. 1–80. Key-relations mapped onto a circle of fifths space.

appear to require greater effort to circumvent, as well as time for the ear to adjust to each shift in the tonal hierarchy as the music approaches each destination within the harmonic space.[26] If we are persuaded by Tovey's position regarding the codependency between harmonic space and form, the onset of the exposition's repeat, or double return of the home key and main theme, would not only serve as a corrective to this apparent tonal drift to the double-flat side of harmonic space—yielding a complete orbital period from the home key—but also help confirm to the ear, retrospectively, that it indeed had traveled to the key of the dominant through an enharmonic juncture.[27] Once this connection has been revealed, the exposition's repeat would invite us to reconfigure our initial conception of the relationships among harmonic regions that unfolded during our first hearing, enabling the possibility for the diatonically indeterminate to become consistent.

Case Study 3: Piano Sonata in B-flat Major, D. 960, i, mm. 216–55

The suggestion that formal ambiguity and cadences in the exposition may not only influence how we group together tonal regions on the local level but also affect our interpretation of them becomes more pronounced when we compare the exposition to the first forty measures of the sonata form's recapitulation. If the recapitulation's main theme (mm. 216–33) and transition, which we might now readily interpret as the b section of a small ternary theme (mm. 235–54), travel through some of the same harmonic regions as those in the exposition (see again, ex. 3.8), how might the change in formal context affect our hearing of these regions?

After the main theme closes (see again, ex. 3.1, mm. 216–33), the anacrusis (m. 234) leads us away from the home key to G-flat major with the same common-tone modulation that was introduced in the exposition (mm. 19–20). The return of the entire G-flat major passage, however, is diverted when the opening four measures (mm. 235–38) are reset in F-sharp (G-double-flat) minor (mm. 239–42). That G-flat major and F-sharp minor sound the same thematic material in such proximity can help unveil their covert relationship in the exposition and draw our attention to the enharmonic juncture that initiated the tonal drift away from the home key. After the modal shift to F-sharp minor, we are similarly led to the relative major, A (B-double-flat) major, albeit now within the time span of the main theme's b section, as opposed to the exposition's first subordinate theme (ex. 3.9, mm. 49–58). When the leading tone of A major, G-sharp, descends a half step to G-natural in the upper voice (m. 253), perhaps we might expect that the A major chord with the added dissonance will similarly function as an augmented sixth chord (m. 34) and usher in a return of the main theme's

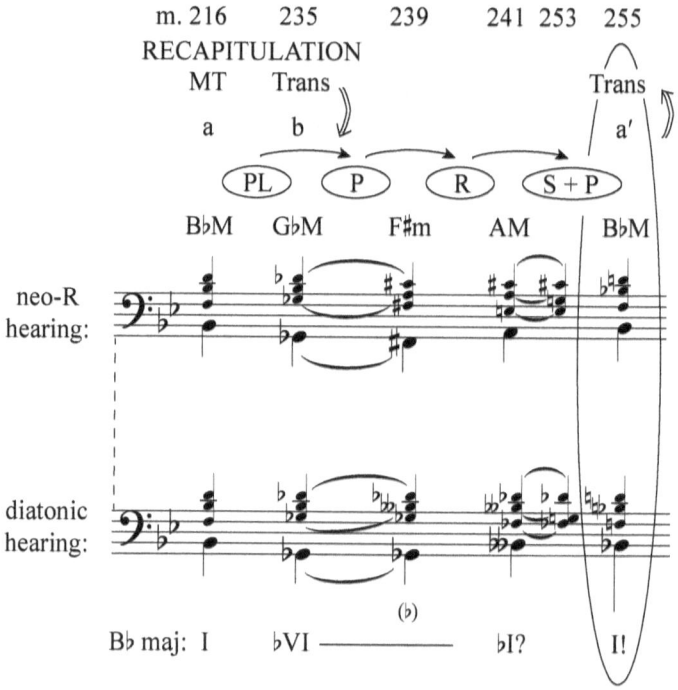

Example 3.16. Piano Sonata in B-flat Major, i. mm. 216–55. Summary.

compound consequent phrase, which would curiously return in the distant key of D-flat major. Schubert instead surprisingly resolves the dissonant chord *up* a half step to B-flat major at the onset of the a' section (m. 255) (which will become the transition), rendering the home key unfamiliar at first. Nicholas Marston (2000), in his article "Schubert's Homecoming," proposes a similar hearing of this resolution to B-flat major, stating:

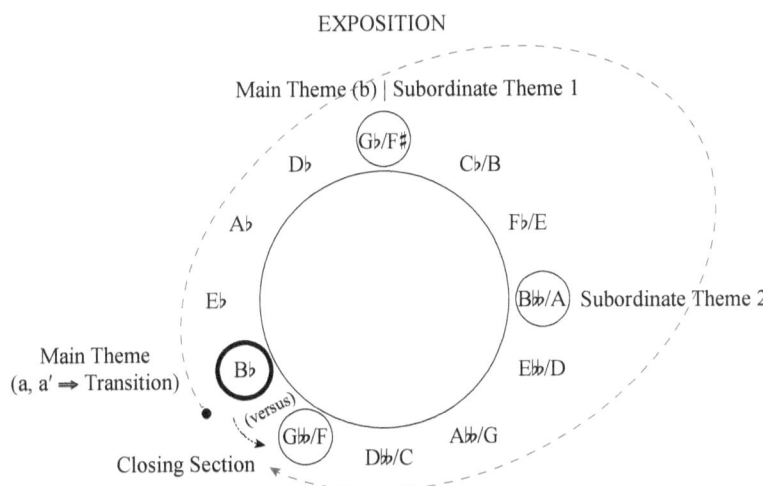

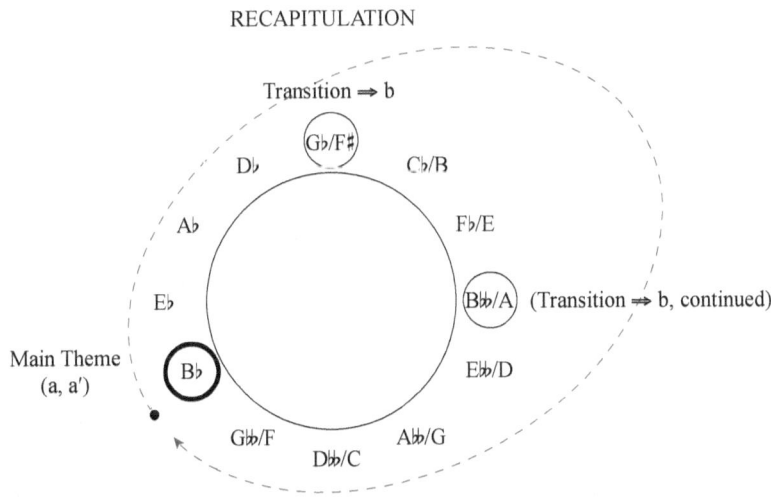

Example 3.17. Piano Sonata in B-flat Major, i. Comparison between orbital periods in the exposition (mm. 1–80) and the recapitulation (mm. 216–73).

The Value of Diatonic Indeterminacy 81

The essence of the deception lies in the defamiliarization of the tonic harmony, which is made to sound other than the tonic.... What is at first taken aurally as an augmented sixth chord (B♭♭–D♭–F♭–G, as it were) at bar 253 is in fact notated as a seventh over A (A–C♯–E–G), the upward semitonal resolution of which to B♭ major is most straightforwardly to be construed, in the immediate aftermath of the surprise, as if it were a deceptive cadence—V⁷–VI—in the mediant key of D. Consequently, whereas the corresponding moment in the exposition brought a return to the tonic following an extended digression to the flattened submediant, here in bars 254–5 Schubert pulls off the feat of "chromaticizing" the tonic, specifically by colouring it as a flat submediant itself. (258)²⁸

The transformation of the home key "into something rich and strange" (263)—here during the return of the compound consequent phrase—might thus be perceived, as Clark (2011a, 158) remarks in her summary of Marston's reading, as "an uncanny homecoming": the once-familiar home key of the double return has been transformed into something foreign. Marston (2000) proposes that the "strangeness or 'ungroundedness' of the recapitulation [continues] beyond the end of the first group," though also suggests that the timespan within which the music's "altered tonal state of the music may be perceived to persist is probably a matter of individual hearing" (267). If the return of the near-complete compound consequent phrase retrospectively confirms that the home key has indeed returned (ex. 3.16), we might then be equally astonished by the notion that we have completed a similar orbital period as the one that we encountered in the exposition (if the exposition is repeated) yet in approximately half the amount of time (ex. 3.17).²⁹

Conclusion

In contemplating the value of diatonic indeterminacy, the reading of the two excerpts from Schubert's Piano Sonata in B-flat Major has attempted to demonstrate a different kind of coherence among the harmonic regions. Rather than show how the local keys (or harmonic regions) unite to express the global tonic, the analyses instead explore the play between synchronic and diachronic perspectives of the harmonic relationships in ways that seek to avoid closure. The proposed hearings trace how the function of the harmonic regions can become amenable to an unbound musical context as they are presented to the ear in time, susceptible to revisions and calibrations, depending on how the relationships among the regions are situated within the formal process and retrospectively conceived or reheard during repetitions and returns. The hearings might thus emphasize the role that listeners may play when attempting to engage with a paratactical musical rhetoric: the juxtaposition of harmonic regions within a musical context that is always in flux can invite listeners to more closely attend to the immediacy of each present moment and imagine, or interpret, their potential connections. An advantage to such a perspective is that it can encourage us to engage with the harmonic regions that unfold within the piece in ways that allow the familiar to transform into something foreign. The exposition, for instance, ends in

Example 3.18. Piano Sonata in B-flat Major, i, mm. 173–219.

Example 3.18. (Continued)

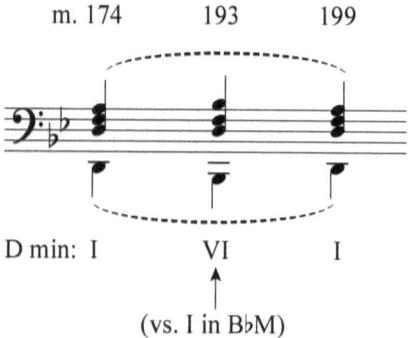

Example 3.19. Piano Sonata in B-flat Major, i, mm. 174–215. Summary.

F major as we might expect from generic norms. Yet the way in which we arrive at this harmonic region may produce an uncanny effect, a strangeness in a repetition. Relatedly, in the recapitulation, the resolution of the A major chord with the added dissonance (mm. 253–55) a half step up instead of down, compared to the exposition (mm. 34–36), can momentarily defamiliarize the sound of the home key within the double return.

The return of the B-flat major region (mm. 193–98) before the onset of the recapitulation (m. 216) may invite a similar reading (ex. 3.18). Although the melodic line from the main theme returns in these measures, the thinner texture, higher register, and triple piano dynamic may suggest that the recapitulation is forthcoming but not underway. In light of the rhetorical emphasis given to the previous harmonic arrival in D minor (m. 173), which marks the boundary point between the end of the development's second core (mm. 159–73) and the beginning of the retransition (m. 174), the D minor context may harmonically render the B-flat major passage as another lowered submediant (here, one of the few diatonic submediant relationships in the movement) instead of as a return to the home key (ex. 3.19).[30] This hearing may be further facilitated by the voice-leading motion from D minor to B-flat major and vice versa. As the bass trill on D quietly descends to B-flat, the uppermost voice in the accompaniment, A, ascends a semitone to B-flat while the inner voices retain F and D (mm. 192–93). Similarly, the bass trill on B-flat rises to D as the accompaniment's upper voice descends from B-flat to A (mm. 198–99). Thus, while the return of the B-flat major passage during this retransition section might call into question whether the home key has arrived prematurely, the resetting of the B-flat major theme's texture, register, and dynamics—coupled with both the D minor harmonic context and the notion that we are in the middle, as opposed to the beginning of a formal process—may instead invite us to interpret the B-flat major passage as another Fremdling.

That the B-flat major tonal region throughout Schubert's piano sonata need not solely be conceived of as a global tonic not only draws our attention to the integral ways that form and harmony intersect, each possessing the potential to animate the other and invite multiple meanings,[31] but also brings to the fore one of the crucial factors that underpin this diatonic purview. If the identity of the B-flat major region is amenable to an unbound musical context as it is presented to the ear in time, altogether preventing this region from expressing an absolute identity as a global tonic, we may speculate that the system that enables this region to express some kind of function is a relational one marked by differences. Accordingly, the B-flat major region, as well as any other region within the chromatic gamut, would not be linked to a predetermined function; rather, each region would obtain a function according to its relation to other regions.

This function, in turn, would be susceptible to multiple revisions, depending upon how the relations among regions or "nodes" are arranged and rearranged throughout the temporal unfolding of a movement or work and how passages are retrospectively conceived or reheard during formal repetitions and returns. In proposing that the B-flat major region and, likewise, any other tonal region, acquires its function from a system of differential relationships,[32] such a relational system marked by negative terms can serve as an alternative form of coherence to a neo-Riemannian system that defines its nodes in positive terms—a repercussion that arises from enharmonic group closure. In the former system, harmonic regions that may be linked to a global tonic can be repositioned or resituated among other harmonic phenomena in such a manner as to allow for a new play among relationships and, consequently, a new function to emerge for each of these regions.[33] This suggests that there may not necessarily need to be a single vantage point from which to organize the harmonic relationships—that we may instead contemplate the harmonic regions that unfold within the piece from multiple angles. Instead of viewing the harmonic regions that unfold in the exposition and recap from a global B-flat major tonic, the formal ambiguities and tonal regions, cadences, and harmonic pathways that lead us from one location in the movement to another can invite us to hear B-flat major differently; from within one set of relationships, it might serve as a tonic function, but within another set, it can become the Neapolitan or lowered submediant. Similarly, a harmonic region previously associated with a dominant function (e.g., F major) may alternatively be heard as a chromatic lowered submediant (♯VI of A major) within a different system of harmonic relationships. Rehearing the exposition during the repeat would enable the initial function of each B-flat major region and final F major region to change once more—the retrospective realization of the modulation to F major serving as a guide for reorganizing the exposition's harmonic regions in the second hearing. The very notion of a global tonic and its respective dominant would thus each be decentered, yielding single "signs" that comprise several functions or internal divisions.

Such an alternative way of engaging with Schubert's sonata would thus invite us to conceive tonal structure differently. In lieu of a single, omnipresent structure that closely depicts the relationships among harmonic regions within a tonal space, structure might be thought of instead as an open, malleable entity that is constantly in flux as the function of each region within a system of differential relationships changes with each perceptual shift in the formal context. Thus, while the unfolding of the harmonic relationships during our entire second hearing of the exposition can invite us to contemplate each diatonic maneuver within the context of our first hearing—to engage with, what Edward T. Cone (1977) refers to as, a "second reading"—in an attempt to decipher how the exposition's tonal denouement is prefigured in earlier events, the potential reinterpretation of the harmonic relationships need not lead us to assert that one of these configurations represents *the* tonal structure of the movement. Nor would such a position require us to conclude that, from a bird's-eye view, the local keys in relation to the global tonic are random. Rather, the position would acknowledge that there may be "other sources of coherence, that may cut across and subvert those we have been trained to recognize," to return once more to Kevin Korsyn's (2003, 38) work. Instead of seeking to puzzle out the ways in which all past and future harmonic phenomena are the expression of an always-already present,[34] we might thus trace in our musical analyses how such phenomena appear to carry new significations as the music unfolds.

Perhaps the primary issue concerning diatonic indeterminacy, then, is not whether coherence is absent within a diatonic perspective or whether one form of coherence is more valid than another. Rather, to what extent do our aesthetic values inform the ways in which we listen and reflect on our journey through Schubert's tonal spaces? That neo-Riemannian perspectives can eradicate diatonic indeterminacy through group closure can promote a sense of security when we engage with Schubert's music. Yet such perspectives need not negate the value of indeterminacy and its potential impact on our musical experiences. To allow ourselves to wander far from the home key to the apparent double-flat side of harmonic space can invoke suspense and surprise when the onset of a double return transforms the foreign into the familiar and when the preparation for a double return renders the home key strange.[35] Such a journey can invite us to engage with a different form of subjectivity, one that embraces the uncanny and the brief experience of being a stranger everywhere.

Notes

1. Whether the term *neo-Riemannian* adequately describes transformational approaches that emphasize voice-leading efficiency or harmonic dualism has been discussed by Dmitri Tymoczko and Richard Cohn in their respective comments on a blog post by Kyle Gann (2009) and, later, by Cohn in *Audacious Euphony* (2012). Cohn (2012, xiii–xiv) expresses a preference for the term *pan-triadic*, after Evan Copley (1991).

2. The nodes on a lattice may represent pitch classes, triads, or keys. As Cohn (2011, 325–29) demonstrates, whereas *Tonnetze* that represent either pitch classes or triads are interchangeable, *Tonnetze* that respectively convey triads and key relations may not be geometric duals. For more on the consequences of shifting from just intonation to equal temperament, see Harrison 2002 and Gollin 2011. Edward Gollin (2011) remarks on Riemann's distinction between equal-tempered tones and "nameable tones" under just intonation, stating that "for Riemann, the equal-tempered

tones are of a different species than the nameable tones, a species that cannot embody musical meanings as do the others, underscoring the importance that Riemann, in the dissertation ["Über das musikalische Hören"], places upon intonation as a signifier of musical meaning" (280). Although neo-Riemannian *Tonnetze* tend to be conceived within equal temperament, it seems plausible that Schubert's harmonic practices were influenced by some form of well-tempered tuning. For a compelling discussion of well-tempered tuning systems, see Gann 2019, 87–101.

3. See also Cohn 1999 for an extended reading of Schubert's Sonata in B-flat Major, D. 960, i.

4. In addition to this analysis in Cohn 1999 and 2012 (125–27), see also Cohn's Weitzmann reading of the same passage (and entire movement) in Cohn 2012, 125–28.

5. Through modal mixture and an enharmonic sleight of hand, F-sharp (G-flat) minor might be conceived of as the lowered minor submediant of B-flat major (♭VI♭).

6. See also Kopp 2002, which adopts a different transformational approach to the key relations in the first movement of Schubert's Sonata in B-flat Major. In David Kopp's analysis of the recapitulation, for instance, the transformations between B-flat major and F-sharp minor are conceived of as **M** + **P** (where *M* denotes one type of mediant transformation—in this case, downward root motion by a major third), as opposed to **PL** + **P** (189–91). Kopp uses italics and nonitalics to distinguish between two different kinds of transformations: chromatic (italics) and diatonic (nonitalics) (166).

7. For further discussions of tonal space, see Proctor 1978; McCreless 1996b; Harrison 2002; Lerdahl 1988, 2011; Clark 2011a; Cohn 2011; and Rusch 2007, 2013b. See also Bharucha 1984, which differentiates between "event hierarchies" (the temporal unfolding of pitch-based material that is specific to a musical work) and "tonal hierarchies" (the atemporal organization of pitch-based material, such as the major and minor modes) (421–22), and McCreless 1991, which further explores this distinction (here, in relation to motivic relations) through the work of Ferdinand de Saussure.

8. Proctor (1978, iv, 138) offers a similar conclusion in his comparison of classical diatonic tonality and nineteenth-century chromatic tonality.

9. See, for instance, Goldenberg 2007 and Rusch 2013b.

10. Kopp (2002) expresses a similar critique of Schenkerian theory in his discussion of *Die Sterne*, D. 939, stating that "a Schenkerian or voice-leading approach might contribute to an understanding of the way in which these unusual harmonic excursions fit into more normative processes by minimizing the strangeness of the mediants by showing how they arise as elaborations of regular structures existing at background levels" (27).

11. On hermeneutic windows, see L. Kramer 1990, 1–20. Here Kramer identifies three different types of windows: textual inclusions, citational inclusions, and structural tropes (9–10).

12. See also Clark 2011a, 157–61; Rusch 2007, 80–85.

13. On the concept of indeterminacy, see especially Hartman 2007, which states: "Indeterminacy, though not an end to be pursued but something disclosed by liberal and thoughtful reading, is more like a traffic sign warning of an impasse. It suggests

(1) that where there is a conflict of interpretations or codes, that conflict can be rehearsed or reordered but not always resolved, and (2) that even where there is no such conflict we have no certainty of controlling implications that may not be apparent or articulable at any one point in time" (265).

14. In addition to Cohn 1999 and 2012, see also Fisk 1997, 2001 (chap. 9); Kopp 2002 (29–32, 189–90); Kessler 2006; Damschroder 2010 (chap. 12); Clark 2011a (146–203).

15. As I attempt to show in Rusch 2013b, parsimonious voice-leading operations approximate Donald Francis Tovey's direct and secondary key relations, albeit within a different tonal space. See especially figure 7, "Comparison between Tovey's key-relations and parsimonious voice-leading operations" (14).

16. On the paradox between equal divisions of the octave, see Cohn 1996, 9–11. Here he clarifies that "a symmetrical division of the chromatic twelve cannot also be a symmetrical division of the diatonic seven without engaging in some enharmonic sleight-of-hand" (11).

17. As an example, whereas Charles Fisk (2001, 254–55) reads the second group as beginning in F major (m. 80ff), Deborah Kessler (2006, 273) interprets this group as beginning in F-sharp minor (m. 48ff).

18. Notwithstanding the early arrival of the cadential dominant in both progressions (my thanks goes to William Caplin for sharing this observation), the cadential progressions seem to approximate those found in the classical style. For more on cadential progressions, see Caplin 1998, 2004, 2010, 2013, 2018.

19. Brian Black (2015) similarly reads a PAC at this point in the form, describing the pathway to harmonic closure in F-sharp minor as a "deflected cadence." As Black suggests, several of Schubert's sonata-form transitions employ this procedure, whereby cadential closure in the home key is averted by a second cadential progression that confirms the subordinate key with a PAC; "the modulation is thus accomplished exclusively by the second cadence, which both ends the transition and ushers in the subordinate-key region" (165).

20. I would like to thank Janet Schmalfeldt for suggesting this hearing to me when I had presented an earlier version of this analysis at the European Music Analysis Conference in 2014.

21. How strikingly different would the key change from G-flat major to F-sharp minor in Schubert's Sonata in B-flat Major have been if the sonata were composed in D major or G major. A sonata in D major would have led to a juxtaposition between B-flat major and B-flat minor, and in G major, E-flat major and E-flat minor. That the enharmonic juncture occurs between G-flat major and F-sharp minor near a significant boundary point in the form may lend further support to the idea that Schubert's harmonic practices were informed by well temperament.

22. A performance of this passage might emphasize either the abandoned cadence reading with a two-beat anacrusis or the dominant arrival reading with a one-beat anacrusis.

23. Cohn (1999, 224–25) observes this relationship as well and highlights additional "transformations of the opening theme."

24. See especially Cohn 2004, which discusses the signifying potential of the progression, described here as a hexatonic pole.

25. As Cohn (2004, 307–8) further explains, the progression may also present a perceptual conundrum from a diatonic perspective, because each chord in the pair contains the other chord's leading tone and lowered sixth degree.

26. That the pathway shown here is elliptical as opposed to circular conveys the effort that it takes to circumvent the circle of fifths, especially the key relations that are furthest from the initial tonic. I would especially like to thank Leslie Blasius for sharing this observation with me.

27. The oft-posed question as to whether to repeat the exposition in this sonata might be answered by considering the function of the final harmonic region in the exposition, F major. As the reading here suggests, repeating the exposition would help emphasize the dual function of F major (♭VI of A major and V of B-flat major), since the development does not begin in the home key. For more on this performance decision, see Macdonald 1984–85; Brendel 2015, 149–52; Frisch 1989; Zaslaw 1989; Schiff 1998.

28. Cohn (1999, 229) similarly suggests that the A major seventh chord resolves "'deceptively' to tonic five-three for the counterstatement."

29. Cohn (1999, 227, figure 7) makes a similar point.

30. Peter Pesic (1999, 141) and Suzannah Clark (2011a, 158) also read this motion to B-flat major (mm. 193–98) as VI of D minor. Cohn (1999, 226) as well posits that "the status [of B-flat major] as a 'real' tonic is undermined" by the higher register.

31. This point recalls Tovey's ([1928] 1949) observation: "Not only do the great masters of tonality not expect us to recognize without collateral evidence, keys that return after intervening modulations, but they rely upon our not doing so" (145).

32. The distinction between a relational system, as opposed to a referential one, recalls Ferdinand de Saussure's (1973) conception of the sign.

33. In his analysis of Wagner's *Tristan und Isolde*, Robert Bailey (1985, 113–146), makes a similar point regarding this play between harmonic relationships: "The older structural polarity of tonic and dominant thus gradually gave way to a new system with polarities based on the interval of a 3rd. . . . In this case, the tonality based on V frequently *functions* not as the dominant but rather as the III of III. Similarly, the tonality based on IV often *functions* not as the subdominant but rather as the VI of VI" (120).

34. On this form of structuralism, see Culler 1973. Here Jonathan Culler cautions that "unless one has postulated some transcendent 'final cause' or ultimate meaning for the work, one cannot discover its structure, for the structure is that by which the end is made present throughout the work" (474).

35. An analogous situation might be when we arrive at a familiar destination by foot or by car through an unfamiliar route.

4 Sonata Forms, Fantasias, and Formal Coherence

Two Frames: The Four-Key Exposition and the Fantasia

Among the scholarship on Schubert's approach to sonata form are brief references to movements that appear to contain a *four-key* exposition. The examples cited include the first movement from the Symphony in B-flat Major, D. 125 (1814) (Webster 1978, 26n18); the first movement from the Piano Sonata in B Major, D. 575 (1817) (Newbould 1997, 105–6; Hunt 2009, 82n39; Brown, Sams, and Winter 2001); and the second movement from the Piano Quintet in A Major, D. 667 ("Trout") (1819) (Hunt 2009, 82n39), the last of which has been described as a sonata form without a development (ex. 4.1). That the concept of a four-key exposition has not been pursued beyond the modest attention afforded to footnotes and short paragraphs suggests that the idea is peripheral to our understanding of Schubert's sonata forms, if not questionable under the rubric of certain approaches to musical form.[1] Furthermore, while the literature on the first movement from Schubert's Piano Sonata in B Major conveys a consensus about its four-key design, analyses of the opening movement from the Symphony in B-flat Major diverge. On the one hand, the form has been interpreted as a four-key exposition and, on the other hand, as an early example of a three-key exposition.[2] With respect to the F major slow movement from the Piano Quintet in A Major, the absence of a development section raises a different set of questions about its four-key design, compared to that of the opening movement from the Piano Sonata in B Major (and potentially the first movement from the Symphony in B-flat Major). For instance, did Schubert decide to modulate to G major instead of C major, the key of the dominant, near the end of the exposition (m. 53) partly because the exposition does not repeat (thereby eliminating the need to reestablish the return of the home key by way of the dominant)? How might delaying the return of the home key during the movement's second half (m. 61ff) affect our perception of its eventual return (m. 96), compared to beginning the

1) Symphony in B-flat Major, D. 125, i (1814)

2) Piano Sonata in B Major, D. 575, i (1817)

3) Piano Quintet in A Major, D. 667 ("Trout"), ii (1819)

Example 4.1. Citations of four-key expositions in Schubert's oeuvre.

recapitulation in the home key—an approach used in the opening movements of the Piano Sonata in B Major and Symphony in B-flat Major? In sum, such differences among sonata form theories and readings of the formal and tonal designs of the three movements mentioned make it difficult to draw broader conclusions about the four-key exposition as a concept in and of itself.

The point at which a theoretical proposition meets skepticism, however, need not deter us from exploring this path altogether. Incertitude about the four-key exposition as a concept can invite us to further probe these formal outliers, if only to consider what they can contribute to our existing knowledge of Schubert's sonata form practices, especially his three-key expositions, which have drawn much attention in contemporary music scholarship since James Webster's two-part study "Schubert's Sonata Form and Brahms's First Maturity" (1978, 1979). Schubert's three-key expositions have often been viewed as an outgrowth or extension of sonata form expositions that contain two keys, because the cadential goals and corresponding interthematic functions (e.g., main theme, transition) are similar. In Schubert's three-key expositions, the home key still tends to be established through a half cadence or perfect authentic cadence at the end of the main theme, and the key of the dominant tends to serve as the cadential goal of a subordinate theme or theme group, even though it is delayed by the appearance of an intermediate, or second key area that is introduced near the beginning of the subordinate theme. This intermediate key area is often conceived of as a transitional one not only because it may lack cadential closure by means of a perfect authentic cadence but also because it appears to be en route to the exposition's final, or third key area (Caplin 1998, 119).[3] The broader question of whether Schubert's three-key expositions arose from an effort to expand the two-key exposition or emerged as a consequence of his experiments with tonality (or both)[4] might thus be revisited by considering the rapport between tonal design and formal process in the movements cited in example 4.1; these movements can alter the context for contemplating Schubert's apparent departures from sonata form practices.

More fundamentally, the suggestion of a four-key exposition can lead us to question the very premises that facilitate our conclusions about Schubert's sonata form procedures, not only by encouraging us to reexamine the musical codes that invite us to read certain movements under the rubric of sonata form but also by prompting us to ask whether there may be other contexts, or frames, for listening. Reevaluating these musical codes and repositioning them within a different frame could lead us to further contemplate (1) how our current frames for listening to Schubert's sonatas can affect the ways in which we think about formal coherence, thereby revealing how these frames tend to promote certain part-whole relationships over others, and (2) what we might gain by bringing other frames into dialogue with that of sonata form, if Schubert's compositional approach appears to straddle the divide between freedom and restraint with respect to our current understandings of sonata form procedure.⁵

One frame that has had a close affinity with sonata form is the fantasia, which resurfaced in late eighteenth- and nineteenth-century compositional thought as both a genre and musical aesthetic.⁶ As a genre, the fantasia offered musicians an opportunity to break away from musical conventions and showcase their command of harmony and voice leading, using originally composed themes, operatic themes, or musical topics as points for departure (Czerny [1829] 1983, chaps. 4 and 5).⁷ As a musical aesthetic, the fantasia could permeate instrumental forms—including the keyboard sonata allegro and rondo—in the tenor of rhetorical pauses and surprising changes of key, texture, and style. While on the surface, it may be possible to separate these two broad conceptions of the fantasia according to the titles of pieces alone, music reviews and historical records suggest otherwise. Of Schubert's first published Piano Sonata in A Minor, D. 845, for example, one critic, believed to be G. W. Fink, writes in his 1826 review of the work: "Many musical pieces nowadays bear the name of Fantasy, though fantasy has had very little share in them, if any at all, and they are so called only because the title sounds well and because the child of the composer's fancy, running off on every side like wild waters, refuses to be fit into any regular form. Here, on the contrary, a composition for once bears the name of Sonata, though it was fantasy, quite evidently, which had the largest and most decisive share in it" (Deutsch 1947, 512).⁸ Editorial decisions made by Schubert's publishers convey a similar ambiguity. Whereas Tobias Haslinger added the heading "Fantasie, / Andante, Menuetto und Allegro / für das Piano-Forte allein" to Schubert's Piano Sonata in G Major, D. 894, in 1827,⁹ Johann Peter (J. P.) Gotthard retitled the Piano Four-Hand Fantasia in C Minor, D. 48, as "Grosse Sonate" for the posthumous publication in 1871 (Deutsch [1951] 1995, 22). The ubiquity of this admix between fantasia-as-genre and fantasia-as-aesthetic is further addressed in one anonymous reviewer's article, "Mittheilungen aus dem Tagebuche eines Tonkünstlers [Notes from the Diary of a Musician]," in the *Allgemeine musikalische Zeitung* (1813): "What we have received, this past year, under the title 'Fantasia' . . . are only a freer type of Sonata" (quoted and translated by Parker 1974, 52).¹⁰ And in music scholar Ernst Ludwig Gerber's letter to composer and organist Christian Heinrich Rinck (1817), he notes: "Finally, it appears to me as if the fantasy, like a despot, has seized absolute power over music. . . . One can no longer perceive either any definite musical forms or any limits to the influence of the fantasy. . . . In such a way we hear and play nothing but Fantasias. Our sonatas are fantasias, our overtures are fantasias and even our symphonies, at least those of Beethoven and his like, are fantasias" (Noack 1953, 326).¹¹ If the fantasia aesthetic mingled with other instrumental genres by the early nineteenth century to the extent that these genres could be interchangeable with the fantasia genre, what purview emerges from this cross-point with respect to the ways in which we think about formal coherence in sonata form movements that appear to convey a four-key exposition and, more broadly, in terms of our overall understanding of Schubert's approach to sonata form?

In contemplating this question, I will begin by exploring the intersection between sonata and fantasia in the exposition from the first movement of Schubert's Piano Sonata in B Major, for which there is a general sense of agreement about its four-key design. Rather than seeking to argue for or against the very concept of a four-key exposition, I will consider instead the consequences that can arise from hearing the exposition from a formal function perspective, on the one hand, and from a fantasia perspective, on the other hand, comparing the kinds of musical relationships and affects that these different frames can highlight. In presenting a formal function analysis of the B major exposition, I do not intend to suggest that Schubert conceived his exposition along these very lines; rather, my turn to formal functions seeks to highlight the listening expectations that can arise within a system that has gained a strong foothold in current Schubert analytical discourse. In attempting to hear the B major exposition from both listening perspectives (formal functions and fantasia), the following discussion acknowledges that the respective vantage points are only two interpretations within a range of many possible hearings and that any conclusions drawn here are provisional owing to the interpretive play among varying conceptions of *Formenlehre* and fantasia. Nevertheless, as I hope to convey, some of the principles associated with each heuristic frame can persuade us to hear certain musical relationships over others, inviting us to not only compare these relationships and observe their interplay but also shift our attention toward the very frames themselves. As I ultimately suggest, the ways in which the two frames overlap and conflict with one another may offer one response to the broader question of why Schubert's approaches to sonata form can be difficult to theorize. The latter part of this chapter addresses how these ideas can enrich our understanding of Schubert's three-key and two-key expositions.

Schubert's Piano Sonata in B Major, D. 575, i, as a Four-Key Exposition

One of the primary advantages to adopting William Caplin's (1998) theory of formal functions and theme types as a heuristic guide for listening to the exposition from the first movement of Schubert's Piano Sonata in B Major is that the theory offers us a way to methodically trace our experience of temporality on multiple levels. We may perceive musical components as expressing a beginning, middle, or end within nested grouping structures in accordance to where we presume to be within the sonata form exposition's formal process (e.g., whether we sense that we are at the beginning of a transition or at the end of a subordinate theme group), as well as explore why the musical content within each timespan appears to convey a specific temporality (Caplin 2010).[12] Also of importance is that the theory takes into account the possibility that our interpretation of a formal function can change, depending on the musical context. The notion that musical contexts are fluid, rather than fixed, as we perceive passages in time can lead us to retrospectively reinterpret these passages.[13] A formal function that connotes a middle timespan, for instance, can appear to evolve into an ending timespan, as when a continuation "becomes" a cadential function during an expanded cadential progression. Similarly, an ending may appear to transform into a beginning when, for instance, the consequent phrase of a compound period "fails" to materialize and becomes the opening of a transition instead. This acknowledgment of the role that context plays when we engage with music temporally, as opposed to spatially, broadly resonates with a revised conception of form proposed by Carl Dahlhaus (1991), Janet Schmalfeldt (1995, 2011), and others—namely that form and, more generally, music may be conceived less "as fundamentally proceeding toward an *outcome*" and more as a process (Schmalfeldt 2011, 35; see also Dahlhaus 1991, 113–20). Accordingly, subjects not only are invited to play an active role in the creation of a structure but may also become acutely aware of their participation in this re-creation (Dahlhaus 1991, 114).[14]

The emphasis on temporality within an ever-shifting musical context bodes well with the kinds of concerns that Schubert's sonata forms have raised in terms of their length and proportion. If the idea of a four-key exposition already suggests a nonesuch in light of prior criticisms of redundancy and excess in the composer's musical reception history,[15] a formal function approach to the B major sonata exposition can offer us one frame for contemplating time, especially with respect to how the exposition's apparent tight-knit and loose-knit constructions relate to those encountered in the repertoire that a formal function approach fundamentally engages,[16] which has often served as a basis for aesthetic judgments of Schubert's sonata forms. Moments when Schubert's formal rhetoric seems to be at odds with this frame will invite us to consider what alternative frames—in this case, the fantasia—can bring to the fore in our hearing of the same exposition.

Example 4.2 shows an annotated score of the exposition from a formal function perspective. The main theme opens with a declamatory arpeggio B-D-sharp–F-sharp that is rhythmically augmented an octave higher before hurtling to the dominant seventh of C-sharp minor at a *forte* dynamic in the lower register. A hushed, falling stepwise melodic line in the higher register (mm. 4–5) answers the opening rising arpeggio gesture (mm. 1–3), leading the main theme

Example 4.2. Schubert, Piano Sonata in B Major, D. 575, i, mm. 1–59. Formal function analysis.

to a perfect authentic cadence (PAC) in B major (m. 5).[17] The varied repetition that follows the opening five-bar theme may initially suggest that a second main theme is underway. Yet the two chromatic pitches that follow—A-natural (m. 9) and a striking C-natural that is rhetorically emphasized by two quarter-note rests (m. 10)—begin to steer us away from the home key. These chromatic

Example 4.2. (Continued)

pitches—coupled with the cadential progression that helps prepare the modulation toward the first subordinate key, G major—might lead us to retrospectively place the beginning of the transition after the initial PAC (m. 6) or perhaps three measures later (m. 8), if we hear measures 6–8 as a truncated version of the main theme. Altogether, the opening measures (mm. 1–14) establish a pattern of one or

Example 4.2. (Continued)

more arpeggios followed by a stepwise descent over a cadential or cadential-like progression. Throughout these varied repetitions, the tonal center abruptly shifts from B major to G major, the lowered major submediant, first with A-natural and then with the unexpected C-natural. The last group of arpeggiations that introduces these two chromatic pitches (mm. 8–10) is answered by a melodic descending scale (here, E-natural–D-natural–C-natural–B-natural–A), which now sounds at a *fortissimo* dynamic, as opposed to *pianissimo* (mm. 4–5 and mm. 7–8).

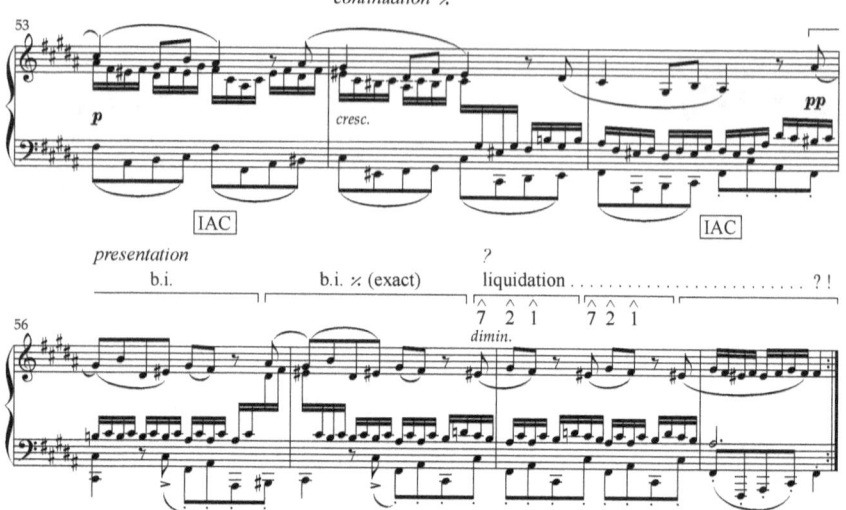

Example 4.2. (Continued)

While motion away from the home key to the first subordinate key in these opening measures is typical of a sonata exposition, the themes that comprise the main theme and transition do not readily correspond to a certain theme type, such as a sentence or hybrid. Here the themes' asymmetrical grouping structures (mm. 1–5 = 3 + 2, mm. 6–8 = 1 + 2, mm. 8–14 = 3 + 4) and tonal instability contribute to the loose-knit design of the entire passage, hindering the possibility of asserting any eight-bar prototype.[18] What may thus appear to emerge from these opening measures, then, is a loose-knit structure that somewhat resembles the silhouette of the first part of a sonata form exposition. The first theme receives cadential confirmation in the home key (m. 5) and the last theme (whether taken to be mm. 6–14 or mm. 8–14) modulates to the dominant of the subordinate key area (V of G major). Collectively, the passage appears to outline a procession from the main theme to the end of the transition.

A lyrical subordinate theme begins in G major (m. 15) with an arpeggiated ascent in the bass, followed by an arpeggiated ascent in the melody that retains the dotted rhythm from the main theme's arpeggio figure.[19] As the subordinate theme's presentation phrase unfolds, the melody and bass's rising and falling gestures combine to form invertible counterpoint at the octave, each rising and falling line imitated in the other voice. When the contrapuntal pattern breaks (m. 20), the presentation phrase's two-bar basic idea is fragmented amid an underlying 6–5 sequential bass pattern, altogether suggesting a continuation phrase. During this model-sequence, G major begins to drift toward its own diatonic submediant (or relative minor), E minor, yet E minor does not achieve cadential confirmation at the end of the continuation phrase. Instead, the expected PAC resolves deceptively to an E major 6/3 chord (m. 27),[20] revealing the parallel major mode instead. This third key area, E major, is finally confirmed by a PAC progression (mm. 29–30).

If the PAC in E major brings the modulating subordinate theme to a close, the passage that follows (mm. 30–37) may at first sound like a closing section. While a closing section in the key of the subdominant (E major) as opposed to the dominant (F-sharp major) may seem strange in accordance with late eighteenth-century sonata form practices, both the temporal position of this E major section within the exposition and the section's musical features may suggest that we have arrived at the tail end of the sonata exposition's dramatic arch.[21] Here the two four-bar codettas (mm. 30–33 and mm. 34–37) in this postcadential section prolong E major in a galant style, alternating between tonic and dominant chords while the melody retraces the melodic idea first heard in mm. 6–8, now expanded to a four-bar symmetrical phrase that repeats. Like many postcadential sections, both the resetting of previous musical material with a lighter musical texture and prolongation of the subordinate key through a simple harmonic progression helps "dissipate the accumulated energy" of the subordinate theme (Caplin 1998, 122). This impression of a closing section is put into question, however, when the codetta's melodic ending (m. 37) forms the basis for the proceeding model-sequence technique (mm. 38–39) that discreetly shepherds us away from E major toward a PAC in the exposition's fourth key area, F-sharp major (m. 41). The initial closing section of the exposition may thus surprisingly become a *second* modulating transition—the two codettas now retrospectively reinterpreted as two compound basic ideas of a compound presentation phrase.

The second subordinate theme that follows this modulating transition curiously averts strong cadential closure, compared to the first subordinate theme (mm. 15–30). After an opening tight-knit eight-bar sentence in F-sharp major closes with an imperfect authentic cadence (IAC) (m. 48), the next six measures feature an extended mini-sentence (mm. 50–55), wherein the proportions of the presentation and continuation are halved and the continuation repeated.[22] That this mini-sentence concludes with an IAC (m. 53; m. 55), as opposed to a PAC, invites one last attempt to achieve strong cadential closure in F-sharp major. The beginning of the mini-sentence sounds once more (m. 56ff) but is then surprisingly liquated—the repetitions of the latter half of the basic idea ($\hat{7}$–$\hat{2}$–$\hat{1}$ over V–I) functioning as a proxy for the PAC in F-sharp major. Altogether, the entire second subordinate theme suggests a gradual foreshortening process—from eight measures (mm. 42–49) to six measures (mm. 50–55) and then finally four (mm. 56–59)—where closure is articulated through liquidation, as opposed to a PAC.

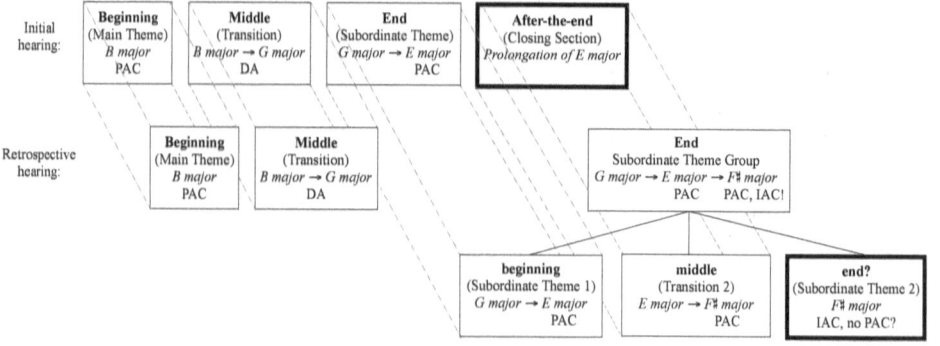

Example 4.3. Piano Sonata in B Major, D. 575, i, exposition. Summary of interthematic formal functions.

If formal functions engage temporality in terms of beginnings, middles, and ends among nested grouping structures, we might initially conclude that the exposition closes in the "wrong" key area (ex. 4.3). The PAC at the end of the first subordinate theme can suggest that we have reached the end of a formal process on the interthematic level. Coupling this PAC with the subsequent closing section—a framing function that connotes a "temporal after-the-end" (Caplin 2010, 29; see also Caplin 2013, 135)—would imply that the tonal goal of the exposition is the key of the *subdominant*, E major, or "under" dominant, as opposed to the key of the dominant, F-sharp major.[23] When the closing section of the B major exposition becomes a second modulating transition, we may be prompted to revise our temporal plan of the exposition's interthematic functions: an after-the-end formal function becomes a middle function nested within a newly formed subordinate theme group that eventually bumps us up a whole step, from E major to F-sharp major.[24] While we do reach the key of the dominant at the end of exposition, both the previous PAC in E major and lack of strong cadential closure in F-sharp major at the very end of the second subordinate theme can strongly suggest that the musical material in the dominant is ancillary to the exposition, as opposed to a goal within a larger formal and tonal process.

From this potential problem of closure in the B major exposition, it may be possible to deduce why there are few comparable examples in Schubert's oeuvre, as well as why the three-key exposition presents a more viable solution—points that I will return to later in this chapter. Such provisional conclusions, however, would still leave open questions concerning the motivation behind the B major exposition's loose-knit organization, including its phrase and cadential deviations, repetitions, and series of modulations—musical characteristics that may align more closely with a paratactic rhetorical style, as opposed to a hypotactic one.[25] That these musical features can seem foreign against the background of more tightly knit constructed sonata form expositions of the high classical style might lead us to consider other frames for which these musical features more readily align. The fantasia, as both a genre and aesthetic, would not only invite us to position these musical codes in the center of our interpretive operations; it would also bring to the fore how a play among key areas, textures, and styles can facilitate freedom from sonata form conventions, suggesting a different way to hear the musical relationships in the exposition.

Schubert's Piano Sonata in B Major, D. 575, I, as a Fantasia

An attempt to hear the exposition from the B major sonata in the mode of a fantasia naturally raises the broader question as to what the fantasia may have meant to Schubert around 1817. By then, he had already composed four named fantasias: in G major for Pianoforte Duet, D. 1 (1810); in C minor for Pianoforte, D. 2e/993 (1811); in G minor for Pianoforte Duet, D. 9 (1811); and in C minor for Pianoforte Duet, D. 48 (1813) (ex. 4.4). As mentioned earlier, the last of these works, D. 48, was renamed "Grosse Sonate" by J. P. Gotthard. All of these piano pieces depart from the eighteenth-century free fantasia in that they are metrically barred. Yet their respective compositional process varies, corroborating Peter Schleuning's (1971) assertion that the fantasia continued to resist a singular design in the nineteenth century and could thus be realized in a number of different ways: "The extent to which the generic name fantasia was used time and again during this period in a manner that tended towards its universal significance is to be noted at this juncture. While this was also very fruitful for the theoretical discussion of the art, it signaled, however, in any consideration of the genre from a musical standpoint, a reversion to the state of widespread indefiniteness with an abundance of synonymous applications and of formal and structural dependence, similar to that observable immediately before the period of the free fantasia" (2:17). The boundless implementations of the fantasia in nineteenth-century compositional practice seem best captured in Carl Czerny's pedagogical treatise *A Systematic Introduction to Improvisation* ([1829] 1983), which explains how one might carry out six different types of "fantasy-like improvisation[s]" on the pianoforte:

a. In the working out of a single theme in all the familiar forms of composition
b. In the development and combination of several themes into a total work
c. In genuine potpourris, or the intertwining of favorite motives through modulations, passage work, [and] cadenzas, without particular development of any single one
d. In variations of all customary forms
e. In improvising in strict and fugal style
f. In capriccios of the most free and unrestrained type (3)

1) Fantasia in G Major for Pianoforte Duet, D. 1 (1810), mm 1–8

2) Fantasia in C Minor for Pianoforte, D. 2e/993 (1811), mm. 1–7

3) Fantasia in G Minor for Pianoforte Duet, D. 9 (1811), mm. 1–7

4) Fantasia in C Minor for Pianoforte Duet, D. 48 (1813), mm. 1–6

Example 4.4. List of Schubert's named fantasias composed before 1817.

Most salient in both Schleuning's summation and Czerny's six types is the latitude of "formal and structural dependence" among nineteenth-century fantasias—from, what Czerny ([1829] 1983, 43, 121) describes as, the "spinning out [of] a theme into an entire piece" in the guise of a first movement sonata to "an arbitrary linking of individual ideas without any particular development" in a capriccio.[26] Czerny further notes that "all [six] types can be combined with one another and employed in one and the same fantasy," emphasizing that the boundaries between these categories are fluid (3). Returning to the four fantasias shown in example 4.4, two of the four-hand piano fantasias, D. 1 and D. 9, and the two-hand piano fantasia, D. 2e/993, do not appear to express a discernible formal plan. Conversely, the first two movements from the four-hand piano fantasia, D. 48, respectively share similar musical features as a sonata allegro and andante from a three-movement sonata, a connection that reflects both J. P. Gotthard's retitling of the work as "Grosse Sonate" and the close alliance between fantasia and sonata form in the nineteenth century. In sum, if, as Leonard Ratner (1980, 314) similarly observed nine years after Schleuning's extensive study, "each composer coordinated standard formula and fantasia in his own way," it is apparent that within Schubert's compositional practice alone, his early engagement with the fantasia was not bound to a single realization.

In light of the fantasia's "widespread indefiniteness" and Schubert's flexible approach, then, how might we hear the exposition from his Sonata in B Major as a fantasia? If we allow the exposition's musical "excesses"—including its thematic

Example 4.5. Piano Sonata in B Major, D. 575, i, mm. 1–59. Fantasia (theme and variations/potpourri) analysis.

Example 4.5. (Continued)

variants and three modulations—to obtain a central position in our interpretation, we might attend to the ways in which the opening five-bar theme is "worked out" or developed across four musical styles and key areas. Example 4.5 provides a summary of this suggested hearing. The five-bar theme is first introduced in a declamatory style, then contracted by two measures (mm. 6–8), and

Example 4.5. (Continued)

finally expanded by two measures (mm. 8–14) during the modulation from B major to G major. Following this expanded version is a subdued, lyrical version of the opening theme in a learned style (mm. 15–30), which features invertible counterpoint at the octave. Similar to the first section, this second section also modulates—in this case, from G major to E minor—leading to an unexpected

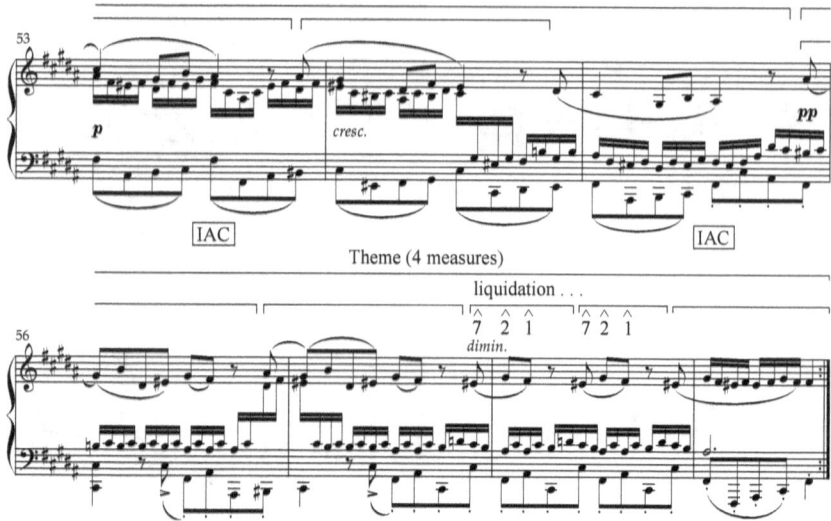

Example 4.5. (Continued)

cadential arrival in the parallel mode, E major (m. 30), that elides with the beginning of the third section. This third section initiates a new area of contrast, where a version of the opening theme (mm. 6–8) is expanded to a symmetrical four-bar phrase and recomposed in a galant style (mm. 30–33; mm. 34–41). The model-sequence technique (mm. 38–41) leads us to a fourth key area, F-sharp major, wherein a final varied repetition of the opening theme is recast in a brilliant style (mm. 42–59). Altogether, this hearing might suggest that the exposition simultaneously approximates a set of variations and a virtuoso potpourri—to refer once more to Czerny's six categories of fantasy-like improvisations—given the thematic variations, four key areas, and stylistic contrasts that unfold in the exposition: the declamatory is juxtaposed with the reserved, the learned with the galant, the public with the private, and the vocal with the instrumental.[27] Aligning the B major exposition with a variation form, or variation cycle, highlights the way in which the exposition's formal sections emerge through topical or stylistic modifications of the opening five-bar theme and how such repetitions appear to convey a paratactic syntax, as opposed to a hypotactic one.[28] Yet mitigating these paratactic juxtapositions and repetitions are moments of caprice near the seams of each section, which transport us from key to key and style to style amid a recurring thematic shape—moments that may be guided by certain principles associated with sonata form.[29] With respect to the potpourri fantasia, Czerny ([1829] 1983) remarks that this type of fantasia catered to public tastes by incorporating "a large assortment of favorite motives and melodies from operas, ballets, folksongs, and all such material that has attained general popularity" (87).

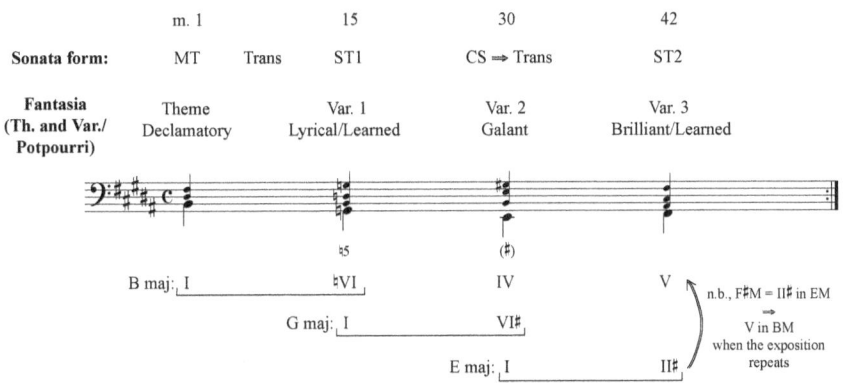

Example 4.6. Piano Sonata in B Major, D. 575, i, mm. 1–59. Summary.

Schleuning (1971) similarly links the menagerie of contrasts to the salon fantasia: "There was a similar variety of the possible manifestations of the salon fantasia, ranging from the treatment of original ideas through the potpourri, consisting merely of a string of tunes, and the free paraphrase to the set of variations preceded by a free section" (2:18). Yet even though Schubert's B major exposition similarly engages an array of musical styles, the broader context within which the exposition appears—within a work titled "Sonata"—suggests that it departs from the potpourri and salon fantasia with respect to matters of style and meter. The B major exposition engages with a higher style than that of the salon, maintains the same meter and tempo throughout, and sounds an originally composed theme that is repeatedly varied, compared to themes typically heard in potpourri fantasias. At most, perhaps, the B major exposition may have its ties to opera overtures, of which Schubert was well-versed after having composed seven theatrical works by 1817, some of which were not completed.[30]

Two significant consequences emerge from our attempt to hear the B major exposition as a fantasia. First, the delineation of thematic groupings by musical style can encourage us to hear the F-sharp major section as an integral part of the exposition, as opposed to a musical appendage; the section forms a complement to the other three styles and provides balance to what would otherwise be an asymmetrical group. Second, the imaginative play and spontaneity from section to section can invite us to temporarily suspend in our hearing the notion of a global tonic. While the third key area, E major, may be construed as the subdominant in relation to B major, the home key, the tonal emphasis afforded to G major in the first subordinate theme may suggest that E major could also be heard as a chromatic submediant of G major (ex. 4.6). A chain of chromatic submediant modulations—from B major to G major and from G major to E major—would thus accompany the contrast between the first three styles. Attending to the drama with which the four key areas unfold on the local level may similarly suggest that the fourth key in the exposition's tonal

Sonata Forms, Fantasias, and Formal Coherence 109

Example 4.7. Piano Sonata in B Major, D. 575, i, mm. 117–30.

plan—F-sharp major—would be first introduced as *the major supertonic* of E major, as opposed to the dominant of B major. While it may be plausible to conclude that the return of B major during the continuation's function (m. 39) encourages us to hear F-sharp major as a dominant, as opposed to a major supertonic, the subdominant recapitulation (m. 88ff), which does not introduce any tonal or thematic adjustments, may call this view into question. In the parallel passage (mm. 125–28) (ex. 4.7), the continuation's model-sequence progression tonicizes F-sharp minor and E major before returning to Variation 3 (or the second subordinate theme) in B major (m. 129). Recalling Donald Francis Tovey's "Tonality" ([1928] 1949, 153) article, a modulation from a tonic to its major supertonic can present a challenge to the ear because of the major II chord's tendency to sound like the dominant of the dominant.[31] The element of surprise in Schubert's modulation from E major to F-sharp major in the exposition, then, would include not only this supposed "false" key relation but also the impending transformation of F-sharp major: what was initially the supertonic of E major *becomes* the dominant of the home key when the entire exposition repeats.[32]

Between Restraint and Freedom, Sonata Form and Fantasia

From our discussion up to this point, we can observe how sonata form and fantasia each provide a frame for construing the musical relationships in the B major exposition. Certainly not all of the analytical statements enabled by one frame are entirely unique to that frame. Within the purview of a sonata form perspective, for instance, we could reach similar conclusions about the ways in which the opening five measures are varied or recomposed throughout the exposition's four-key plan and array of musical topics or styles.[33] The sonata form and fantasia perspectives appear to diverge when we consider the potential unity of the exposition and its dramatic trajectory. As the analyses suggest, each frame serves as a guide for interpreting the exposition's part-whole relationships and for experiencing the exposition's dramatic trajectory as it unfolds in time. What may sound superfluous to the exposition within the context of one frame may be heard as a necessary component within the context of another frame; what may appear to be the wrong key area may instead be rationalized within a different network of tonal relationships.

Given these two possible ways to hear the exposition, how might we approach this fork in the road if traveling down one path appears to run the risk of excluding some of the experiences and insights afforded by the other path? If the musical codes in Schubert's Sonata in B Major invite us to read the exposition from a sonata form perspective and from the perspective of a fantasia, we might instead consider the cross-point between the two frames. Such a position would invite us to contemplate the ways in which one frame delimits the other—how expectancy may be met with surprise and freedom with restraint. When we hear the B major exposition in the mode of a sonata form, the fantasia can emerge as a loosening device, lending a sense of unpredictability with respect to the exposition's thematic unfoldings, harmonic path, cadences and grouping structures. The fantasia appears to invite development in the guise of thematic repetitions and cadential and phrase deviations, unraveling the tight-knit design characteristic of sonata form expositions in relation to their development sections. The fantasia can also motivate modulations to several key areas, enabling key relations in the sonata exposition to obtain multiple meanings. E major, for instance, might be locally interpreted as the major submediant of G major and, from a more global perspective, as the subdominant of B major. When we hear the same B major exposition as a fantasia, sonata form may conversely impinge on the freedom with which the fantasia appears to operate, lending a form to a seemingly formless genre and carving out a tonal destination for which the series of modulations will eventually reach. Or put differently, sonata form offers a covert order for the thematic variations that unfold on the musical surface. Altogether, the ways in which the two frames overlap would suggest that the B major exposition is a sonata *and* fantasia while also being neither at the same time.

It is at this cross-point where the compositional advantages to positioning sonata form alongside the fantasia become clearer. If, around the turn of the nineteenth century, sonata form patterns had begun to crystallize into more permanent, fixed structures, the fantasia provides a solution to reviving their dramatic action.[34] In facilitating a sense of uncertainty, the fantasia can challenge expectancies and transform the familiar into something foreign. Just as the fantasia can upend our sense of location within the exposition and, relatedly, disrupt our perception of musical time, it can also introduce new harmonic paths to old destinations, thereby encouraging us to become reacquainted with these destinations.

Fundamentally, the fantasia can make us more aware of the epistemological frame(s) at play when formal coherence is sought. By breaking the set of expectations that a frame engenders and thus putting into question the very frame itself, the fantasia brings to the fore not only the frame's heuristic principles and value thereof for which the element of surprise ultimately relies on but also the frame's conditions of possibility for which certain statements about Schubert's expositions can be made.[35] Although the B major exposition falls less within the genre of the free fantasia, it nonetheless appears to draw attention to the ways in which we make sense of its musical relationships. The observation that the opening measures in the first movement from Schubert's B major sonata convey a four-key exposition is partly informed by the impression that certain musical components express the codes of a sonata form trajectory—a determination that may be revisited altogether if the notion of a four-key type seems questionable. If the fantasia invites this kind of reflexive turn, we need not entirely refute the value of hearing the B major exposition in the mode of a sonata form. What we might consider instead is the fantasia's capacity to call into question whether compositional freedom—a semblance of the imagination—can be wholly theorized, not only because of the multiple ways in which a fantasia can be realized in a musical setting, but also because of the ways in which its musical codes can be seamlessly woven with sonata form procedures, Schubert's B major exposition offering us one example within a wider compositional practice. This intersection can suggest that the compositional challenge with respect to Schubert's sonata form practices may revolve less around the antiquated question of whether he was capable of adhering to the principles of sonata form (however these are defined), and more around the question of how such associated works balance freedom with restraint, especially with respect to the recapitulation, where prior moments of caprice run the risk of becoming determinate.

Finally, such apparent efforts to bring sonata form and fantasia together may offer one clue as to why there are so few examples of these four-key types in Schubert's oeuvre. Returning once more to the B major exposition, the formal function reading suggested that the first modulating subordinate theme and closing section that follows can compromise the need for a second subordinate theme (see again, ex. 4.3). That is, if the modulating subordinate theme initially expresses an end temporality and achieves strong cadential closure in E major and the closing section initially expresses an *after-the-end* temporality and prolongs this subordinate key, the retrospective reinterpretation initiated by the modulation away from E major can skew the temporal process by "relocating," as it were, the exposition's final harmonic goal to a later time point.[36] Although this unexpected undoing and postponement of the final tonal goal resonates well with the fantasia's ability to undermine convention, the modification can contribute to the overall impression that the exposition, as the initiating unit of a sonata form, may be too long. To alleviate this potential problem, yet preserve some of the musical codes that align with the fantasia, one could omit the second subordinate theme in F-sharp major and recompose one or both of the previous modulations so that they end in the key of the dominant, a solution that altogether would yield a three-key exposition. Or if the exposition from the first movement of Schubert's Sonata in B-flat Major, D. 960, seems to similarly express a four-key design as the B major exposition, with its four PACs in B-flat major, F-sharp minor, A major, and F major (see again, chap. 3, ex. 3.9), another solution to remedying the temporal "lapse" in the B major exposition would be to convey the passage between the third and fourth key areas (E major and F-sharp major) as a second subordinate theme rather than as a closing section that becomes a transition, as suggested in the B-flat major exposition (see especially mm. 59–80). Both solutions may help support the broader conclusion that Schubert's three-key expositions not only developed from an expansion of two-key types but also emerged from an effort to address the question of temporality while attempting to balance freedom with restraint, or fantasia with sonata form—especially with respect to the tonal plan and the treatment of thematic material. While this balance may vary from movement to movement, given the differences in tonal plans and formal designs among Schubert's three-key expositions,[37] the loose-knit features that often render these expositions unusual or strange within the mode of a sonata form can put into question whether certain musical codes characteristic of fantasias are similarly operative.[38]

The opening measures from the last movement of Schubert's Piano Sonata in A Minor, D. 537 (1817),[39] a work that was composed five months before the Sonata in B Major, offers us one example. Compared to the movement's interthematic formal functions, which, when put together, invite us to hear the movement as a

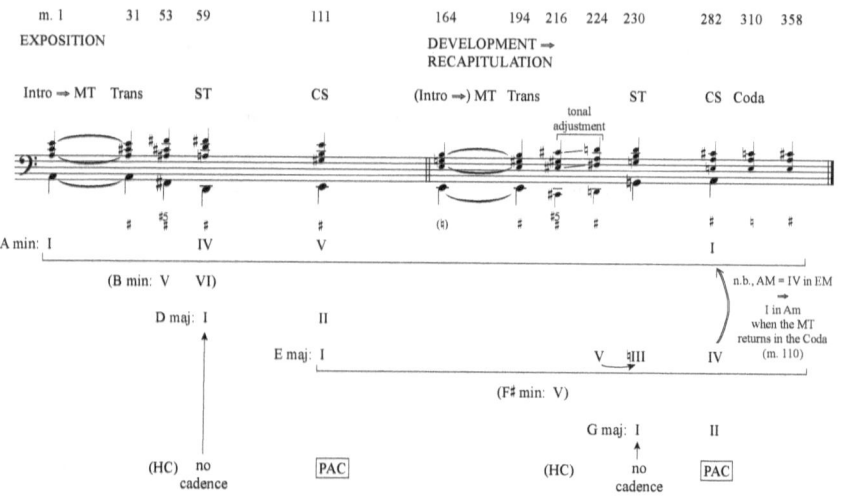

Example 4.8. Piano Sonata in A Minor, D. 537, iii. Summary.

sonata form without a development section (ex. 4.8),[40] the intrathematic functions seem less clearly defined (ex. 4.9). If the opening eight measures unfold as a compound antecedent phrase that reaches a dominant arrival (m. 7), the compound phrase that follows might initially be heard as a compound consequent that then surprisingly averts stronger cadential closure.[41] Not only does this phrase introduce the dominant seventh chord of B-flat major, the Neapolitan, as a harmonic goal (mm. 14–17), but it also readjusts this goal shortly thereafter by repeating a truncated version of the contrasting idea, leading us to a dominant arrival in the home key (mm. 19–20). Similar to the previous compound phrase (mm. 10–17 + 18–20), the next compound phrase returns to the basic idea and remains harmonically open, this time presenting a variant of the first cadential progression (mm. 5–8) in the major mode (mm. 26–29). Altogether, the opening measures can present an enigma to a formal function reading, retrospectively suggesting a string of compound antecedent phrases that lead to dominant arrivals, for which there is no stronger cadential reply. Yet within the mode of a fantasia, the three-fold statement of "beginnings," coupled with the fermatas, full measures of rest, and striking departure to the Neapolitan, readily align with the genre's improvisatory rhetoric. From a formal function perspective, the improvisatory passage may altogether initially convey an introduction that becomes the exposition's main theme,[42] a retrospective hearing that one might similarly experience in the opening movements from Schubert's Piano Sonata in A Minor, D. 845, and String Quintet in C Major, D. 956 (ex. 4.10).[43] In those two movements, an apparent introduction, seemingly unbound in its rhetorical play, may become the main theme of a sonata exposition. Here the crux of each retrospective

Example 4.9. Piano Sonata in A Minor, D. 537, iii, mm. 1–32. Formal function analysis.

reinterpretation appears to lie in the fantasia's capacity to infuse itself within sonata form processes to the point of interrupting our hearing of them as sonata forms. In sum, the opening measures in all three respective first movements (D. 537, D. 845, and D. 956) may not exclusively express a fantasia, introduction, or main theme but rather a play among all three.

Conclusion

In exploring the potential intersection between sonata form and fantasia in Schubert's expositions, my discussion has primarily aimed to understand how both frames can affect an interpretive act. Studying the space between these frames can invite us to contemplate (1) the musical codes that enable us to

a) Piano Sonata in A Minor, D. 845, i

Example 4.10. Additional examples of movements that suggest a hybrid between sonata and fantasia (n.b., introduction becomes the main theme).

b) String Quintet in C Major, D. 956, i

Example 4.10. (Continued)

Example 4.10. (Continued)

recognize when a particular frame may be operative; (2) how each one of these frames distinguishes the central from the peripheral; and (3) how both components—musical codes and frames—can affect our hearing and conception of part-whole relationships in the expositions. A formal section's capacity to seemingly sound superfluous under the principles of sonata form, on the one hand, and integral to those of the fantasia, on the other hand, can point to the possibility that the B major exposition, along with Schubert's other expositions, is not necessarily the execution of one or more master formal archetypes but rather fusions of several interrelated compositional processes that, when closely examined from the perspective of musical composition, pose new challenges when these processes are combined.[44] The combination of sonata form and fantasia—each of which has been realized in a number of ways that prevent them from being singularly defined—may thus serve as only one of several possible fusions.[45] Attempting to inhabit the space between these two frames whose codes appear to intersect can invite us to further reflect on the ways in which we have made sense of Schubert's sonata forms and, more broadly, creative acts of the imagination, which may ultimately resist explanatory closure.

Notes

1. Caplin (1998, 119), for instance, suggests that three-key expositions can be conceived of as two-key expositions with a modulating subordinate theme, since the subordinate theme's first tonal region (or "second key area") seldom achieves cadential closure: "This initial [second] key functions more as an emphasized tonal region in the broader modulatory processes from the home key to the true subordinate key

(dominant)" (119–20). Following Caplin's position (1998), one might posit that a four-key exposition constitutes a three-key exposition with two modulating subordinate themes.

2. On the former view, see Webster 1978, which suggests that similar to the first movement of Schubert's Piano Sonata in B Major, I, the opening movement from the Symphony in B-flat Major "bring[s] three keys in the second group" (26n18). On the latter view, see Newbould 1999, 105–6; Hunt 2009, 82–86; Hunt 2014, 263–64. The two views appear to depart in their respective readings of the subordinate theme group—whether this group begins in C minor in measure 49 or in E-flat major in measure 80. Graham Hunt (2009, 82) proposes that the C minor section functions as "a continuation of the transition zone."

3. Cf. Black 2015, which introduces the possibility of cadential closure in the first subordinate key area through the concept, "deflected cadence." A deflected cadence contains "two successive cadential progressions," the second of which leads to a perfect authentic cadence in a subordinate key at the end of the exposition's transition (165).

4. On this latter view, see Feldman 2002 and 2007. Another hypothesis regarding the genesis of Schubert's three-key expositions is that they emerged from his efforts to appropriate Beethovenian models. For further discussion, see Webster 1978; Longyear and Covington 1988; Hunt 2009.

5. Several authors have recently debunked the notion of a normative type of sonata form. Charles Rosen (1988), for instance, suggests that "it is very dubious that a unique sonata form can be so defined even for a single decade of the late eighteenth-century" (2) and that "the specific model of sonata form which crystallized at the end of the century represents the narrowing of a very much wider range of possibilities" (13). See also Rosen 1972; Horton 2005. On the dialectic between "freedom and restraint" as it relates to art and nature in late eighteenth-century fantasias, see especially Richards 2001 (quote appears on 25n37).

6. Annette Richards (2001) similarly interprets "'fantasia' to mean not only the genre itself, but a musical aesthetic that enters into, destabilizes and complexifies other genres of instrumental music" (18). On the relationship between fantasia and sonata form during this time frame, see Schleuning 1971; Parker 1974; Ratner 1980; Mak 2016; Rusch 2016.

7. On the fantasia as a genre and its relationship to improvisation in the nineteenth century, see especially Gooley 2018, which clarifies that "by 1810 the older type of free fantasia had largely been converted into a rhetorical style or genre of composition. As a genre, it was now developing with little direct interface with improvisational practice, and few players after Beethoven pursued the older free fantasia aesthetic when improvising" (10). As Dana Gooley continues in an accompanying footnote, "the older free fantasy style appears occasionally in printed compositions," the F-sharp minor movement from Schubert's Piano Sonata in A Major, D. 959, offering us one example (23n28).

8. For a related example, see Robert Schumann's 1838 review of Schubert's last set of Impromptus, D. 935, in the *Neue Zeitschrift für Musik*, wherein he suggests

that nos. 1–2 and no. 4 in the set (numbered 5–8 by Schubert) approximate a multimovement sonata: "Yet I can hardly believe that Schubert really called these movements 'Impromptus'; the first is so obviously the first movement of a sonata, so perfectly executed and self-contained [*so vollkommen ausgeführt und abgeschlossen*] that there can be no doubt. I consider the second Impromptu to be the second movement of the same sonata; in the key and character it is closely related to the first. . . . One might perhaps regard the fourth Impromptu as the finale, but while the key confirms this supposition, the rather casual design speaks against it" (translated in Daverio 2002, 49; see also Daverio 2000, 606n6; Schumann 1838, 193). John Daverio proposes that, while the first Impromptu in F minor "is hardly devoid of features generally encountered in sonata-form movements," its lack of a development section and episodic section (mm. 69–111 and 182–224) depart from the sonata-allegro design (52).

9. Otto Erich Deutsch (1947) notes that "the original title, 'Sonata,' was avoided by the publisher, who wished to give a distinctive name to the work; but on the inside heading it is described as 'Fantasy or Sonata'" (627). Richard Kramer (2016) further clarifies: "On the title page of the autograph, Schubert wrote merely 'IV. Sonata fürs Pianoforte allein'" (114n7). See also Deutsch (1951) 1995, 432–33; Hatten 2004, 65.

10. The review appears in the *Allgemeine musikalische Zeitung*, Leipzig, 1813, col. 732.

11. Quoted and translated by Parker 1974, 51; Richards 2001, 199. On the relationship between Beethoven's symphonies and the fantasia, see, for instance, the review of his Symphony no. 3 in E-flat Major ("Eroica") in the *Allgemeine musikalische Zeitung* 7/20 (February 13, 1805), col. 321.

12. Here William Caplin (2010) states: "Musical form directly engages our temporal experience of a work inasmuch as its constituent time-spans have the capacity to express their own location within musical time. . . . And it is precisely the attempt to differentiate just how such spans express their temporality that is the goal of a theory of formal functions" (23, 25).

13. On retrospective reinterpretation and its relation to Hegelian dialectics, see Schmalfeldt 1995, 2011. See also Lewin 1986, which draws from Husserl's writings on phenomenology.

14. Here Carl Dahlhaus (1977) proposes: "[Music] positively challenges the listener who plays an active part in re-creating it as a coherent unity, instead of allowing it to roll past him like an acoustic movie, to be conscious of his activity, and of the conditions in which he is doing it" (114).

15. With respect to nineteenth-century music criticism, see, for instance, Ludwig Bischoff's 1859 review of Schubert's Symphony in C Major ("Great"), D. 944 (Curtis 1979, 193; Messing 2007, 247n60), quoted in chapter 1, which presents a stark contrast to Schumann's ([1840] 1965) celebratory review of the work's "heavenly lengths." Similar reservations about the proportions of Schubert's sonata forms have been raised in twentieth-century music scholarship, including Tovey (1927) 1949, (1928) 1949; Cone 1970; Rosen 1972, 451–60. On the tendency of Schubert's sonata forms to gravitate toward lyricism and stasis, see especially Salzer (1928) 2015; Mak 2015.

16. Tight-knit phenomena include "harmonic-tonal stability, cadential confirmation, unity of melodic-motivic material, efficiency of functional expression, and symmetrical phrase groupings" (Caplin 1998, 17). Loose-knit phenomena include "harmonic-tonal instability, evasion or omission of cadence, diversity of melodic-motivic material, inefficiency or ambiguity of functional expression, and asymmetrical phrase groupings (arising through extensions, expansions, compressions, and interpolations)" (17).

17. In an effort to be consistent with Caplin's theory of formal functions, my criteria for cadences align with his definition in *Classical Form* (1998, 26–29). Accordingly, my analyses take into account the three basic cadence types—half cadence (HC), imperfect authentic cadence (IAC), and perfect authentic cadence (PAC)—that occur at the end of a formal process, as well as the three types of cadential deviations (deceptive, evaded, and abandoned) that may supplant an authentic cadence. I interpret a modulation to a secondary key area as that which is confirmed either by one of the three basic cadences or by a dominant arrival (DA) (a dominant seventh chord in root position or in inversion). Although Schubert's cadential progressions do not always conform to the syntactical patterns that we often find in the music of Haydn, Mozart, or Beethoven, they generally share the same cadential arrivals, enabling us to consider how the composer's approach to formal closure compares to his predecessors. For more on the classical cadence, see Caplin 2004; Burstein 2014; Bergé and Neuwirth 2015.

18. On the topic of "originary repetition," see Korsyn 2003, 91–123.

19. The notated dotted eighth-note plus sixteenth-note rhythm may be performed as a quarter-note plus eighth-note under a triplet rhythm.

20. On this particular type of deceptive cadence, where a root-position dominant resolves to a tonic in first inversion via a passing $\hat{4}$ in the bass (i.e., $V-V^{4/2}-I^6$), see Caplin 1998, 28–29.

21. On the closing section, see especially Caplin 2013, which proposes: "Since every subordinate theme is required to end with a PAC, the potential for the appearance of a closing section regularly arises" (388). See also Caplin 1998, 122.

22. In Caplin's (1998, 51) theory, an antecedent function can be structured as a mini-sentence—the first two downbeats comprising two one-bar basic ideas, and the next two downbeats, a two-bar continuation. While we might construe measures 50–55 as an extended antecedent phrase with an internal mini-sentence that cadences with an IAC and measures 56–59 as a consequent phrase that gradually dissolves, the curtailing process that unfolds over the course of the second subordinate theme (mm. 42–59) seems to suggest otherwise. Measures 50–55 seem more suggestive of a genuine sentence (albeit, in "miniature") and measures 56–59 a liquidated version of this sentence.

23. A similar situation occurs in Schubert's Symphony in B-flat Major, where, following the first subordinate theme in the key of E-flat major, the subdominant (mm. 80–126), a second modulating transition follows (mm. 126–83) that leads us to the key of F major, the dominant (m. 184ff). Unlike the second subordinate theme from the Piano Sonata in B Major, however, the symphony's second subordinate theme curiously reprises the melodic content from the main theme.

24. An analogous temporal revision occurs in the slow movement from Schubert's "Trout" Quintet, D. 667. The first subordinate theme (mm. 24–36) modulates from F-sharp minor to D major and closes with a PAC that elides with what at first sounds like a closing section in D major (m. 36ff). As in the exposition from the Sonata in B Major, the modulation after the two codettas in the quintet (m. 40ff) suggests that the closing section becomes a second transition that leads to a second subordinate theme in G major. Unlike the B major exposition, however, the quintet's second subordinate theme seems more indicative of a closing section as it unfolds, yielding a *second* retrospective reinterpretation of the initial closing section in D major—as a second subordinate theme (mm. 36–53):

Schubert, Piano Quintet in A Major, D667 ("Trout"), ii,
retrospective reinterpretations

mm. 36–53	mm. 53–60
1. Closing Section (CS) ⇒ Transition (Trans)	ST2
2. Trans ⇒ Subordinate Theme 2 (ST2)	ST2⇒CS
(D major -> G major)	(G major)

Compared to the B major exposition and the slow movement from the "Trout" Quintet, the exposition from Schubert's Symphony in B-flat Major does not seem to introduce a postcadential function after the first subordinate theme in E-flat major (mm. 80–126). While the first four-measure group (mm. 126–31) that follows the first subordinate theme prolongs the tonic, the next group (mm. 132–35) initiates a modulation to the dominant of F major, the key area of the second subordinate theme, suggesting that a second modulating transition is already underway.

25. As Bas Aarts (2014) summarizes, the paratactic style is characterized by the "juxtaposition of units of equal status," whereas the hypotactic style entails "the subordination of one linguistic unit to another in a relationship of inequality." While an in-depth study of the relationship between the paratactic style and the fantasia exceeds the scope of this chapter, I briefly address the intersection between the two at a later point in the discussion. For more on the paratactic style with respect to Schubert's sonata forms, see especially Mak 2004, 2006, 2010; Hyland 2014; Martinkus 2017, 2018, 2021.

26. Czerny ([1829] 1983) includes the following types, in addition to an "Allegro (probably as the first movement of a sonata)": "Adagio (in the serious style); Allegretto grazioso (unadorned, or with embellishments in the gallant style); Scherzo presto (à capriccio); Rondo vivace; Polacca; Theme for variations; Fugue (also Canon frequently); Waltz, Ecossaise, March, and the like" (43).

27. On topics and style (including registers), see especially Ratner 1980; Agawu 1991; Hatten 1994, 2004; Monelle 2000, 2006; Mirka 2014.

28. On the intersection between sonata form and variation cycle, see especially Dahlhaus 1986; Wollenberg 2011; Hyland 2016a; Martinkus 2017, 2018, 2021. On the relationship between formal functions and musical topoi, see Caplin 2005. Here Caplin concludes that while some musical topics may more typically appear within a beginning, middle, or end timespan, compared to other topics, the correlation

cannot be easily substantiated (120–24). In terms of the order of presentation of topics in the B major exposition, my analysis seeks to focus more on the contrast between topics rather than on their temporal placement within the exposition. Nonetheless, that the movement begins with a declamatory topic before proceeding to a lyrical one (as opposed to the reverse), may further suggest that certain topics are more suitable as beginnings, middles, or ends and thus help convey the exposition's dramatic arch.

29. Dahlhaus (1986) makes a similar observation in his reading of the first movement from Schubert's String Quartet in G Major, D. 887: "Each variation breaks off more because of the constraint of sonata principles—a constraint that Schubert called to mind late enough—than because it points beyond itself and pushes ahead to the next 'station' of the form" (1–2).

30. These works are *Der Spiegelritter*, D. 11 (1811–12/13); *Des Teufels Lustschloss*, D. 84 (1813–15); *Der vierjährige Posten*, D. 190 (1815); *Fernando*, D. 220 (1815); *Claudine von Villa Bella*, D. 239 (1815); *Die Freunde von Salamanka*, D. 326 (1815/16); and *Die Bürgschaft*, D. 435 (1816).

31. One exception that Donald Francis Tovey cites is the opening measures from the slow movement of Schubert's Quintet in C Major, D. 956. Here he states: "Schubert in the slow movement of the Quintet produces a mysterious brightness by going from E to F# (II) and refusing to explain it away as the dominant of V" ([1928] 1949, 153).

32. The exposition from the first movement of Schubert's Symphony No. 2 in B-flat Major features a similar relationship among key areas:

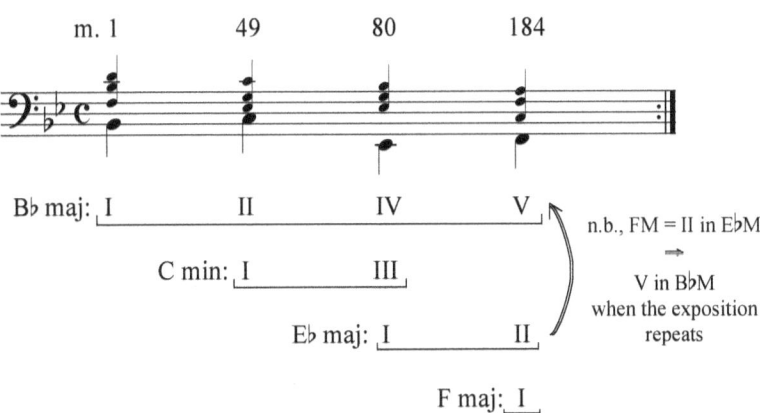

Example endnote 4.33a. Symphony in B-flat Major, D. 125, i. Summary.

After having modulated from the home key to C minor (m. 49) and then to E-flat major (m. 80), Schubert concludes the exposition in F major. E-flat major might be heard as the relative major of C minor, and F major as the supertonic of E-flat major. When the exposition repeats, F major might then become the dominant of B-flat major. The key relations in the slow movement from the "Trout" Quintet, F major–F-sharp major–D major–G major, could be construed along similar lines:

All four tonal regions are confirmed by a PAC, except F-sharp minor, which is established by a deflected cadence.

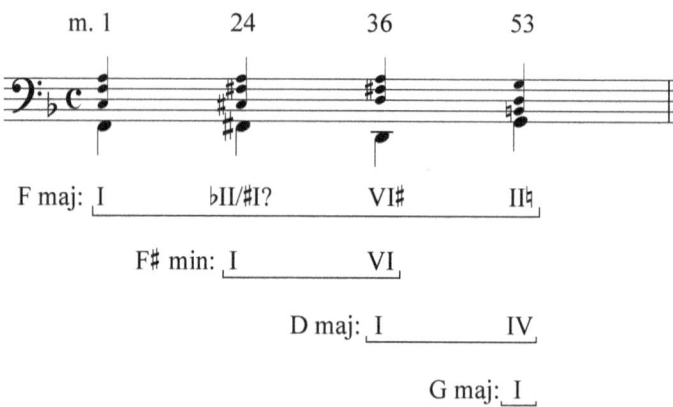

Example endnote 4.33b. Piano Quintet in A Major, D. 667 ("Trout"), ii. Summary.

33. Regardless of whether the B major exposition's topics are better conceived of as styles or vice versa, they can be readily incorporated into a formal function analysis and are not intended to be discrete to interpreting the exposition as a fantasia. On the relationship between topics and styles, see especially Mirka 2014, which defines topics as "*musical styles and genres taken out of their proper context and used in another one*" (2, italics in the original).

34. This point is similarly made by Drabkin, in his entry on the nineteenth- and twentieth-century fantasia (Field, Helm, and Drabkin 2001).

35. In her study of the relationship between the eighteenth-century free fantasia and the aesthetics of the picturesque in English landscapes, Annette Richards (2001) similarly proposes: "In its picturesque dialectic between freedom and constraint, its disguised connections and hidden lines of demarcation, the musical fantastic draws attention to the act of interpretation, of reading itself, and threatens to undermine, and render impossible, the naive engagement of sensibility" (26).

36. On false closing sections, see Caplin 1998. Caplin suggests that a false closing section can occur after the PAC of a main theme in an exposition (i.e., the closing section that follows the PAC becomes the beginning or "initiating unit" of a transition) (129; see also Caplin 2013, 320) or after the PAC of a subordinate theme (i.e., the closing section becomes the beginning of a second subordinate theme) (1998, 123; Caplin 2013, 389). Unlike the latter scenario, where the retrospective reinterpretation remains in the same subordinate key, the retrospective reinterpretation in the B major exposition involves a modulation near the time point where the exposition

could have come to close, suggesting that what was initially heard as the final tonal goal of the exposition has, in effect, not been attained after all.

37. See Hunt 2009, which outlines these variants in detail according to Hepokoski and Darcy's *Elements of Sonata Theory* (2006). Grant (2022) discusses the common features of Schubert's three-key expositions and "proposes a new form-functional model for Schubert's expository practice" (64).

38. With regard to the exposition from the first movement of Schubert's Piano Sonata in B-flat Major, D. 960 (discussed at length in the previous chapter), the thematic relationships, rhetorical pauses (mm. 94–117/119), series of modulations, and changes in texture may also encourage us to hear the exposition in dialogue with the fantasia.

39. Hunt (2009, 83, "Example 7") lists this movement under the category "early three-key expositions."

40. Brian Newbould (1997) refers to this movement as "an abridged sonata form," observing that "there is not even a short link to replace the development: Schubert goes directly from the end of the exposition into the recapitulation, which begins in the dominant" (100).

41. It seems unclear whether a real measure encompasses one or two notated measures (R=N or R=2N). Regardless of whether we hear the movement as R=N or R=2N, the phrases seem to resist a formal function reading. Perhaps the entire exposition (mm. 1–163) might be interpreted, then, as a written-out improvisation with the overall design, sonata form without development, becoming more apparent when the music that follows the exposition (m. 164ff; transposed a fourth down) replicates the same content from the exposition until m. 220.

42. With respect to formal functions, the suggestion that a fantasia-as-introduction can readily become the main theme of a sonata form exposition seems to resonate with Caplin's (1998) observation that "the beginning of the transition is often the moment when the movement seems to be 'getting under way'" (125). See also Czerny ([1829] 1983), who relatedly shows how a slow introduction (and in other cases, a prelude) may precede an allegro.

43. For a formal function reading of these works, see Schmalfeldt 2002, 2011 (113–32), and Martin and Vande Moortele 2014, respectively. Both analyses suggest that the introduction becomes the main theme. Reading the first movement from Schubert's Sonata in A Minor, D. 845, in the mode of a fantasia would comport with G. W. Fink's review of the sonata (Deutsch 1947, 512), quoted in the first section of this chapter. Beethoven's Sonata in D Minor ("Tempest"), op. 31, no. 2, which has been read from a formal function perspective (Schmalfeldt 1995, 2010; Bergé, Cample, and D'hoe 2009; see also Dahlhaus 1978, 9; Dahlhaus 1991, 116–18), might also be seen as work that fuses together sonata form and fantasia principles.

44. Roland Barthes (1971) offers a similar point, concluding that "the text is ceaselessly and through and through traversed by codes, but it is not the accomplishment of a code" (44, cited in Culler 1975, 242).

45. One might also explore, for instance, the potential kinship between fantasias and rondos.

5 Biography, Music Analysis, and the Narrative Impulse

Schubert's Illness and the Promissory Note: A Case Study

Toward the end of his article "Schubert's Illness Re-examined," Eric Sams (1980, 21) poses the following question: "What would be the consequences for musical and biographical studies if Schubert were not only mortally ill for his last six years but also aware of the extreme gravity of his condition?" The condition that Sams refers to is Schubert's bout with syphilis, a diagnosis that had been concealed, if not ignored, in biographies and research on the composer's life throughout most of the nineteenth and twentieth centuries.[1] Aiming to dispel previous doubts about the cause of Schubert's death, Sams (1980) closely examines the medical timeline of the disease in tandem with Schubert correspondence, medical records, and memoirs by Schubert's friends and concludes that the composer's death was more likely caused by tertiary syphilis than by typhus or typhoid fever.[2] Although Sams does not ultimately confirm whether Schubert contracted syphilis in late fall of 1822 or early 1823, he posits that "1823 would mark a decisive crisis in his [the composer's] music as in his life" (21).[3]

Sams's article only briefly comments on the potential links between this aspect of Schubert's biography and his music,[4] though other writings that have appeared after his reappraisal have speculated on these connections in more depth. One well-known and celebrated example is Edward T. Cone's "Schubert's Promissory Note: An Exercise in Musical Hermeneutics" (1982). Published two years after Sams's reassessment,[5] Cone's article explores the potential link between Schubert's illness and music through a close reading of the composer's *Moment musical* in A-flat Major, D. 780, no. 6.[6] Using Wilson Coker's (1972) semiotic approach to musical meaning and aesthetics as a point of departure, Cone (1982) outlines a hermeneutic model for music analysis, stipulating that a work's extrageneric meaning—"the supposed reference of a musical work to non-musical objects, events, moods, emotions, ideas, and so on" (234), which gives each work

Example 5.1. Schubert, *Moment musical* in A-flat Major, D. 780, no. 6, mm. 1–16 and mm. 40–60, after Cone's (1982) "Schubert's Promissory Note: An Exercise in Musical Hermeneutics," *19th-Century Music* 5 (3): 235–39.

a unique expression—must be conceived of in terms of its congeneric meaning, which "depends on purely musical relationships: of part to part within a composition and of the composition to others perceived to be similar to it. It embraces the familiar subjects of syntax, formal structure, and style" (234).[7] According to Cone, it is this unilateral relationship between the extrageneric and the congeneric that grounds a work's individualized expression and discourages the possibility of mistaking a generic description of the work's mood or character for an explanation of its content.

To demonstrate the relationship between the two axes of his hermeneutic approach, Cone first discusses the congeneric meaning of the *Moment musical*, examining the work's musical structure. Focusing on a series of musical events put into motion by a seemingly innocuous E-natural, which he identifies as the promissory note (ex. 5.1), Cone shows how this note pervades the ensuing melodic and harmonic content throughout the large A section (mm. 1–77) of the *Moment musical*'s ternary design to ruinous proportions, despite the notion that the note (and the C major or V/VI chord that lends harmonic support to the promissory note) has been "paid" by the F minor 6/3 harmonies (mm. 48–49) that occur before the onset of the reprise (m. 54). Turning to the extrageneric meaning of the work, Cone then asks:

> What, then is the expressive potential of *Moment musical* No. 6? What kinds of human situations present themselves as congruous with its structure? . . . As I apprehend the work, it dramatizes the injection of a strange, unsettling element into an otherwise peaceful situation. At first ignored or suppressed, that element persistently returns. It not only makes itself at home but even takes over the direction of events in order to reveal unsuspected possibilities. . . . In dealing with the relation of music to its composer's own emotional life, I realize that I can put forward only the most tentative of hypotheses. . . . It is well

Table 5.1. Comparison of Linguistic Descriptions

"Schubert's Promissory Note" (Cone 1982), congeneric reading	"Schubert's Promissory Note" (Cone 1982), extrageneric reading	"Schubert's Illness Re-Examined" (Sams 1980)
At last, then, the promise of E♮ as a leading tone has been kept. (238)	When the normal state of affairs eventually returns, the originally foreign element seems to have been completely assimilated. (239–40)	For a time, indeed, he believed himself cured. (16)
What does occur, as Elizabeth Bowen says of a well-constructed novel, is unforeseen in prospect yet inevitable in retrospect. . . . For the E♮ has returned once more, now as an F♭ that replaces the F (m. 62). (238)	But that appearance is deceptive. The element has not been tamed. (240)	But whatever his condition in March 1824, and however it was treated, the cure was short-lived. (17)
The result is an expansion of the consequent phrase [mm. 62–70] that is terrifying in its intensity. . . . The harmonic material of the development, then, has infiltrated the reprise with devastating effect. (239)	It bursts out with even greater force, revealing itself as basically inimical to its surroundings, which it proceeds to demolish. (240)	It was not continuous or violent until the evening of 17 November. On 19 November, at three o'clock in the afternoon, Schubert died. (19)

established now that Schubert, too, suffered from syphilis. The disease was probably contracted late in 1822; and although it was ameliorated by treatment, or perhaps just by time, it was, of course, in those days incurable. (239–41)

As Cone suggests, the melodic E-natural that encroaches on the work's A-flat harmonic structure may denote a distressing personal circumstance in Schubert's life, perhaps the syphilitic disease that had gradually afflicted the composer's health. The most persuasive element of Cone's argument is the way in which his linguistic description of the *Moment musical*'s congeneric meaning matches his account of the work's extrageneric meaning.[8] With Cone's reading of the *Moment musical*'s comprehensive design in place, his interpretation of the work's expressive potential becomes imminent by way of substitution: the two axes of the hermeneutic model are conjoined by the same narrative reading, or emplotment, of events. This blurring of the boundary between a description of Schubert's illness and Cone's structural analysis of the *Moment musical* seems most apparent when positioning excerpts from Cone's congeneric and extrageneric readings alongside snapshots from Sams's portrait of Schubert's deteriorating health (see table 5.1.).

Cone's hermeneutic model and resulting view of the *Moment musical* might thus be read as a response to Sams's query regarding Schubert's condition and its consequences for musical and biographical studies. His reading of the E-natural that progressively disfigures the work's A-flat major tonal landscape appears to evolve into a tragic narrative account of Schubert's syphilis.

Lived Experiences, Music Analysis, and the Role of Narrative

Cone's view of the relationship between the congeneric and extrageneric in his reading of Schubert's *Moment musical* might be seen today as an early attempt to balance two burgeoning approaches to music criticism in the 1980s. The first approach, which gained a foothold in North American music theory research programs after the inception of the Society for Music Theory (1977–78), bears ties to the New Criticism of literary theory (c. 1938), which proposed that "a text is, in itself, sufficient material for sound critical analysis" (Johnson 2014, 492).[9] The second approach, which may be seen as an outgrowth of the "new musicology," offers a critical response to the first approach, contending that such a focus on the music itself runs the risk of uprooting a work from its social, cultural, and historical context.[10] Rejecting the idea of the autonomous work, proponents advocated for a form of music criticism that views musical compositions as cultural artifacts, bound to the very circumstances from which they emerged. In aiming to demonstrate the relevance of gender, sexuality, and politics, among other related matters to music, this second approach to music criticism offered scholarship not only an alternative way to make sense of musical passages or entire works that appear to depart from convention but also a way to connect the historical past to the present: compositions could be conceived as unique expressions of a shared, diverse sociocultural history rather than as abstract musical structures. Cone's (1982) hermeneutic model, when viewed in this light, might be read, then, as an attempt to show how one might harmonize "non-musical objects [and] events" (234) with a close reading of a work's musical structure. In asking with respect to Schubert's *Moment musical* "what kinds of human situations present themselves as congruous with its structure" (239), his analysis demonstrates how the work's expressive potential (the different stages of Schubert's syphilis) arises from its structural content (the various manifestations of the E-natural, from a surface chromatic pitch to a structural component that undermines the A-flat major tonality).

Further study of the analytical prose that one might adopt to explain the relationship between musical phenomena may lead us to question whether an account of the comprehensive design of a musical work may also be viewed as a cultural, literary artifact.[11] As Marion Guck (1994) has proposed, analytical discourse may not only reveal something about a musical work that had been previously unknown; it may also reflect an analyst's involvement with a work. With respect to Cone's reading of the *Moment musical*, for instance, she writes: "The composer, rather like a novelist, creates a persona whose mental experiences the music depicts. The listener tries to read the protagonist's mind through the musical events, to imagine from them his mental struggle with being trapped and killed by a compulsion. Cone's analyst interprets the work, rather like a literary critic, and listeners (readers), including the critic, psychologically participate in the mental life depicted, whether through identification or empathy" (220). As Guck further proposes in a later article, "Analysis as Interpretation: Interaction, Intentionality, Invention" (2006), analytical discourse also has the capacity to reflect "intellectual, social and disciplinary commitments" (197) and different experiences of a work—"experiences [that] happen in the imaginative space between the interacting human agent and the music" (201).[12]

Conceiving a work and a music analysis as related forms of human expression resonates with the epistemological framework that Wilhelm Dilthey (1833–1911) envisioned for the human sciences. Dilthey, who had written his dissertation on Friedrich Schleiermacher's (1768–1834) ethics, edited his letters, and authored a biography on the philosopher, shared some of Schleiermacher's views on hermeneutics, including the idea that matters concerning the interpretation of specialized texts of religion, law, and classic literature extend to all writings, and the idea that a text may be conceived as an expression of the internal made external.[13] His perspective of the human sciences can help us further contemplate how one might obtain a more comprehensive knowledge of our historical world and the lived experiences that have come to pass. In his *Introduction to the Human Sciences* ([1883] 1989) and, later, in *The Formation of the Historical World in the Human Sciences* ([1910], 2002), Dilthey maintains that the natural sciences generally aim to show through empirical observation how the disparate parts of our universe obtain an order through causal laws or general principles. Because this representation of reality can differ from conceptions of reality that arise from lived experience (*Erlebnis*), Dilthey suggests that it is also imperative to understand the lived experiences of human beings: "The human sciences rely on the relationship between lived experience, expression, and understanding.... What we grasp through lived experience and understanding is life as it encompasses the human race. When we first confront this vast fact, which we consider the starting point not only for the human sciences but also for philosophy, we must go behind its scientific elaboration and grasp life in its natural state" ([1910] 2002, 153).[14] For Dilthey, such lived experiences can be conveyed through what he calls *Erlebnisausdrücke*, expressions of lived experiences, which for him constitute one of three different classes of expressions.[15] On an *Erlebnisausdruck*, Rudolph A. Makkreel (1975) further clarifies that while "Dilthey does not make clear what it consists of . . . we know from other parts of the text ["Das Verstehen anderer Personen," in "Entwürfe zur Kritik der historischen Vernunft"] that facial expressions and gestures, artistic and reflective writings can be considered *Erlebnisausdrücke*. . . . This class of expressions is most often assumed to arise from emotive or imaginative experience" (323–24). In differentiating the goals of the human sciences from those of the natural sciences, Dilthey thus suggests that the human sciences should aim to understand the expressions of others' lived experiences, which in turn will enable us to comprehend our historical world and its values (Makkreel 2021). Additionally, understanding all expressions of lived experiences—especially those of artists, who he views as having the ability to creatively synthesize their lived experiences into unified, self-contained expressions—can inform the ways in which we understand individual lived experiences, which he sees as limited (Makkreel 1975, 326).

In outlining a hermeneutics for understanding expressions of lived experiences, Dilthey distinguishes between expressions that require an elementary form of understanding and those that require a higher form of understanding. Expressions that are understood to belong to what he calls the "objective spirit" require only an elementary form of understanding to determine their common meaning.[16] Comparatively, expressions that seem ambiguous or contradictory require a higher form of understanding. This higher form of understanding will not only attempt to uncover the implicit meaning of the expression by appealing to the context within which the expression emerged; it will also seek to reexperience (*Nacherleben*) this lived experience (Makkreel 2021). Here Dilthey clarifies that this process of reexperiencing should not merely aim to recreate another's lived experience, as such recreations are impossible (Makkreel 1975, 324). Rather, he proposes that one should first imagine how the parts of a lived experience may have come together in what he perceives as a unified expression, or self-contained whole, and then relate this expression to its author in a way that offers insight into the author's lived experience, an operation that can draw attention to something that might have been hidden or perhaps unknown. As Makkreel summarizes of Dilthey's conception of *Nacherleben*: "*Nacherleben* is a *creative* understanding which may go beyond the original. Its task is to understand a text as an unfolding continuity whereby the fragments of life that an author selects are articulated into a unified theme. The *creativity* of *Nacherleben* is specifically what makes it possible to understand an author better than he understood himself" (Makkreel 1975, 329, emphases mine). For Dilthey, the process of situating an expression within its context and then reexperiencing or imagining how the expression distinctly articulates a unified whole through a creative form of understanding can enable us to comprehend expressions of lived experience that seem more perplexing or equivocal.

Dilthey's epistemological framework for the human sciences in tandem with his conception of *Nacherleben* can offer us a point of departure for thinking about the relationship between musical works and our analyses thereof, and about what our analyses may collectively convey about our historical world and its values. That is to suggest that, in drawing from Dilthey's conception of *Nacherleben*, an analysis of a musical work may not only offer insight into how a composer may have synthesized the particulars of a lived experience; it may also be construed as a creative understanding of a work. Along these lines, we might conceive of an analysis not only as a reexperience (*Nacherleben*) of a lived experience, as Dilthey suggests, but, on another level, as a kind of *Erlebnisausdruck*—a reflective writing that conveys an analyst's lived experience of the work which, like the composer's *Erlebnisausdruck*, has been synthesized into a self-contained response.

If an analysis can be conceived as a creative understanding of a composer's expression of a lived experience, how might we synthesize our respective experiences of this expression into unified, self-contained expressions? Returning to Cone's article, his analysis of the *Moment musical*'s structural content appears to discriminate among all of the musical events in the work and determine how the perceived interrelationships that involve E-natural ("the strange unsettling element") and its enharmonic counterpart, F-flat, express a greater unity. As briefly suggested above (and further elaborated below), *narrative* appears to play an imperative role in conceiving the "text as an unfolding continuity,"[17] to refer once more to Dilthey's conception of *Nacherleben*, carrying out at least three functions (a fourth one will be discussed in the penultimate section of this chapter). First, narrative can help one determine which events are more important and how such events relate to one another in terms of cause and effect. Second, narrative can bring closure to a temporal process. Individual musical moments can be woven into a plot that expresses the totality of a work's beginning, middle, and end—the most common plots being romance, tragedy, comedy, and satire.[18] Third, as Kevin Korsyn (1993b) proposes in "J.W.N. Sullivan and the *Heiliger Dankgesang*: Questions of Meaning in Late Beethoven," narrative can serve as "a vehicle for moving between biography and music" (143).[19] Like Sams's exegesis of the primary, secondary, latent, and tertiary stages of Schubert's illness, Cone's analysis of the *Moment musical* weaves together selected events into a similar narrative. Their shared, verbal structure helps facilitate a connection between Schubert's illness and the *Moment musical*.

In light of Dilthey's hermeneutics, Cone's analysis thus not only invites readers to temporally reexperience the horror incited by the strange, unsettling disease that gradually consumed Schubert's life; his written analysis also offers readers an opportunity to reexperience his lived experience of *Moment musical*. As this discussion further suggests with respect to Cone's analysis, narrative provides a way to structure the musical events in the *Moment musical*, convey his experience of these events as a self-contained, unified expression (here, in the form of a music analysis), and unite Schubert's music and biography.

Music and Narrative Revisited: Between Description and Creation

Before exploring further how our readings of Schubert's music and life may collectively convey information about our historical world, the suggestion that narrative can help us organize our experience of a musical work as it unfolds in time naturally calls into question whether we can distinguish between what is inherent to a work and what emerges from the imagination. To what extent are our explanations of causation and the part-to-part relationships in a musical work susceptible to variation among different analyses of the same work?[20] Do some musical moments carry intrinsic or shared meanings within our historical world that invite more stable descriptions from narrative to narrative, compared to other musical moments?

Such points of inquiry can invite us to revisit the broader question of whether music has the capacity to narrate or tell stories, a concern that emerged in response to some of the ideas introduced in writings on music and narrative in late twentieth-century music scholarship. Much of the ambivalence surrounding this issue has tended to revolve around three related questions: (1) whether music can express a past tense, conveyed by a surviving, fictional narrator who is able to recount the tale; (2) whether music can define actants, agents, and functions with the same level of semantic detail as that found in literary narratives; and (3) whether music can directly communicate its own set of causal relationships to listeners.[21] Proponents of narrativity in music have responded to reservations by respectively positing that (1) certain musical phenomena and combinations thereof—especially moments of contrast—make possible a narrative grammar that can alert listeners to shifts in temporality as the music unfolds, regardless of the contention that our experiences listening to music tend to unfold in the present; (2a) a musical work can direct listeners to its subject matter by engaging certain cultural codes such as styles and topics; (2b) meaning may also arise from the relationships between cultural signifiers or, in some cases, between more generically defined musical phenomena, than from individual phenomena alone; and (3) while a musical work may be able to narrow the range of possible listening strategies, the determination of causal relationships ultimately depends on the kind of listening strategy adopted and is thus open to several readings, some of which may be deemed more plausible than others. To speak of narrativity in music along these lines may thus be conditional on the extent to which a work invites a narrative reading and the contexts that listeners bring to their hearing of a work (e.g., music theories or heuristic frameworks for listening).

If different listening contexts can influence how one emplots, or weaves together, musical events into a narrative form, the act of determining which relationships are essential to understanding the work as a unified expression may be more flexible than fixed. Furthermore, a musical work may be open to multiple conceptions of cause and effect with respect to the same sequence of musical events, even under the same motif or unifying idea. David Beach's (1998) reading of the same *Moment musical* analyzed by Cone offers us one example. His analysis retains Cone's idea of the promissory note as a metaphor for causality of the work's part-whole relationships. But the Schenkerian context that informs his reading of these relationships leads him to identify the promissory event and payment differently, partly because the theory distinguishes between chords that arise from voice leading and those that arise from inversion. Quoting Beach at length:

> This passage (mm. 10–12) provides the focus for a very interesting article by Edward Cone, who refers to this motion toward F minor (the submediant) as Schubert's "promisory [sic] note." The idea is that this motion, which is not completed here, must eventually be realized, just as a promissory note must eventually be paid—a wonderful analogy. It is Cone's contention that this promise is fulfilled in mm. 48–9 with the F minor chord in first inversion. The problem with this interpretation, it seems to me, is that we do not hear this chord as an independent harmony but as an extension (involving an implied 5–6 motion) of the preceding tonic harmony—a reference to the covering f^2–$e\flat^2$ motive of mm. 2–3, which here is extended. Perhaps Cone makes

too much of the unfulfilled motion toward the submediant in mm. 10–12. Another way to interpret the C major harmony here is that it provides consonant support for the chromatic passing tone e♮ within an expanded statement of the f²–eb² covering motive . . .

The initial phrase of the B section opens with an augmented sixth chord, which is transformed into a supertonic harmony in six-five position by means of a chromatic voice exchange (where d♯ becomes d♭) before progressing to the dominant. Clearly, we have moved into the realm of the parallel minor, and our expectation as the answering phrase begins is that this will be confirmed. Instead Schubert redirects the motion toward the lowered submediant (F♭ major, which is rewritten as E major). Though this key is confirmed by a strong cadence and an accompanying descent to closure from b♯, which enharmonically equals ^♭3 in the main key, *the stability of the E major harmony is undermined by our memory* of the harmony that initiated both this and the preceding phrase—the augmented sixth chord with the d♯. Perhaps this chord, with its potential dual function, is the real promissory note, *a point to which we will return later*. (85–86; emphasis mine)

Rather than interpret the C major harmony (mm. 11–12) as an unresolved applied dominant of F minor and the F minor harmony (mm. 48–49) as the resolution, as in Cone's reading (see again, ex. 5.1), Beach's reading, by contrast, proposes that both harmonies arise from voice-leading phenomena: the chromatic E-natural (m. 12) receives consonant support during a composing-out of the f²–eb² melodic dyad (cf. mm. 2–4), and the F minor harmony (mm. 48–49) arises from a contrapuntal 5–6 motion above a stationary A-flat in the bass (ex. 5.2). Compared to Cone's analysis of the C major harmony and F minor 6/3 chords, the same two musical events in Beach's reading are thus viewed as less marked. The promissory note is instead recast as the augmented sixth chord (m. 17), a chord that invites cadential confirmation in A-flat minor instead of A-flat major. As Beach's analysis proposes, this anticipated cadence in the parallel minor mode is intercepted by a cadence in E major, an enharmonic respelling of the lowered submediant of A-flat major (F-flat major). His reading then links the sound of the augmented sixth chord (m. 17) to the $V^4/^2$ of the Neapolitan (mm. 65–67), the latter of which serves as a reminder of the deferred cadence in A-flat minor:

> First, Schubert reintroduces the opening gesture the f♭ and the passing c♭ [m. 62], elements of the parallel minor mode, a gesture that he repeats immediately, *as if to confirm that something momentous, perhaps even ominous, is about to happen*. He does not disappoint us, though I doubt we are prepared for the sudden outburst that follows, which I have shown structurally as the parenthetical insertion (an expansion) of an underlying eight measure phrase. This aside, which is introduced *fortissimo* on the third beat of the measure, as if to emphasize its *violent intrusion*, opens with a $V^4/^2$ of

♭II, enharmonically the same chord, though in different position, as the augmented sixth chord that opened the initial two phrases of the B section. Here finally the full implications of this harmony are realized, its promisory [sic] note paid in full, to borrow Ed Cone's analogy. This $V^{4/2}$ of ♭II moves on to the Phrygian II (here rewritten as an A major chord instead of B♭♭) on its ways [sic] to the dominant in mm. 69–70. *Instead of closing, the intrusion is repeated in a lower register, which finally leads to closure, now in the minor mode and in a much darker register than at the beginning,* in mm. 74–77 (87; emphasis mine).

Example 5.2. *Moment musical* in A-flat Major, D. 780, no. 6, after Beach's (1998) "Modal Mixture and Schubert's Harmonic Practice," *Journal of Music Theory* 42 (1): 88–89.

Example 5.2. (Continued)

Whereas Cone's interpretation posits that the final cadence at the end of the large A section of the ternary form hovers between an ambiguous A-flat major-minor tonality, Beach's analysis suggests that the promise of the A-flat minor cadence is finally fulfilled at this very same juncture. In his analysis, then, the deferred resolution of the C major harmony (mm. 11–12) is interpreted as an unmarked event compared to the cadence in A-flat minor that was initially promised by the augmented sixth chord (m. 17).

Though the main objective of Beach's analysis seems to lie in elucidating Schubert's approach to mixture, as opposed to making a hermeneutic claim about the relationship between the promissory chord and Schubert's illness, his explanation appears to emplot the *Moment musical*'s sequence of events as a tragedy, enabling the events in the work to acquire certain meanings.[22] The return of the promissory event (mm. 65–67), for instance, acquires the values "momentous," "ominous," and "violent intrusion," and the fulfillment of this promise (mm. 74–77) is described as foreboding. Considering Beach's direct reference to Cone's promissory note, how might his rewriting of the promissory note (or chord) and

Biography, Music Analysis, and the Narrative Impulse 137

resolution alter the dramatic arch expressed in Cone's narration of events? Both authors' analyses appear to emplot the work's sequence of events as a tragedy, a decision that may primarily be influenced by the large A section's gradual shift from the major to minor mode. But whereas the payment of the promissory note in Cone's story feigns a triumphant outcome when the F minor chord sounds in measures 48–49, the payment in Beach's reading only leads to a tragic denouement. The strange, unsettling element that seems to have been momentarily tamed in Cone's reading appears to shed its deceptive quality in Beach's reading.

Positioning Beach's analysis alongside Cone's may thus not only begin to highlight the variance with which the *Moment musical*'s sequence of events can be emplotted within the same narrative archetype but also the role that both authors seem to play in their respective analyses: as narrators who appear to convey their lived experiences of the work in the form of a reflective writing—in this case, a music analysis. While we could attempt to identify all the narrative aspects of the authors' respective analyses of the *Moment musical*'s events, let us for now consider those features that relate to the concerns aforementioned, with respect to music's capacity to narrate: (1) the use of the past tense or narrative grammar, (2) semantic specificity, and (3) causal relationships. First, temporality seems to function as the "ultimate referent" in both authors' verbal accounts of the sequence of musical events,[23] a temporality that can be viewed as separate from any kind of narrative grammar perceived to be inherent (or not inherent) in the *Moment musical*. Both analyses seem to be told from the standpoint of an author who has already experienced the series of moments unfold and who now recounts how the work's part-whole relationships temporally convey a unique, complex unity. The denouement has been prefigured before the written account begins. Just as Cone's (1982) analysis employs a narrative grammar in the phrases "As we shall see" (236) and "That chord is foreshadowed in the opening" (236), as well as in parenthetical asides that explain the purpose of a promissory chord and how it differs from a deceptive cadence, Beach's (1998) analysis uses such phrases as "undermined by our memory" (86) and "a point to which we will return to later" (86), weaving into his prose parenthetical asides that refer to Cone's article and to certain aspects of the work's metric organization. Lending support to both authors' narrative grammar are pictorial musical examples or figures that allow the analytical act to become unbound to the work's experienced "piece" time. Cone's example 3 (summarized in ex. 5.3), for instance, shows how the promissory chord connects with its F minor 6/3 resolution. Beach's figure 7 (summarized in ex. 5.2) illustrates the striking tonicization of the Neapolitan (♭II) as a parenthetical insertion nested within a normative, eight-bar phrase. Second, both discussions view the modal shift(s) from A-flat major and A-flat minor as significant; yet whereas Cone's (1982, 239) reading construes the final octave (m. 77–78) as

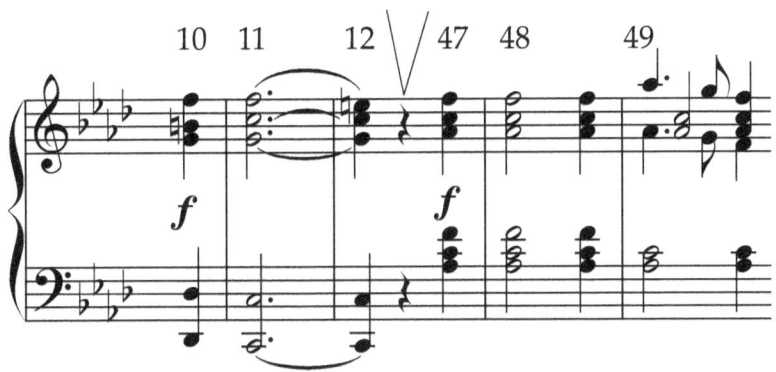

Example 5.3. *Moment musical* in A-flat Major, D. 780, no. 6, promissory chord (m. 12.1) and resolution (m. 47.3), after Cone 1982, 238.

"a neat tactical device," suggesting that neither a major- nor minor-mode ending would have been satisfactory, Beach's (1998, 87) reading maintains that the work's tragic outcome is finally realized "in the minor mode and in a much darker register than at the beginning." Finally, both analyses draw our attention to the musical moments that relate to the authors' individual hearings of the promissory event and to its respective consequences that lead to the work's tragic outcome.

In proposing that narrative helps facilitate an explanation of a work's structural content and impart meaning to musical events, the current discussion does not intend to suggest that the *Moment musical* is open to any kind of narrative reading. It would seem difficult, for example, to emplot the piece's sequence of events as a comedy; the shift from A-flat major to A-flat minor alone appears to narrow the range of possible narrative archetypes, if we accept the sign system associated with the major and minor modes.[24] What I hope to have suggested up to this point instead is that music analysis can serve as the site through which lived experiences of musical works can be expressed. Synthesizing this lived experience in the form of a self-contained written account (or expression) would appear to necessitate a prior working out or determination of which musical events or moments are essential to one's impression of the work and how they relate to one another in terms of cause and effect. Narrative can not only help structure this experience but also serve as a way to communicate this experience in a manner that approximates one's perception and understanding of the work as an unfolding continuity.

The Role of Narrative in Moralizing Reality

If a narrative account of a work's structural content invites us to imagine Schubert's lived experience on one level and reexperience a music analyst's lived experience of Schubert's expression on another level, what might our analyses of Schubert's instrumental works collectively reveal about our historical world? What values can be gleaned from our analyses and what might they disclose about the sociocultural contexts that have helped shape the reception history of Schubert's music and life? As previously suggested, narrative can help us discriminate among musical events and determine how they relate to each other in terms of cause and effect, provide closure to this sequence of events as well as to our explanations thereof, and facilitate a connection between music and biography. Hayden White's (1973, 1987) assessment of the ways in which historians may similarly employ narratives in their representations of reality can lead us to identify a fourth way that narrative can function in a music analysis. As White (1987) remarks, "If every fully realized story, however we define that familiar but conceptually elusive entity, is a kind of allegory, points to a moral, or endows events, whether real or imaginary, with a significance that they do not possess as a mere sequence, then it seems possible to conclude that every historical narrative has as its latent or manifest purpose the desire to moralize the events of which it treats. . . . Narrativity, certainly in factual storytelling and probably in fictional storytelling as well, is intimately related to, if not a function of, the impulse to moralize reality" (14).[25] If the act of emplotting musical events entails determining an outcome, or deciding what the sequence of events collectively convey, narrative can also serve as a way to assign a moral meaning to the totality of musical events in a work and, by way of substitution, an event or series of events in a composer's life. In Cone's analysis of the *Moment musical*, the moral meaning arises from reading the piece and Schubert's disease in the mode of a tragedy: the E-natural/syphilis that refuses to be tamed cataclysmically pervades the A-flat major tonality/body to devastating results. Assembling a work's sequence of musical events into narrative form might be driven, then, not only by a desire to show how the temporal unfolding of events may coalesce into a unified whole but also by an impulse to explain the moral meaning of biographical events.

Examining the moral meanings that our narrative analyses assign to musical and biographical events may enable us to come to a provisional understanding of the historical world within which we have interpreted Schubert's music, particularly the values of our sociocultural communities. These values and the extent to which they change over time can especially be observed by comparing writings about Schubert's instrumental works from different moments in the composer's reception history. Discourse that includes references to gender and sexuality offer us a principal example, with Robert Schumann's ([1838] 1965) "Schubert's Grand Duo and the Three Last Sonatas" serving as a starting point. Although this publication from the *Neue Zeitschrift für Musik* may fall more readily into the category of an evaluative essay than a music narrative analysis, its metaphorical comparisons, which verge on a character study (or brief narrative sketch) of two protagonists who are situated within a monumental history,[26] nonetheless appear to carry a historical index, one that outlines a kind of patriarchy familiar to domestic settings in the nineteenth century: "Compared with Beethoven, Schubert is a feminine character, much more voluble, softer and broader; or a guileless child romping among giants. Such is the relationship of these symphonic movements [from the Grand Duo] to those of Beethoven. Their intimacy is purely Schubertian. They have their robust moments to be sure, and marshal formidable forces. But Schubert conducts himself as wife to husband, the one giving orders, the other relying upon pleas and persuasion" (142). Schumann's writing entwines a gendered description of the two composers with characterizations of their music, using the social and power dynamics of marriage as a metaphor to compare their compositional aesthetics and relationship to one another. At the same time, his likening of Schubert to a child contextualizes the composer's position in history; Schumann appears to place Schubert in a story world inhabited by giants (*Riesen*), or monumental figures, including Beethoven.[27] That music critics continued to characterize Schubert's instrumental works in relation to Beethoven's music along similar gendered lines throughout the nineteenth century—viewing Schubert's compositional approach to harmony and large-scale forms as rambling, passive, and weak and associating his more successful works with domestic environments—suggests that such constructions of femininity were habitual.[28] Given that gendered descriptions like Schumann's have become less prevalent, if not taboo, in contemporary discourse can suggest that our conception of gender and gender roles in our historical world has changed. Indeed, more recent writings in feminist theory scholarship have shown how gender may be performative rather than biologically determined (Butler 1990) and how gender may be conceived less as a binary opposition between masculinity and femininity and more as a spectrum of identities. This rethinking of gender can naturally invite us to ask how more recent narrative analyses reconceive Schubert's musical aesthetic (a question that I will return to shortly) and how this change in understanding can affect the value that we place on this aesthetic.

Where differences among the values of our sociocultural communities seem equally pronounced, if not more so, are in writings about Schubert's illness and sexual orientation. Sams, in his article "Schubert's Illness Re-Examined," appears to have been the first to offer a detailed account of Schubert's medical condition in an effort to confirm the cause of death, remarking in the antepenultimate section that "it seems strange that both [Schweisheimer 1921 and Deutsch 1947] should have overlooked the possibility of tertiary syphilis, which would be entirely consonant with their own views" (1980, 19–20). If Schubert's first biographers appeared tentative in disclosing this aspect of his life, their hesitancy may have been informed by the social stigma associated with the sexually transmitted disease;[29]

linking Schubert's cause of death to a disease affiliated with immorality and deviance would have likely transformed the public's conception of the composer's image and music. The ramifications of this once buried aspect of Schubert's biography especially come to the fore when coupled with the responses to Maynard Solomon's (1989a, 200) assertion in "Franz Schubert and the Peacocks of Benvenuto Cellini"[30] that the composer's, as well as those in his social circle's "primary sexual orientation was a homosexual one" (table 5.2). Of central concern among the responses to this revelatory disclosure is the extent to which musical

Table 5.2. Chronicle of selected publications in Schubert scholarship.

1980	Eric Sams, "Schubert's Illness Re-Examined."
1981	Maynard Solomon, "Franz Schubert's 'My Dream.'"
1982	Edward T. Cone, "Schubert's Promissory Note: An Exercise in Musical Hermeneutics."
1989	Maynard Solomon, "Franz Schubert and the Peacocks of Benvenuto Cellini."
1989	Donal Henahan, "The Dark Side of Schubert."
1989	Maynard Solomon, "Schubert's Sexuality: The Findings Clarified."
1993	Lawrence Kramer, ed., "Schubert: Music, Sexuality, Culture":
	Rita Steblin, "The Peacock's Tale: Schubert's Sexuality Reconsidered."
	Maynard Solomon, "Schubert: Some Consequences of Nostalgia."
	Kristina Muxfeldt, "Political Crimes and Liberty, or Why Would Schubert Eat a Peacock?"
	David Gramit, "Constructing a Victorian Schubert: Music, Biography, and Cultural Values."
	Commentary
	Kofi Agawu, "Schubert's Sexuality: A Prescription for Analysis?"
	Susan McClary, "Music and Sexuality: On the Steblin/Solomon Debate."
	James Webster, "Music, Pathology, Sexuality, Beethoven, Schubert."
	Robert S. Winter, "Whose Schubert?"
1994	Charles Rosen, "Music à la Mode."
1994	Rita Steblin, "Schubert à la Mode."
1994	Charles Rosen, Reply to Steblin's response to "Music à la Mode."
1994	Susan McClary, "Constructions of Subjectivity in Schubert's Music."
1997	Philip Brett, "Piano Four-Hands: Schubert and the Performance of Gay Male Desire."

structures and other related phenomenon can signify sociocultural ones, whether the composer's sexual orientation should be relevant at all to our understanding of his music and whether the heated reactions are fueled by a covert homophobia. Donal Henahan's (1989) article for the *New York Times* "The Dark Side of Schubert" alludes to the latter concern, remarking that Solomon's findings "are likely to distress pious Schubertians, both in and out of the scholarly community" (23).[31] Susan McClary's (1994, 206) prefatory remarks in her article "Constructions of Subjectivity in Schubert's Music" similarly broach the issue, recounting several instances when audience members "made pronouncements in 'defense' of Schubert's reputation."[32] If narrative plays a central role in linking together biographical accounts of Schubert's life and his instrumental works in ways that organize and explain the moral significance of events in one or both domains, then what can appear to be at stake in these exchanges, in addition to the hermeneutic frameworks used to interpret his biography and music, is the kind of protagonist that is permitted to be at the center of the story.

Based on these revisions to our conception of gender in tandem with revelations about Schubert's illness and sexual orientation, we might further contemplate, then, how such shifts in thought have affected the ways in which we emplot and explain the significance of musical events in our narrative analyses of his instrumental works. Whereas Cone's re-presentation of the events in the *Moment musical* invites us to view Schubert's illness as a tragedy, or "defeat of a transgression by order" (Almén 2003, 18),[33] other music analyses since the publication of Sams's and Solomon's articles have rewritten prior tragic narratives of defeat, reconceptualizing, at the same time, nineteenth-century constructions of masculinity and femininity that have tended to inform prior perceptions of Schubert's musical aesthetic. Susan McClary's (1994) analysis of the second movement from the Symphony in B Minor, D. 759 ("Unfinished"), offers us one example of how we might rethink prior conceptions of gender and sexuality in music that appears to deviate from more conventional late eighteenth- and early nineteenth-century formal and tonal practices. As McClary (1994, 213–15) proposes, Schubert's narrative strategy in the second movement as well as in other instrumental works may depart from the bildungsroman—a self-formation or education novel that traces the development of a protagonist (usually male) within middle-class society—not because he was incapable of generating such narratives or because he was more feminine compared to other male composers, but rather because he may have been exploring an alternative form of masculinity. As McClary remarks of this second movement: "Schubert conceives of and executes a musical narrative that does not enact the more standard model in which a self strives to define identity through the consolidation of ego boundaries. Instead, each of several moments within the opening theme becomes a pretext for deflection and exploration" (215). McClary additionally cautions that Schubert's turn to narrative archetypes that depart from more "aggressive formulations" does not confirm in any way that the composer was gay; rather his decision to promote "a sustained image of pleasure and an open, flexible sense of self" in the symphony's second movement may have been motivated by a deliberate effort to expand more rigid formulations of masculinity (223). In situating the second movement of the symphony against the background of conceptions of gender and sexuality in nineteenth-century culture and music criticism, and of more recent debates surrounding Schubert's homosexuality, McClary's emplotment of the movement's musical events invites music scholarship to broaden its understanding of gender and sexuality in art works in ways that go beyond the more restrictive binary oppositions masculinity/femininity and straight/gay, thereby suggesting a different way to rationalize his music aesthetic. Her portrayal of the second movement as "utopian"—an ideal social state where the flexible self, as represented by the opening theme, need not be subjected to domination or violence—might thus be read as an allegory not only of the kind of society or version of moral reality that Schubert may have envisioned but also one that we, too, might strive toward.[34]

With respect to the Symphony in B Minor's unfinished state, McClary (1994) suggests: "Because the conventional return to the overarching tonic B minor for subsequent movements would have returned us necessarily to 'miserable reality,' would have canceled out the g♯/a♭ so tentatively established at the end of the movement, Schubert may well have been reluctant to complete this symphony" (227). Here her analysis appears to emplot Schubert's approach to the B minor symphony as a romance, ascribing to his compositional process a narrative outcome that markedly departs from prior explanations of the symphony's incomplete form. As one comparative example, Martin Chusid's essay "Beethoven and the Unfinished" in the Norton Critical Score, *Franz Schubert: Symphony in B minor ("Unfinished")* (1968), appears to emplot the same events in the mode of a tragedy, proposing that Schubert may have no longer been able to finish the symphony once he realized that removing the resemblances between the symphony's third movement and the trio from Beethoven's Symphony no. 2 in D Major, op. 36, would have destroyed the melodic coherence among the movements (109–10). Eduard Hanslick's ([1870] 1968) review of the first performance of the Symphony in B Minor in 1865 offers us an additional example where McClary's account departs from prior narrative readings:

> As if he could not separate himself from his own sweet song, the composer postpones the conclusion of the [andante], yes, postpones it all too long. One knows this characteristic of Schubert: a trait that weakens the total effect of many of his compositions. At the close of the Andante his flight seems to lose

itself beyond the reach of the eye, nevertheless one may still hear the rustling of his wings (350–51, translated in Chusid 1968, 114–15, and quoted in McClary 1994, 227)

In response to Hanslick's remarks, McClary (1994) instead proposes, "Here once again we find the most loving of insights ruptured by a disclaimer that attempts to distance the anxious critic from the object of desire. I would prefer to say that Schubert concludes with a gentle yet firm refusal to submit to narrative conventions that would have achieved closure only at the expense of his integrity" (227). In suggesting that the utopian narrative prevails because the symphony remains incomplete, McClary's emplotment of the symphony's musical events and compositional process transforms the tragic into the triumphant: like the hero of a romantic narrative, Schubert appears to transcend the world that imprisons him by subverting nineteenth-century conceptions of gender and male subjectivity. Altogether, her discussion explains both the moral significance of the symphony's musical events and unfinished state in a way that markedly departs from prior narrative analyses of the same musical and historical moments.

A similar revamping of prior narratives of defeat can be observed in several of Charles Fisk's analyses of the composer's instrumental works. In *Returning Cycles* and elsewhere, Fisk (2001) suggests that the allegorical tale *Mein Traum*, dated July 3, 1822, could be read as "a secret psychological manifesto and thus as potentially revelatory of affective dispositions and emotional upheavals that might have found expressive correlates in Schubert's music" (9).[35] Such correlates include the Symphony in B Minor, the *Wanderer Fantasy* (D. 760), the second *Moment musical* in A-flat Major (D. 780, no. 2), and the last two piano sonatas in A major (D. 959) and B-flat major (D. 960). When comparing Fisk's analyses of these works to other scholars' respective readings in Schubert's reception history, we can detect a significant departure in the ways in which his analyses emplot the same musical events in each work and explain their moral significance. To take one example, let us briefly consider Charles Rosen's (1972) reading of the rondo finale from the Sonata in A major, which positions Schubert's handling of the formal structure in opposition to that of Beethoven's, in the finale from the Piano Sonata in G major, op. 31, no 1:

> But Schubert's imitations are too often more timid, less disturbing than the originals. For this reason, the structures of most of his large forms are mechanical in a way that is absolutely foreign to his models. They are used by Schubert as molds, almost without reference to material that was to be poured into them.... The nature of Schubert's dependence on classical models can be seen most clearly in the last movement of the late A major Sonata which is based on the rondo finale of Beethoven's G major Sonata op. 31, no. 1 (1972, 456)

Fisks's (2001) discussion of the same movement (here contextualized within the entire multimovement work) instead defines the narrative as one of "integration, of the finding of a home hospitable enough to be a haven for the protagonist's dreams and a refuge from his nightmares" (276). Quoting Fisk at length:

> With respect to Schubert's own project of musical rediscovery and rebuilding of himself in the aftermath of *Winterreise*, the A major of this sonata is perhaps most aptly understood simply as home. At the beginning it is a home that the protagonist who is individuated in the second phrase must encounter and question: he cannot sing in it, and for this reason cannot fully live in it. He explores his own imagination—his own subjectivity, his own pleasure gardens—and derives new approaches to home from these explorations. By the first movement's end, its opening idea has already become singable, and in this way it is far more accessible now than at first. . . . Only the Rondo takes full lyrical possession of home territory and finds ways within that territory to embrace both the dream and the terror to which the dream's pursuit has led. The home that Schubert created in this finale is perhaps utopian, but this is a utopia that he deeply wins and one, accordingly, that comes to life as though it were animated by his own breath and blood. (235–36)

Although both Rosen and Fisk conclude that Schubert prevails in the rondo finale, their respective emplotments of events leads them to ascribe a different moral outcome, suggesting two very different ways of conceiving the composer's relationship to his sociocultural context. Rosen (1972) at first places Schubert in Beethoven's shadow by pointing out the similarities between their handling of the ritornello's diminutions and musical textures but then draws our attention to musical passages where Schubert's "lack of constraint" results in "a work that is unquestionably greater than its model" (456–58).[36] Comparatively, Fisk (2001) positions the composer as an outsider who, through his music, "create[d] for himself the home to which he never entirely found his way in actual life" (268). Even though Schubert's rondo effectuates a utopian homecoming, one that resonates with McClary's analysis of the second movement from the Symphony in B Minor, Fisk ultimately suggests that the hard-won victory that Schubert obtained in his music is a fiction that could not be fully realized (268).

The Value of Narrativity in Music Analysis

If our analyses of Schubert's instrumental music can be construed as a form of creative understanding that contains traces of our lived experiences, it seems possible, then, to view them less as neutral objects that offer impartial accounts of reality (whether musical or sociocultural) and more as cultural artifacts that convey certain values of our historical world. Positioning these artifacts side by side, especially those from different points in time, can highlight changes among our values and perceptions of reality; differences among our metaphorical descriptions and narrative analyses of the same musical works may reflect revisions to our understanding of not only Schubert's music and life, but also the subject matters that his music and life invite us to explore. While the foregoing discussion has tended to focus on some of the discourse surrounding gender and sexuality in Schubert's reception history—here with an aim toward understanding how the proposed revisions to the composer's biography amid a burgeoning cultural pluralism have modified our emplotment of musical events in his instrumental works—other comparative studies of our narrative analyses can allow us to identify additional ways in which our perceptions of reality have changed. Such studies include Schubert's relationship to Beethoven, originality, and history, topics that are further addressed in the next chapter.

What these shifts among our narrative discourses of Schubert's instrumental music and life can also draw our attention to is the extent to which our contexts for reading may be unstable and, as Jonathan Culler (2007, 123) summarizes, "unmasterable, both in principle and in practice."[37] On the one hand, while our current historical situatedness may afford us some distance to reevaluate prior readings of Schubert's instrumental music and identify the sociocultural conditions that inform certain perspectives, it can lead us to question whether our understanding of these same works today are also provisional. When we take into account the number of readings that have accumulated over time, each of which were formulated during a temporal moment that was once deemed a present, the contexts that have and continue to inform our understanding of various aspects of Schubert's music can appear to forever remain in flux. Although narrative may offer some kind of closure to these multiple "nows," every present has the capacity to become a past that can be historicized. Notwithstanding this inability to obtain complete closure, the very notion that Schubert's instrumental music has remained open to different causal explanations and moral outcomes suggests, on the other hand, that such works have resonated with a panoply of life experiences in our historical world and will continue to be socially and culturally relevant.

In addition to questioning what our narrative analyses can reveal about our historical world, we might also ask why in contemporary Schubert scholarship we have been more drawn to certain instrumental works in the composer's oeuvre compared to others.[38] Scholarship's gravitation toward certain impromptus (D. 899, no. 2 in E-flat major and no. 3 in G-flat major), *Moment musicals* (no. 2 in A-flat major and no. 6 in A-flat major), piano sonatas (D. 845 in A minor, D. 894 in G major, D. 958 in C minor, D. 959 in A major, and D. 960 in B-flat major), chamber works (string quartets D. 804 in A minor ["Rosamunde"], D. 810 in D minor ["Death and the Maiden"], and D. 887 in G major; String Quintet in C

Major, D. 956; and Piano Trio in E-flat Major, D. 929), and symphonies (D. 759 in B minor ["Unfinished"] and D. 944 in C major ["The Great"]), for instance, may suggest a shared affinity for works that appear to convey either a romantic or tragic narrative. Both narrative archetypes place the individual at the center of the drama and involve plots that revolve around the individual's ability or inability to transcend a world that threatens to imprison them. That scholarship has tended to return to these same works may indicate that such narratives resonate more deeply with our individual lived experiences compared to others.[39]

Finally, if part of the impetus for emplotting Schubert instrumental works is to try to explain the meaning of musical, biographical, or historical events, to what extent is narrative valuable to analyzing Schubert's music, if the realities that such accounts generate may be partial to our individual lived experiences and the contexts that inform these experiences? One way to answer this question would be to consider what we might lose if narrative were wholly absent or suppressed in our verbal accounts of Schubert's music. Using a similar procedure adopted by Hayden White in his essay "The Value of Narrativity in the Representation of Reality" (1987), let us briefly consider two different verbal representations (or realities) of the opening movement from Schubert's Piano Sonata in A Minor, D. 784. One possible form of representation would be to depict the events in the movement as a list of measure numbers with corresponding musical content. Such a representation, shown in table 5.3, approximates what we might record in writing if we were to assume the role of an annalist. While the measure numbers lend an order to the sequence of events in the sonata's first movement, the annals as a whole do not discriminate among or determine the significance of any of these musical events.

Were we to represent the musical events in the same movement as a chronicle, we might convey them along the lines shown in table 5.4. Like the annals, the chronicle would present the events of the first movement in chronological order but discriminate among them by assigning a central subject for which the events are perceived to revolve around. While both representations of reality shown in tables 5.3 and 5.4 appear to offer a more objective account of the movement's musical events than a narrative analysis—the annals more so, perhaps, than the chronicle, which designates Schubert as the acting subject[40]—neither seeks to explain the significance of these events. It is only when we emplot these events in a narrative form—where the opposed outcomes, victory and defeat or triumph and tragedy, hang in the balance—that we can begin to ascertain the music's social relevance not only in relation to the composer's life but also in terms of our individual lived experiences. The narrative expresses a "moralism that alone permits the work to end, or rather to conclude" (White 1987, 23). The movement's tonal path from A minor to A major, for instance, seems especially marked

Table 5.3. Piano Sonata in A Minor, D. 784 (February 1823), i, annals

m. 1	In octaves: A, half note. E, half note.
m. 2	In octaves: D♯, half note. E, eighth note. C, dotted-eighth note. B, sixteenth note.
m. 3	A octave, half note. E major triad, half note.
m. 4	In octaves: C, half note. A, eighth note.
...	...
m. 286	In double octaves: C♯ whole note.
m. 287	(as before, m. 286)
m. 288	In double octaves: A, whole note.
m. 289	(as before, m. 288)
m. 290	A major chord, half note x2
m. 291	A major chord, whole note, with fermata.

Table 5.4. Piano Sonata in A Minor, D. 784, i, chronicle

m. 1	Schubert begins the first movement in A minor,
m. 61	introduces a new theme in E major,
mm. 94–103	and then transforms E major into the dominant of A minor in preparation for the repeat of the exposition.
mm. 104–65	After he develops the material from measures 1–103,
m. 166	he returns to the opening theme in A minor, which signals the beginning of the recapitulation.
m. 205	Schubert begins to depart from the exposition's tonal design by gradually transposing the music up a perfect fourth (cf. m. 40ff).
mm. 213–18	He then reintroduces the melodic minor thirds from the exposition (now transposed; cf. mm. 47–48), Measures 51–60 do not immediately return.
m. 219	Schubert recapitulates the exposition's E major theme (m. 62ff) in A major
mm. 260–63	before returning to a varied restatement of the E♭–C melodic minor third passage (m. 213ff).
mm. 268–77	He reintroduces the material from measures 51–60, transposing it up a fourth (from E major to A major), and
mm. 278–91	concludes the first movement in A major.

Biography, Music Analysis, and the Narrative Impulse

(ex. 5.4), as does the omission of a transposed version of measures 51–60 in the recapitulation and eventual return of this material in the coda (mm. 268–77) (ex. 5.5). The gradual shift from the minor to the major mode throughout the course of the movement might signify transcendence, an outcome characteristic of romantic narrative archetypes, and the return of measures 51–60 in the coda (m. 260ff) might suggest one final struggle before ultimate victory. Were we to expand our narrative reading to the entire multimovement sonata, we might conclude that the hard-won A major mode victory obtained at the very end of the first movement was only temporary; the first movement's ominous, chromatic neighbors (mm. 1–2 and mm. 5–6) return in the second movement (m. 4 and m. 8) (ex. 5.6), and the final movement's whispered return to the minor mode signifies the peripeteia (ex. 5.7)—the thick, aggressive A minor chords at the end of this last movement resolutely confirming the tragic ending (ex. 5.8). Situating our emplotment of this sonata within the context of events that surround the date of composition, February 1823, might invite us to read this sonata in relation to the peripeteia in the composer's life—his contraction of syphilis and its early signs. Such an interpretation may be supported by appealing to Schubert's request in his letter to Ignaz Franz Elder von Mosel—"Kindly forgive me if I am compelled to incommode you with another letter soon, the circumstances of my health still forbidding me to leave the house"—on February 28 (Deutsch 1947, 269–70). As Deutsch comments of Schubert's letter, "We here for the first time learn something of an illness, which seems to have attacked Schubert already at New Year" (270). Or as an alternative to this reading, we might interpret the

Example 5.4. Piano Sonata in A Minor, D. 784, i. Modal shift from A minor (mm. 1–8) to A major (mm. 282–91).

entire sonata within the context of our individual lived experiences, using as a framework our emplotment of the work as a tragedy. In doing so, we may come to understand, as Robert Hatten (2016) suggests more broadly of Schubert's late instrumental works, the expressive meaning of the composer's musical symbols: "We discover Schubert's move from traditional communicative signs to more ineffable symbols of interiority. We can confidently trace the rhetorical markers for these shifts and note the rarefied effects of their sonic textures. But as the symbolic takes on mythic dimensions, its immediate meanings are revealed to each of us in ways that are highly personal, and for which terms like tragic or transcendent can provide only the most general of labels" (110). That Schubert's symbols have the capacity to resonate with our individual lived experiences in ways that are most unique, yet at the same time familiar speaks to the extent to which his instrumental works—as expressions of his own lived experiences—resonate with different sociocultural communities across different time points and continue to affect us in deep and meaningful ways.

In closing, if my own emplotment of selected writings on Schubert's instrumental music has been driven by an effort to further contemplate the moral

Example 5.5. Piano Sonata in A Minor, D. 784, i. Omission of mm. 51–60 and return in the coda, mm. 268–77.

Biography, Music Analysis, and the Narrative Impulse

Example 5.5. (Continued)

Example 5.6 Piano Sonata in A Minor, D. 784. Motivic connection between the first and second movement.

Example 5.7 Piano Sonata in A Minor, D. 784, iii, mm. 1–4.

Example 5.8 Piano Sonata in A Minor, D. 784, iii, mm. 260–69.

meaning(s) of our music-analytical discourses, then I hope to have shown how our analyses may be conceived as self-contained expressions of lived experiences, ones that offer us an opportunity to further understand our historical world and its evolving values. In addition to inviting us to empathize with those who have either encountered a desperate situation, felt socially marginalized, or both, our analyses may teach us that the hero of a story need not always conform to dominant constructions of masculinity and encourage us to imagine a utopian state where cultural pluralism, in its truest sense, prevails. In sum, our analyses may have the potential to reveal to us both our past and present condition in order to help us determine how we might collectively live a productive future.

Notes

1. Sams confirms that Otto Erich Deutsch (1907) provides "the earliest musicological intimation that Schubert was syphilitic" (Sams 1980, 15). In Deutsch 1907, see especially p. 231 ("Noch weniger dürfen wir glauben, daß Schuberts herz bei einer der namenlosen Liebeleien affiziert wurde, deren eine im Jahre 1823 mit ihren bösen folgen sein Leben bedrohte. Nicht in der Höldrichsmühle bei Mödling, auch nicht in der Schubertmühle bei Zseliz, wie die Sage will, sondern im Spital hat Schubert damals, an einer schweren venerischen Krankheit daniederliegend, die ersten "Müllerlieder" komponiert"). See also Deutsch 1947, 287 ("After a few earlier hints we find here the first definite mention of a serious illness suffered by Schubert. There is no doubt that it was venereal, probably syphilis"). Maurice Brown (1958) clarifies that "the conventions of the nineteenth-century [sic] forbade any reference to the disease in the biographies of the composer; the complete absence of contemporary references, although the trouble was known to all his friends, suggests that documents, letters and so on, have been destroyed. Schubert's illness is mentioned, if at all, as a passing indisposition" (127).

2. See also McKay 1996, Gibbs 2000, and Byrne Bodley and Horton 2016b, which respectively offer different perspectives on the cause of Schubert's death. Elizabeth Norman McKay (1996) suggests that "all available evidence seems to point to the ultimate cause of Schubert's death being typhoid fever in a man afflicted with active tertiary syphilis and compounded by the toxic effects of treatment and self-neglect" (331). Christopher Gibbs (2000) proposes that "the diagnosis is not settled. Tertiary syphilis is one possibility, or complications from the condition (undoubtedly his immune system was weakened by the disease), or typhoid fever, or something else" (168). Lorraine Byrne Bodley and Julian Horton (2016b) conclude that "given the pace of Schubert's work, it is unlikely that he died of tertiary syphilis or neurosyphilis, the onset of which is characteristically between seven and thirty years of infection. The record of Schubert's symptoms, however, relates directly to *Typhus abdominalis*, a bacterial infection (*Salmonella typhi*) which was extremely common in nineteenth-century Vienna and from which Schubert's mother had died" (5).

3. As Sams remarks, the fall of 1822 is suggested by Brown (1958, 126), even though biographical documents more strongly support the hypothesis that the composer contracted primary syphilis in early 1823 (Sams 1980, 15). On Schubert's "year of crisis," expressed in his letter to Leopold Kupelwieser on March 31, 1824, see especially Gingerich 2014, 41–58, which discusses in depth the setbacks that Schubert faced during this timeframe. As John Gingerich suggests, this year of crisis "was the catalyst for the completed works from 1824 and after" (2014, 40).

4. Here Sams refers to the Symphony in B Minor, D. 759 ("Unfinished") (October 1822), the two Müller song cycles—*Die schöne Müllerin*, D. 795 (May–November 1823) and *Winterreise*, D. 911 (February–October 1827)—and the String Quintet in C Major, D. 956 (ca. August–September 1828) (1980, 17).

5. Sams's (1980) article is cited by Edward Cone in footnote 14 (Cone 1982, 241).

6. No. 6 was first published by Sauer & Leidesdorf in December 1824 with the added title, "Plaintes d'un Troubadour" (Complaints of a Troubadour) (Deutsch [1951] 1995, 360–61).

7. Cone (1982) clarifies that his hermeneutic model seeks to revise Coker's definition of extrageneric meaning by positing that it can only be built upon "a close structural analysis": "The locus of expression in a musical composition is to be sought neither in its wider surfaces nor in its more detailed motivic contours, but in its comprehensive design, which includes all the sonic elements and relates them to one another in a significant temporal structure" (235).

8. Aware of this similarity, Cone (1982) writes: "An astute reader will have noticed that my analysis has not been wholly objective. I have insinuated a few leading phrases to suggest to him the kind of expression I find in the work, and to encourage him to hear it in the same way" (239).

9. See also Christensen 2001, which similarly suggests: "Other potent influences on music analysis (particularly in the 1960s) were developments in literary theory and specifically the movements of 'New Criticism' and structuralism, by which texts were analysed as discrete autonomous objects standing apart from questions of historical origin or authorial intention" (497).

10. For further discussion on these two views, see especially McCreless 1996b, 1997, 2000.

11. This is not to suggest that Cone views the congeneric as wholly objective. See, for instance, p. 234, wherein he states: "Whereas the relative stability of congeneric interpretations has tempted some analysts to claim that their conclusions are objectively demonstrable, it is hard to reach any consensus about the expressive or other extrageneric significance of even the simplest composition, save perhaps in the broadest terms."

12. In addition to Guck 1994, 2006, see especially Maus 1988, 1993, 2004; Cusick 1994.

13. On the emergence of a generalized hermeneutics, see Szondi 1995, which proposes that the writings of Johann Martin Chladenius (1710–1759), Georg Friedrich Meier (1718–1777), and Georg Anton Friedrich Ast (1778–1841)—which raise

questions about historical objectivity, semiology, and the concept of the spirit—may be read as precursors to Schleiermacher's and Dilthey's hermeneutics.

14. As Rudolf Makkreel (1975, 307) summarizes of Dilthey's position, "Man knows abstractly that he is a part of nature, but he can intuitively understand his participation in the transformation of nature as it is objectified and preserved in the products of his activity and understanding."

15. The other two classes of expressions are (1) *concepts, propositions,* and *larger thought-structures,* which maintain their identity irrespective of the context within which they emerged (Makkreel 1975, 322), and (2) *actions,* which are understood to carry out a goal (323). For a summary of Dilthey's three classes of expressions, see Makkreel 1975, 322–24; Dilthey 1959.

16. For further clarification on Dilthey's concept of "objective spirit," especially as it relates to Hegel's initial formulation, see Makkreel 1975, 305–14. As Makkreel remarks of Dilthey's use of the term, *objective spirit* does not "posit any ideal communion of spirit, but designates the plurality of objectifications that can be empirically discovered through the study of history. It is a covering term for *all* modes of expression of human life as they manifest themselves in the external world" (Makkreel 1975, 308).

17. This chapter focuses on the role that narrative plays in music analyses of Schubert's instrumental works, though a similar study could be undertaken with respect to biographical accounts of the composer. Heinrich Kreissle's *The Life of Schubert* (1869), for instance, may be viewed as a literary biography, a genre of writing that similarly uses narrative to discriminate among a series of historical events and explain their significance. For a related discussion, see Gibbs 1997b. On the literary biography, see Benton 2009.

18. For more on these four plots, or "narrative categories," see especially Frye (1957) 2000.

19. Of J. W. N. Sullivan's reading of the third movement of Beethoven's String Quartet in A Minor, op. 132, Korsyn (1993b) states: "Sullivan's desire for a reconciliation of opposites, for organic continuity, determines every aspect of his approach. The Romantic *Bildungsgeschichte* becomes a vehicle for moving between biography and music: the same poetic models that underlie Sullivan's interpretation of Beethoven's life are appropriated to describe the spiritual content of his music" (143).

20. See especially chapter 1 in Burnham 1995, which offers a critical overview of the analytical stories told of Beethoven's Eroica symphony.

21. These concerns are voiced in Abbate 1989, 1991; Nattiez 1990. Almén 2003, 2008, and Klein 2004 summarize and address these reservations.

22. On "explanation by emplotment" with respect to the historical field, see White 1973, 7–11.

23. On narrative and time, see especially Paul Ricoeur (1980), who states: "I take temporality to be that structure of existence that reaches language in narrativity and narrativity to be the language structure that has temporality as its ultimate referent" (169).

24. See especially Robert Hatten (1994, chap. 2), who discusses the notion of markedness in relation to the major and minor modes. As Hatten summarizes, the

relationship between the two modes is asymmetrical, because the minor mode "has a narrower range of meaning than major" (36).

25. See also White 1973, which suggests that "providing the 'meaning' of a story by identifying the *kind of story* that has been told is called explanation by emplotment" (7).

26. References to "monumental history" can be found in Nietzsche's essay, "On the Uses and Disadvantages of History for Life" ([1874] 1997), which is further discussed in chapter 6.

27. Scott Messing (2006) explores in detail Schumann's gendered depiction of Schubert and Beethoven in the 1838 essay and the long-standing repercussions for the reception history of Schubert's music and image. As Messing confirms, "Schumann's invention of Schubert's *Mädchencharakter* came at a time when gendered descriptions of music were aesthetic constructions common enough to find their way into the composer's prose" (56). Shortly thereafter, Messing similarly suggests that "Schumann often served as the authoritative touchstone for the early attempts to place Schubert in a historical context" (56).

28. See, for instance, Sir George Grove's (1883) entry "Franz Peter Schubert" in the first edition of *Grove Dictionary of Music and Musicians* ("Another equally true saying of Schumann's is that, compared with Beethoven, Schubert is a woman to a man. For it must be confessed that one's attitude towards him is almost always that of sympathy, attraction, and love, rarely that of embarrassment or fear" [364]); and Christopher Gibbs (1997b), who summarizes these gendered depictions of Schubert and Beethoven. Suzannah Clark (2011a) relatedly shows how "Schubert's physique was pressed into service to explain the diffuseness in his instrumental music" (45), referring to multiple writings by biographers and historians, including Hutching 1945; Mason 1906; C. Gray 1928. See especially Clark 2011a, 39–52, "From Vogl's voice to Schubert's body."

29. See again Brown 1958, 127.

30. See also Solomon 1981, which discusses Schubert's sexual orientation within the context of the composer's tale, "Mein Traum": "All of this—fear of female sexuality, thinly disguised matricidal impulses, passivity towards the father, libidinal union with idealized male figures, identification of love with pain, fantasies of feminine transformation—implies that Schubert's oedipal conflict did not have a traditional resolution. And indeed, the facts of his lifestyle, his bachelorhood, his intense and loving male relationships, his reported antipathy to women, and multiple reports of his disordered sexual behavior, are strongly suggestive of a homosexual orientation" (146).

31. Donal Henahan (1989) infers from Maynard Solomon (1989a) that "the unorthodox lifestyle" that Schubert admirers found repugnant may not have been the composer's homosexuality but rather the "connotations of child molestation." In his rebuttal, Solomon (1989b) clarifies that "Schubert was by no means a 'child molester,' for that phrase has implications of compulsion and malevolence. . . . There is not the slightest sign that Schubert ever molested anyone."

32. Here Susan McClary (1994) discusses the reactions of attendees at an AMS session on Schubert in 1991 and at the Y on Ninety-Second Street in 1992. See also

Charles Rosen's (1994b) reply to Rita Steblin (1994), which, in turn, is a response to Rosen 1994a.

33. On the possible hierarchical configurations of transgression and order as they relate to the four narrative archetypes (romance, comedy, tragedy, and satire), see Almén 2003, 2008. Byron Almén further adds that readers' sympathies lie with the victors in the case of a comedy and romance, and with the conquered or overpowered in the case of a tragedy and satire (2003, 18; see also 2008, 64–67).

34. Toward the end of her essay, McClary (1994, 225) suggests that Schubert also appears to have "produced victim narratives, in which a sinister affective realm sets the stage for the vulnerable lyrical subject, which is doomed to be quashed" and refers to the first movement of the Symphony in B Minor as an example. Cone's (1982) hermeneutic reading of the last *Moment musical* might also comport with McClary's description of victim narratives. On McClary's discussion of Cone 1982, see p. 226.

35. See also Fisk 2000a, 2000b, and the discussion of Fisk's reading of the second *Moment musical* in A-flat Major in chapter 2 of this monograph, which also includes a brief summary of the tale.

36. See also William Kinderman's (2016) discussion of this movement. Here Kinderman proposes that the F-sharp major passage (mm. 211–20) "offers a transfigured vision of the tonality of the tragic slow movement glimpsed through the veil of the rondo theme. Beethoven's works offered models for this procedure . . . but Schubert's execution of this artistic device displays a subtle and profound character, which belongs to him alone" (54).

37. Jonathan Culler (2007) further states in this regard, "Meaning is context-bound, but context is boundless" (123). Although Culler's remarks are given in response to J. L. Austin's (1975) theory of speech acts, as read through the lens of Derrida's writings, his conclusion regarding the formation of meaning in relation to a given context seems relevant to the current discussion.

38. I would like to thank Kevin Korsyn for posing this question in his comments on an earlier essay that I wrote on the role of romantic narrative archetypes in contemporary Schubert music criticism.

39. On the reception history of Schubert's image, see Gibbs 1997b. Here Gibbs concludes that "the image of Schubert changes in response to the culture that perceives him. The Biedermeier Schubert, the Romantic Schubert, and now a Postmodern Schubert are creations of periods that approach historical documents and musical compositions with changing expectations, seeking new information, and asking different questions" (55). See also Clark 2011a, 6–55.

40. Both representations of reality would nonetheless seem to rely on a perceiving subject to determine how to parse and describe musical events.

6 Beyond Homage and Critique: Rethinking Musical Influence

Schubert's Approach to Composition through the Lens of Beethoven's Music: Homage or Critique?

It would be difficult to draw conclusions about Schubert's reception history without taking into account the role that Beethoven's music has played in shaping our understanding of Schubert's approach to composition.[1] Among the composers whose works Schubert also engaged, including Handel, Gluck, Haydn, Mozart, Zumsteeg, Hummel, and Rossini, Beethoven has figured the largest in scholarship's evaluations of Schubert's music, from the earliest reviews in the *Allgemeine Musikalische Zeitung* to more recent publications. As Christopher Gibbs (1997b) summarizes, "Much of Schubert's image was created in counterpoint to Beethoven's.... The two are opposed in terms of a supposed 'work ethic' and characteristic genres (Lied versus symphony), as well as in fame, personality, lifespan, and so on" (50).[2] Scott Messing (2006) similarly concludes, "A writer could be sympathetic to and even perceptive about the composer's gifts, but the case for Schubert was often characterized in terms of a relationship with Beethoven" (61).[3] When one engages with the writings on Schubert's music and his life, one is likely to encounter Beethoven.

Such consensus of Beethoven's prominent presence in Schubert's reception history notwithstanding, assessments of Schubert's compositional abilities in relation to Beethoven's have tended to differ. Whereas one anonymous reviewer from the Leipzig *Allgemeine Musikalische Zeitung* remarked in 1820 that "in this first dramatic essay [*Die Zwillingsbrüder*] he [Schubert] seems to attempt to fly as high as Beethoven and not to heed the warning example of Icarus" and that "little true songfulness is to be found, whereas hardly any repose is to be met with in confused and surcharged instrumentation, anxious striving after originality and continual modulation" (Deutsch 1947, 139), Josef Hüttenbrenner declared in a letter to Carl F. Peters two years later that "among the newer local composers

Vienna again possesses a talent to-day which has already attracted general attention and enjoyed the resident public's favour—in short, and without exaggeration, we may speak of a 'second Beethoven.' Indeed that immortal man says of him: 'This one will surpass me'" (Deutsch 1947, 232).[4] Offering a more middle-ground appraisal of Schubert's talents, Joseph von Spaun, in a letter to Eduard von Bauernfeld penned shortly after the composer's death, conceded: "In spite of all the admiration I have felt for my dear friend, for years, I am of the opinion that, in the field of instrumental and church music, we shall never make a Mozart or a Haydn out of him, whereas in song he stands unsurpassed. It was in this type of composition that he made his name, and in it he knows no peer. I believe, therefore, that Schubert must be approached by his biographer as a song writer" (Deutsch 1958, 30).[5] As John Gingerich (2014, 48–49) points out, Spaun would revise his initial assessment of Schubert's instrumental music approximately thirty years later in his "Notes on my association with Franz Schubert" (1858): "There is a prejudice that Schubert was born only to be a song writer. His pianoforte pieces are wonderful. His splendid D minor Quartet, his magnificent Symphony in C were failures in Vienna and it is only due to Mendelssohn and Schumann, who knew better how to value Schubert, that the fame of these wonderful compositions reached us from Leipzig; to Hellmesberger and to the Müller brothers went the merit of making us acquainted with the splendid quartet, and to Kapellmeister Eckert the merit of obtaining recognition for the glorious symphony" (Deutsch 1958, 140).[6] That Spaun's impression of Schubert's legacy appears to have shifted around this time resonates with the public's gradual exposure to the composer's longer instrumental works.[7] By midcentury, several of Schubert's piano sonatas, chamber works, and symphonies had already been posthumously performed and published, including the Piano Sonatas in A Major, D. 664 (pub. 1829); A Minor, D. 784 (pub. 1839); C Minor, D. 958 (pub. 1839); A Major, D. 959 (pub. 1839); B-flat Major, D. 960 (pub. 1839); B Major, D. 575 (pub. 1846); and A Minor, D. 537 (pub. 1852), as had the Piano Quintet in A Major, D. 667 ("Trout," pub. 1829); the String Quartets in D Minor, D. 810 (pub. 1831), and G Major, D. 887 (pub. 1851); the Piano Trio in B-flat Major, D. 898 (pub. 1836); and the String Quintet in C Major, D. 956 (pub. 1853), and the two Symphonies in C Major, D. 589 ("Little") (perf. 1828), and D. 944 ("Great") (perf. 1839; pub. 1840). Notwithstanding earnest efforts to bring to the public's attention Schubert's larger, unknown works, comparisons to Beethoven's music still abounded, with Schumann's discovery and review of the Symphony in C Major ("Great") for the *Neue Zeitschrift für Musik* ([1840] 1956) offering a notable case in point.[8]

    Schubert's own writings about Beethoven contain a nonesuch about his view of the older composer's music, raising the question of whether his opinion was always a positive one. In a diary entry dated June 16, 1816, wherein Schubert reflects on the celebration of Antonio Salieri's fiftieth-anniversary year in Vienna, he states:

> It must be beautiful and refreshing for an artist to see all his pupils gathered about him, each one striving to give his best for his jubilee, and to hear in all these compositions the expression of pure nature, free from all the eccentricity that is common among most composers nowadays, and is due almost wholly to one of our greatest German artists; that eccentricity which joins and confuses the tragic with the comic, the agreeable with the repulsive, heroism with howlings and the holiest with harlequinades, without distinction, so as to goad people to madness instead of dissolving them in love, to incite them to laughter instead of lifting them up to God. To see this eccentricity banished from the circle of his pupils and instead to look upon pure, holy nature, must be the greatest pleasure for an artist who, guided by such a one as Gluck, learned to know nature and to uphold it in spite of the unnatural conditions of our age. (Deutsch 1947, 64)

Identifying the German artist in the diary entry has proven to be less of a question in music scholarship than puzzling out the rationale for Schubert's unfavorable view of Beethoven's music.[9] Deutsch (1947, 64), for instance, attributes Schubert's disapproval to Salieri's influence, to which Maynard Solomon (1998) adds, "Salieri could not accept Beethoven's later works, and it was during Salieri's tutelage of Schubert that the young composer became for a short while so heated an opponent of Beethoven's music" (98).[10] Offering a more sympathetic reading of the diary entry, Gibbs (2003) suggests that Schubert's remarks may not necessarily "indicate an 'early repudiation' of Beethoven" (118) as much as reflect "important musical and aesthetic issues current around 1816" (133). As Gibbs continues, "It seems quite a stretch for Schubert's diary entry to serve as the basis for positioning overt hostility on his part toward Beethoven, especially when every other primary and secondary source, his every other action, and a good amount of musical evidence suggest just the opposite" (135).

Such sources, actions, and musical evidence have indeed helped confirm Schubert's admiration for Beethoven and his music, lending support to the long-standing conclusion that Schubert's instrumental works attempt to emulate, if not imitate, his predecessor's. When Schubert's instrumental works seem to allude to Beethoven's compositional techniques or directly quote from the older composer's music, writings throughout the majority of Schubert's reception history have proposed that these forms of appropriation can be interpreted either as a musical homage or as evidence that Schubert modeled several of his works on Beethoven's out of a lack of formal training or skill—a view that generally positions Schubert as a passive participant within a history comprised of musical monuments and monumental figures.[11] It is only recently that such conclusions

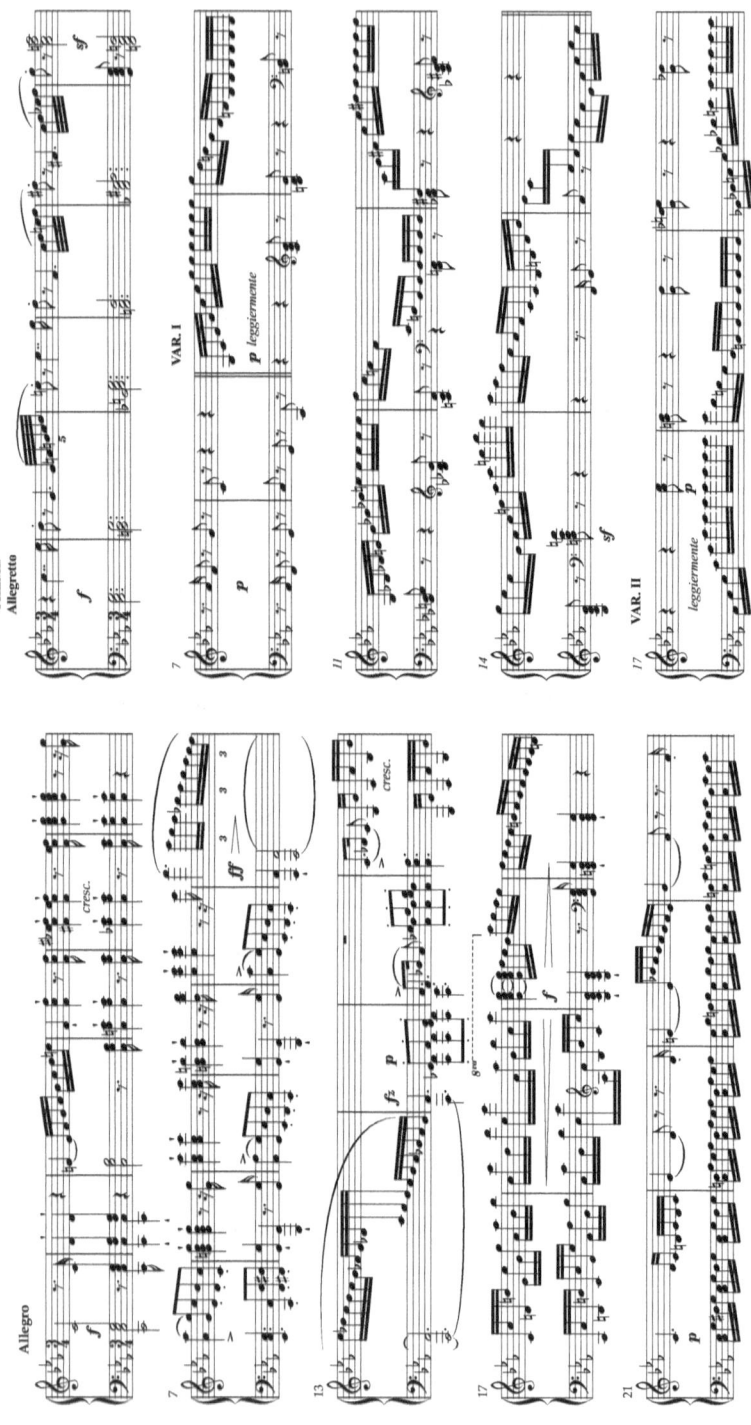

Example 6.1. Schubert, Sonata in C Minor, D. 958, i, mm. 1–24 (left). Beethoven, Thirty-Two Variations in C Minor, WoO 80, theme and variations 1–2 (right).

about musical influence and, more specifically, the meaning of certain musical repetitions between Schubert's and Beethoven's works have been called into question. Several contemporary writings have encouraged us to rethink these perspectives of musical homage and model composition, suggesting instead that the same kinds of musical appropriations can be read as responses or, in some cases, antipodes to Beethoven's music; if Schubert's instrumental music invokes Beethoven's, it is only because the composer sought to critically engage with the same models in an effort to transcend them. Here Schubert is positioned as an active participant within this history of monuments, a move that, in effect, reverses the active-passive dynamic between predecessor and latecomer.

The opposing views seem most visible when engaging with different readings of the first movement from Schubert's Piano Sonata in C Minor, D. 958 (1828), which is believed to contain a reference to the theme from Beethoven's Thirty-Two Variations in C Minor, WoO 80 (c. 1806) (exs. 6.1 and 6.2; the rationale for why the two themes are shown twice in reverse order will be clarified shortly). Both pieces share the same tonic and 3/4 meter and feature a minor sixth chromatic ascent from C to A-flat in the right hand. Conclusions regarding the meaning of Schubert's apparent repetition of Beethoven's theme, however, tend to diverge. In his article "Schubert's Beethoven" (1970), for instance, Edward T. Cone (1970) renders Schubert's sonata as a musical homage:

> Thus, when one finds in each of the last three piano sonatas, composed almost simultaneously during the summer of 1828, a reference to the music of the master, then one begins to suspect that Schubert may have been deliberately trying to pay tribute to the memory of the illustrious colleague who had died only a short time before.
>
> The C minor Sonata makes only a bow in Beethoven's direction, but it is one that reveals more than mere politeness. Schubert's opening is taken almost note-for-note from the theme of Beethoven's Thirty-Two Variations in C minor. (780)

Arthur Godel reaches a similar conclusion about the same work in *Schuberts Letzte Drei Klaviersonaten* (1985): "Für den Schubert von 1828, der in diesem Werk seinem Beethoven so deutlich die Reverenz erweist, war ein Sonatensatz ohne ein sehr fein geknüpftes Netz motivisch-thematischer Beziehung wohl kaum vorstellbar" (124) [For Schubert in 1828, who in this work so clearly pays reverence to Beethoven, a sonata movement was hardly conceivable without an intricately woven network of motivic-thematic relationships].

Other writings appear to convey a general reluctance to explain Schubert's reference to Beethoven's Variations in C minor as an overt gesture of reverence. Instead, they suggest that the same iteration can be interpreted as a critique, or response, to Beethoven's work. In his two essays on Schubert's piano sonatas,

Example 6.2. Beethoven, Thirty-Two Variations in C Minor, WoO 80, theme and variations 1–2 (left). Schubert, Sonata in C Minor, D. 958, i, mm. 1–24 (right).

Alfred Brendel (2015) posits: "It seems to me that the similarities of these two openings are less revealing than their differences. . . . Schubert relates to Beethoven, he reacts to him, but he follows him hardly at all. Similarities of motif, texture, or formal pattern never obscure Schubert's own voice. Models are concealed, transformed, surpassed" (130 and 197). Hans-Joachim Hinrichsen, in his discussion of Schubert's sonata forms in *Untersuchungen zur Entwicklung der Sonatenform in der Instrumentalmusik Franz Schuberts* (1994), also expresses some skepticism toward understanding Schubert's apparent reference to Beethoven's Theme and Variations as a musical homage:

> Gegen die ältere Literatur, die eine Anlehnung an Beethovensche c-Moll-Vorbilder wie op. 10 Nr. 1 oder op. 13 unterstellte, hat Arthur Godel auf ein anderes Modell für das Initialthema der Sonate aufmerksam gemacht: Es handelt sich um eine erstaunlich präzise Kontrafaktur des Themas der c-Moll-Variationen WoO 80. Gerade diese Beobachtung aber legt es nicht zwingend nahe, diese Übernahme ganz auf der Linie der älteren Interpretation einfach als 'Reverenz' an Beethoven zu deuten. Ob nämlich die erstaunliche Entscheidung, ein beethovensches Variationenthema zum Hauptthema eines Sonatenkopfsatzes umzufunktionieren, unmißverständlich die Absicht einer Anlehnung ausdrückt oder aber im Gegenteil die entscheidende Markierung einer selbstbewußten Gegenposition, läßt sich nur durch die Berücksichtigung der Formanlage des ganzen Satzes klären. (1994, 322–323) [In contrast to the older literature, which insinuated (Schubert's) dependence on Beethoven's C minor models like op. 10, no. 1, or op. 13, Arthur Godel has called attention to a different model for the first theme of the sonata: it is a remarkably accurate contrafactum (*Kontrafaktur*) on the theme of the C minor Variations WoO 80. But precisely this observation does not necessitate this appropriation to be read entirely along the line of the older interpretation simply as homage to Beethoven. Whether the surprising decision to change a Beethoven variation theme into the main theme of the sonata's opening movement unmistakably expresses the intention of dependency or, on the contrary, the decisive mark of a self-confident counterposition, can only be clarified by considering the formal plan (*Formanlage*) of the entire movement.]

Hinrichsen's (1994, 323) analysis suggests that Beethoven's theme functions as a reservoir of chromatic material that Schubert's sonata both draws from and modifies throughout its formal sections. He concludes that there is no substantive reason why the sonata should be interpreted as subordinate to Beethoven's Theme and Variations.

From this very brief survey of some of the discourse surrounding the opening measures from Schubert's Piano Sonata in C Minor, we can already begin to observe the variance at which its apparent repetition of Beethoven's theme has been understood,[12] differences that raise questions about what kind of historical consciousness we should adopt to explain this repetition and others in Schubert's music. If the repetition can be interpreted as a musical homage in one reading and as a musical critique in another, what are the advantages to and disadvantages of these different forms of remembering (and forgetting)?[13] Moreover, if we were to rethink certain oppositions that can inform conclusions about musical influence, such as text and context, and original and copy, what are some alternatives to homage and critique, and how might they affect our understanding of the relationship between these two musical passages?

In an effort to address some of the challenges that revolve around the topic of musical influence, this chapter will further explore the two constructs mentioned above, homage and critique, which have tended to frame discussions of Schubert's music as it relates to Beethoven's. My motivations for revisiting homage and critique stem from broader ontological questions about repetition (What constitutes a repetition? How do repetitions mean?) and, more specifically, from a desire to probe the interpretive pathways that lead discussions of the same musical work to part ways in their conclusions about a certain iteration. In contemplating homage and critique—here, with respect to Schubert's Sonata in C Minor and Beethoven's Theme and Variations in C Minor—I will use as a point of departure Jacques Derrida's writings on grafting, discussed and exemplified in both *Dissemination* ([1972] 1981) and *Glas* ([1974] 1986). Grafting is a technique commonly associated with horticulture and generally refers to the inosculation or joining together of vascular tissues between two plants. Derrida uses this notion of grafting metaphorically to describe the insertion of one text into another by means of a scission. The act of "cutting" a prior text and transplanting it into another text—a procedure that can be repeated infinitely so as to yield a graft within a graft within a graft (and so forth)—permeates, according to Derrida ([1972] 1981), the very act of writing, which depends on repetition. As I hope to convey in the following pages, grafting has the potential to restructure the ways in which we think about origin and repetition in music, and can thus help unravel the binary oppositions that weave history into a linear and continuous form. Put succinctly by Gayatri Chakravorty Spivak, Derrida's study of "the interweaving of different texts (literally "web"-s) [is] . . . an act of criticism that refuses to think of 'influence' or 'interrelationship' as simple historical phenomena" (Spivak 1997, lxxxiv). Derrida's intertextual "model" is similar to those cultivated by other French post-structuralists who also wrote about intertextuality in the late 1960s, such as Julia Kristeva and Roland Barthes.[14] Just as Kristeva ([1969] 1980) views a single text as a permutation of multiple discourses from several different social and cultural contexts, Derrida also recognizes a text to be, as Jonathan Culler (2007, 135) summarizes, "the product of various sorts of combinations or insertions." Derrida's subversion of binary oppositions—such as inside/outside, text/context, and center/margin—through deconstruction, however, sets him apart from other post-structuralists who generally rely on the reader to activate a text's meaning. Deconstruction's ability to displace the very ground that supports statements about meaning prohibit the possibility that meaning can be represented univocally, either by the reader's experience of a text or by the author's intentions (Culler 2007, 131).

A number of music scholars have explored the potential of Derrida's work for understanding music.[15] Among these discussions, I find Kevin Korsyn's "Beyond Privileged Contexts: Intertextuality, Influence, and Dialogue" (2001) to be especially suggestive, and I will build on that essay here.[16] In exploring discursive space from one of several post-structuralist positions,[17] I propose an alternative frame for thinking about musical influence with respect to Schubert's Sonata in C Minor. As such, my discussion will consider the following two ideas: (1) if, as Derrida ([1972] 1981, 355) suggests, "to write means to graft," Schubert's Sonata in C Minor and Beethoven's Theme and Variations contain a heterogeneity of texts, raising the question of whether either work can solely function as an original text, and (2) matters concerning appropriation do not lie entirely within a musical text but rather between texts, inviting us to reconsider how constructions of both history and originality can affect music-analytical readings of influence in musical works.

Grafting Schubert's Sonata in C Minor, mm. 1–21, and Beethoven's Thirty-Two Variations in C Minor, mm. 1–8

In conceiving musical influence from an alternative perspective, let us begin our discussion by returning to example 6.1, which sets both themes in motion by grafting them together on the same page.[18] In an effort to dismantle any notion of *paragon* (model) and *parergon* (supplement) that may be suggested by such a typographic setting, example 6.2 shows the same pair of musical excerpts in the reverse order.[19] I will first summarize some observations that we might draw about each musical excerpt (which, in the spirit of Derrida's writings, could be conceived as containing grafts of prior analyses, including my own [Rusch 2013a]), and then explore how this joining together of Schubert's and Beethoven's themes can encourage us to hear each theme as a reversal of the other theme's characteristic features and, more broadly, as offshoots of other branches or permutations of other musical discourses. Even though the analytical discussions of Beethoven's and Schubert's themes appear in the left-hand and right-hand columns, respectively (table 6.1), and are respectively accompanied by exs. 6.3 and 6.4, and exs. 6.5, 6.6, and 6.7, readers are encouraged to imagine the reverse orientation with renumbered examples, following the rationale of the repeated pair of musical excerpts shown in examples 6.1 and 6.2.

Table 6.1.

The C minor theme (annotated in ex. 6.3) that serves as the basis for the thirty-two variations features a chromatic descending bass line paired with thick chords in the lower register and an ascending chromatic line in the melody. The expectation of an eight-bar sentence may arise after the basic idea (mm. 1–2) is followed by a varied repetition (mm. 3–4).[1] During the continuation phrase (mm. 5–8), Beethoven first elides the basic idea's thirty-second-note run (here, from C to F) with the descending octave leap (from F-sharp to F-sharp) (cf. mm. 2.3–4.1). He then foreshortens the basic idea again (m. 6); the right-hand's thirty-second-note run that leads to the G on the next downbeat (m. 6.1) is not followed by the octave descent that we might expect at this point (see ex. 6.4, "Beethoven, theme recomposed," m. 6). Instead, the G surprisingly ascends to A-flat, a melodic goal that is emphasized by the thick F minor chords in each hand and the *sforzando* dynamic. While the metric placement of the F-minor chord comports with the theme's recurring accent on beat 2, the denial of the G melodic octave leap (see ex. 6.4, m. 6) nonetheless creates the effect of a double accent: the A-flat appears to have entered too soon. This second foreshortening of the basic idea extends the bass's descending chromatic tetrachord by one step, from C–G to C–F: the suggested cadential 6/4 becomes a passing chord, and the contrapuntal focus retrospectively shifts to the unfolding of the subdominant harmony (F minor, mm. 4–7) (cf. 6.4). The F minor harmony lingers in the following measure amid the registral and textural shift (m. 7), threatening to disrupt the 3/4 meter by denying a change of harmony across the bar line. The right hand's registral shift down an octave to A-flat and then G (now accompanied by a lone A-flat and G in the bass) recovers the denied octave leaps suggested in the second and third fragmentations	The C minor theme (annotated in ex. 6.5) functions as the main theme of a sonata form movement and features a chromatic ascending melody that is paired with thick chords and a c-pedal in the bass. The varied repetition of the basic idea (mm. 3–4) may initially suggest that an eight-bar sentence is underway. The sweeping scale (m. 3) that breaks up the blocked chords in the presentation phrase (mm. 1–4) and that facilitates a register transfer to the higher octave introduces the fantasia topic to this sonata allegro movement—one that becomes increasingly prominent as the sentence's eight-bar, tight-knit structure begins to unravel. Here the potential for cadential closure (mm. 7–8) is undermined by two phrase extensions that lead to a striking, climactic point of arrival on bare A-flats, which are emphasized by their extreme registral placement in the upper and lower registers and by the *fortissimo* dynamic (m. 12). In leading up to this climax, Schubert composes a varied repetition of the two-bar segment (compare mm. 9–10 with mm. 7–8), suggesting that the second repetition (mm. 11–12) will continue the reaching-over pattern in the upper voice ([A-flat]–G, C–B-natural, E flat–D) and the hypermetric trochaic pattern of strong and weak beats (ex. 6.6). Both patterns are usurped by the A-flats (m. 12), which interrupt the completion of the last pair in the reaching-over pattern (E-flat–D) and transform a hypermetric weak beat into a strong beat, causing two consecutive, hypermetric strong beats. Accompanying this climatic point is a reversal between consonance and dissonance with respect to G and A-flat. Whereas A-flat first sounds as a dissonant upper neighbor to a consonant G in both the melody and the bass during the tonic prolongation

(see the dotted arrows in ex. 6.3, mm. 6–7). Although the theme attains melodic, motivic, and harmonic closure, it does not achieve the kind of registral, textural, or dynamic closure that the opening measures may warrant. The variations that follow might be heard, then, as a response to the open-ended musical "questions" posed by the theme.

(ex. 6.7, mm. 7–16), this dissonant-consonant relationship is reversed during the tonicization of A-flat major (mm. 12–16), where G temporarily functions as the leading tone. The D-natural (ex. 6.5, m. 17; cf. mm. 15–16) embedded within the broken octave ascending scale begins to undo the tonicization of A-flat major, and the cadential 6/4 chord (m. 19) restores the initial consonance-dissonance relationship between G and A-flat. Motion toward a perfect authentic cadence is then confirmed in m. 21, with the cadential arrival eliding with the beginning of the transition.

---

[1] I would especially like to thank Alexander Rehding for sharing his reading of the Beethoven theme, in response to a different version of this paper that was presented at the Université de Montréal (Rusch 2009) in celebration of his book launch, *Music and Monumentality: Commemoration and Wonderment in Nineteenth-Century Germany* (2009). See also, Caplin 2014, 444–47, which offers a similar formal function analysis of this theme.

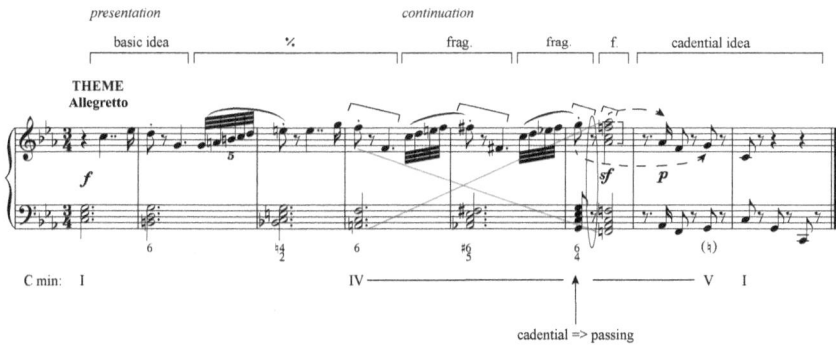

Example 6.3. Beethoven, Thirty-Two Variations in C Minor, WoO 80, theme.

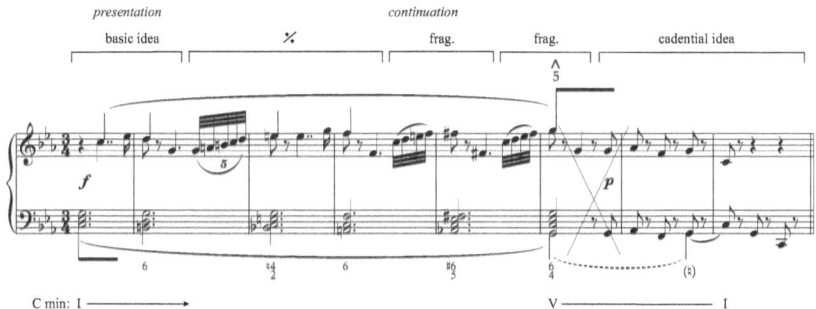

Example 6.4. Thirty-Two Variations in C Minor, WoO 80, mm. 6–8 recomposed.

Example 6.5. Schubert, Piano Sonata in C Minor, D. 958, i, mm. 1–24.

Example 6.6. Piano Sonata in C Minor, D. 958, i, mm. 7–12 recomposed.

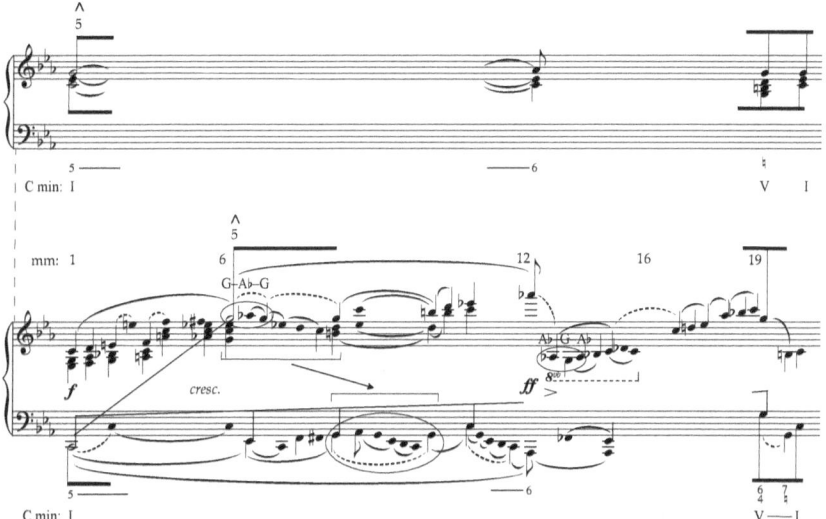

Example 6.7. Piano Sonata in C Minor, D. 958, i, mm. 1–24. Voice-leading sketch.

While each musical excerpt and corresponding analytical discussion could be read independently of the other excerpt and discussion, positioning the two scores and discussions side by side can facilitate a reciprocity among musical properties, whereby each excerpt appears to permeate the boundaries of the other theme and embed itself in the other's "discourse." As one example, just as the chromatic counterpoint between the outer voices in Beethoven's theme can draw our attention to the chromatic counterpoint between the melody and inner voice in Schubert's theme,[20] so, too, can the tonic pedal in the first six measures of Schubert's theme point us to the presence of the tonic pedal in one of the inner voices of Beethoven's theme (with exception to m. 2), as well as

Beyond Homage and Critique 171

direct us to Schubert's reharmonization of the chord in measure 2, which allows the pedal tone to sound throughout the first six measures. Similarly, the repeated Gs that are harmonized with the two C minor chords in Schubert's theme (m. 6) can highlight the way in which the F minor subdominant chord in Beethoven's theme (m. 6) disrupts the completion of the melodic motive (G–G) and transforms the cadential 6/4 into a passing chord, just as Beethoven's eight-bar, tight-knit theme can emphasize in Schubert's theme how the fantasia unravels the cadential idea and arrival (mm. 7–8) and, hence, the potential completion of an eight-bar, tight-knit theme. As one final example, the broader formal context within which each composer situates his theme can draw our attention to the conditions of possibilities of the other theme. A theme and variation form and a sonata allegro form can each raise certain expectations for how the opening theme will develop in relation to the entire work or movement, especially with respect to the kinds of repetitions and musical contrasts (harmonic, melodic, formal, and textural) that are likely (or less likely) to occur. Altogether, if Schubert's theme appears to graft certain musical attributes from Beethoven's theme and reconstitute them in a new context, Beethoven's theme can appear to anticipate how these musical attributes in Schubert's theme may be reconstituted.

This graft of Beethoven's and Schubert's themes and analytical descriptions can also create a chiasmus, one that highlights how the apparent repetitions among them are rhetorical inversions of one another. Both composers, for instance, pair a chromatic descending line with a chromatic ascending line, yet each composer situates this counterpoint among the voices differently. By positioning the chromatic counterpoint between the outer voices, Beethoven facilitates harmonic motion toward a goal. Conversely, Schubert grounds the chromatic counterpoint with a tonic pedal in the bass, rendering the harmonic progression less mobile. In addition, while Beethoven's theme conveys a tight-knit, sentence theme type within the boundaries of eight measures, Schubert transforms a potential eight-bar, tight-knit theme into a twenty-one-bar, loose-knit one. Finally, whereas Beethoven's sentence is situated within the broader context of a theme and variations form, welcoming thematic and harmonic stasis with each variation that follows, Schubert's sentence is situated within a sonata form, inviting thematic contrast and tonal motion by way of the impending subordinate theme group and development section.[21]

Were we to consider additional reverberations that arise from this typography, perhaps we might recall other works within the Schubert-Beethoven/Beethoven-Schubert graft that bear a strong relationship to Schubert's Sonata in C Minor and Beethoven's Theme and Variations, such as Beethoven's Piano

Example 6.8. Beethoven, Sonata in C Minor, op. 13 ("Pathétique"), i, m. 1 (upper left and lower right). Schubert, Sonata in C Minor, D. 958, i, m. 1 (upper right and lower left).

Example 6.9. Schubert, Sonata in C Minor, D. 958, i, mm. 20–21 (upper left and lower right). Beethoven, Sonata in C Minor, op. 13 ("Pathétique"), iii, mm. 209–10 (upper right and lower left).

Sonata in C Minor, op. 13 ("Pathétique").[22] When playing the first C minor chord in Schubert's sonata (m. 1) on the piano, for instance, we may be reminded of the embodied feeling of playing the opening C minor chord from the first movement of Beethoven's sonata (m. 1) (ex. 6.8). The experience of playing either opening chord might feel simultaneously foreign and familiar—foreign in that each musical context invites us to perform the chord differently (the beginning of a main theme in an allegro tempo versus the beginning of an introduction in a Grave tempo) and familiar in that the position of the hands and fingers in each sonata's opening gesture are analogous. In a similar vein, both the descending harmonic minor scale that sounds above the dominant chord and the subsequent tonic resolution in Schubert's sonata (mm. 20–21) may recall a similar passage that recurs in the sonata rondo movement of Beethoven's sonata (mm. 209–10) (ex. 6.9).[23]

Schubert's and Beethoven's Themes as Countersignatures to the Passacaglia

From our discussion up to this point, we might begin to deduce that the potential connections between Schubert's and Beethoven's themes may be located in the space between the respective texts. It is arguably this location where conceptions of history and musical influence can also linger as silent, yet guiding contexts for which to frame these connections. As one way to approach and possibly reconstitute these contexts, let us further explore how this graft of the two themes can offer us one way to rethink the hierarchies implicit in homage and critique (e.g., predecessor and latecomer, original and copy). To graft, once more, Culler's (2007) comment on textual grafts in our current discussion: How else might each musical excerpt be conceived "as the product of various sorts of combinations or insertions" (135)?

Returning to Schubert's and Beethoven's themes, their minor mode, 3/4 meter, and descending chromatic line can suggest that they both engage with an earlier form of writing initially associated with improvisation, the passacaglia,[24] which garnered renewed attention in late eighteenth- and nineteenth-century music. While the passacaglia overlaps with other closely related historical practices such as cantus firmus improvisations and chaconnes,[25] which vary with respect to compositional approach and social function, certain musical attributes associated with its manifestations in seventeenth- and eighteenth-century baroque music appear to become reinscribed within the context of late eighteenth- and early nineteenth-century compositional writing. These combined attributes include the passacaglia's triple meter; the descending diatonic or chromatic tetrachord in the minor mode, which functions as a ground bass; and the elision between the bass's resolution to ^1 at the end of the ostinato pattern and the ^1

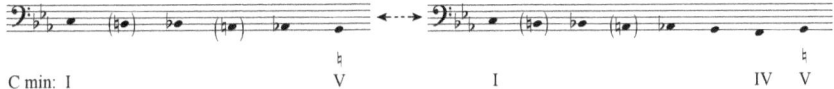

Example 6.10. Two passacaglia bass ostinato patterns (after Hudson 1981).

that begins the next iteration. If the passacaglia, as a kind of predecessor, materializes in the margins of the Schubert-Beethoven/Beethoven-Schubert graft, questions concerning the meanings of these repetitions would seem to shift, from asking whether Schubert's approach to his Sonata in C Minor can be read as an active or passive response to Beethoven's Theme and Variations, to asking how both composers engage with a compositional practice that came before them. If Beethoven and Schubert each graft a passacaglia in their respective themes, how might they reinscribe it within the context of their own beginnings? What "countersignatures" do they offer to a compositional practice whose associated patterns have been countersigned numerous times by composers who came before?[26] Furthermore, how might previous countersignatures anticipate Beethoven's and Schubert's reinscriptions?

The very notion of a countersignature may naturally call into question which version of the passacaglia bass served as a potential model for Beethoven's and Schubert's themes. Such a determination may be especially difficult to make with respect to Beethoven's theme, due to variances with which the 6/4- and F minor chords (m. 6) appear to function in the initial and retrospective hearing. As the previous analysis and recomposition of Beethoven's theme suggest (see again exs. 6.3 and 6.4), the thick, subdominant chord that provides harmonic support for the melody's A-flat (m. 6.2) presents a paradox in that it may be heard as lying both outside and inside of the descending bass progression. The F minor chord can seem to lie outside of the progression because it follows what may at first sound like a cadential 6/4 chord (m. 6.1), breaking the expectation of a complete repetition of the basic idea's fragmentation. Yet the F minor chord may also seem to lie inside the descending bass progression in the retrospective hearing, because it transforms the cadential 6/4 chord into a passing chord within a prolongation of the subdominant harmony via a chromatic voice exchange before the "second" cadential dominant arrival (m. 7.3).[27] Example 6.10 introduces at least two potential candidates relative to Beethoven's ground bass, then, notated in C minor for comparison. The bass pattern on the left-hand side descends a chromatic fourth, from ^1 to ^5, and the pattern on the right-hand side, a chromatic fifth, from ^1 to ^4, before ascending by step to ^5. Conceiving Beethoven's theme as containing a graft of the pattern shown on the left would appear to align with the initial hearing of the 6/4 chord (m. 6), that it functions as a part of the cadential dominant harmony (see again ex. 6.4). Accordingly, the proceeding motion to the

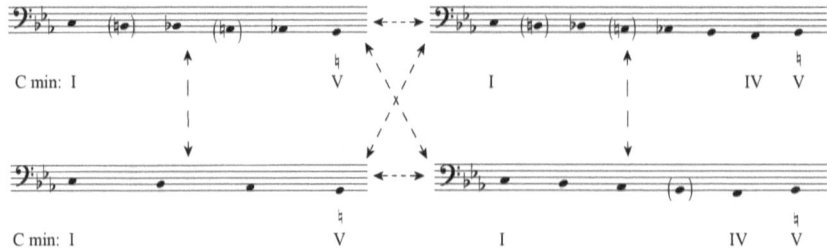

Example 6.11. Four passacaglia bass ostinato patterns (after Hudson 1981).

subdominant might be construed as an anomaly, one that rewrites the descending chromatic tetrachord by extending it downward by one step. Taking into account a retrospective hearing of the same 6/4 chord, however, where the chord now functions as a passing chord en route to the F minor subdominant (m. 6.2), we might imagine that the bass pattern on the right-hand side of example 6.10 may have also served as a potential model for Beethoven's theme. Even though this pattern could be interpreted as an embellished version of the descending chromatic tetrachord on the left-hand side (whereby the melodic motion down to ^4 delays the motion to ^5), its potential realization in the retrospective hearing suggests that it, too, may also function as a beginning, or ground bass, for the variations.

In addition to these two ostinato bass patterns, we might also consider as possible models for Beethoven's theme, the diatonic versions of these patterns. Example 6.11 adds to example 6.10 two additional bass patterns (all of which are arranged in a matrix that highlights their relationships), yielding four potential models relative to Beethoven's ground bass. The top staves reproduce the chromatic versions of example 6.10, and their respective diatonic versions are shown in the bottom staves. The left-hand side includes those patterns that descend a melodic fourth, and the right-hand side, patterns that descend a melodic fifth and then ascend by step. Consistent with the reading of the relationship between the two patterns shown in example 6.10, the chromatic patterns in the top staves of example 6.11 may each be interpreted as embellished versions of either diatonic pattern shown in the bottom staves, and each pattern on the right-hand side may be an embellished version of either pattern on the left-hand side. Such a view may suggest that the pattern that appears in the lower left-hand corner serves as the primary form of the other three patterns.[28] Yet as Beethoven's theme appears to demonstrate, complex patterns that may be heard as embellishments of simpler ones can nonetheless be used as a ground bass for a passacaglia and may thus serve as a beginning, or primary form, in and of itself.

The ambiguity that arises from our efforts to identify the model on which Beethoven's theme (and, by default, Schubert's theme) is based—especially in light of the retrospective reading of the cadential 6/4 as a passing 6/4 chord (m.

6)—can also draw our attention to the apparent discord between the descending chromatic bass lines of early eighteenth-century compositional practices and archetypal bass progressions associated with the eight-bar sentence theme type of the classical style (Caplin 2014, 415).[29] As William Caplin notes in "Topics and Formal Functions: The Case of the Lament" (2014), it is less common to begin a classical theme with a descending bass line, as such themes tend to prolong the tonic harmony during the beginning of a formal process:[30]

> By the later decades of the eighteenth century, this preponderance of bass descents, particularly at the very opening of a theme, had largely run its course, and the high classical style sees a marked change in bass line structure ... a fundamentally ascending bass motion. ... As a result of this change in practice, the lament topic, with its striking descending bass motion is not so suitable for use at the opening of a thematic unit, unlike the case for earlier styles, where such a bass descent is appropriate to general stylistic norms. Thus in classical themes, the lament tends to appear in a medial formal context, typically as a continuation following a solidly expressed initiating idea or phrase supported by a root-position tonic prolongation. (436)

In an effort to illustrate Caplin's point with respect to Beethoven's theme, example 6.12 shows a second recomposition that uses the same, two-bar basic idea as a point of departure and that preserves the theme's sentential structure (cf. ex. 6.4). In this version, the basic idea's I–V motion, or tonic statement (mm. 1–2), is answered by a V–I motion, or dominant response (mm. 3–4), which facilitates a prolongation of the tonic harmony (mm. 1–4). The continuation phrase (mm. 5–8) features an expanded cadential progression with a bass that ascends stepwise from ^3, which signals the onset of the cadential progression, to ^5, the cadential dominant. Altogether, the bass line's calculated melodic ascent from ^1 to ^5 by way of ^3 would appear to unfold along the lines of its classical precedents.[31]

In Beethoven's theme (see again ex. 6.3), the two-bar response that follows the initial two-bar basic idea might thus appear to betray the more familiar statement-response pair by continuing its chromatic bass descent past the B-natural, surrendering instead, as it were, to the passacaglia as it makes its way to ^4. The extent to which Beethoven's theme suppresses this implicit clash between the descending bass line and tonic prolongation can be observed in his harmonization. As Caplin (2014, 446) remarks, Beethoven sets the B-flat with a V$^{4/2}$ of IV (m. 3),[32] which permits a concealed, tonic prolongation in an inner voice during the presentation phrase. In some of the variations that follow (nos. 5, 7, 8, 10, 17, 18, 19, 20, 26, 27, and 28), this third chord in the descending chromatic tetrachord is supported by ^1 (C) in the bass, as opposed to ^♭7 (B-flat), which may help further convey the temporal quality of "being in the beginning" of a formal process.

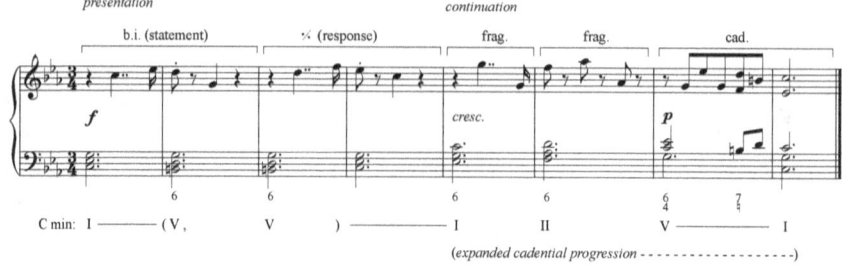

Example 6.12. Beethoven, Thirty-Two Variations in C Minor, WoO 80, mm. 3–8 recomposed.

Schubert's countersignature, in comparison, appears to side-step this form-functional dissonance by grafting the passacaglia in an inner voice over a tonic pedal point in the opening measures (see again ex. 6.5, mm. 1–6), thereby prolonging the tonic harmony during the initiating idea as well as extending this prolongation well into the continuation phrase.[33] Moreover, the interplay between sonata form and fantasia appears to erode not only the promise of a complete passacaglia "text," but also the theme's initial tight-knit design and clear sense of being either in the middle or near the end of a formal process. The arrival on I⁶ and motion toward what may at first sound like a cadential dominant (mm. 7–8), for instance, may initially suggest the end of a formal process. The subsequent varied repetitions of the cadential gesture (mm. 9–10 and m. 11ff), however, appear to undermine the initial sense of cadential closure (m. 8), transforming the end of a formal process (mm. 7–8) into a pseudo beginning. Similarly, the arrival on the A-flat major octaves (m. 12) may simultaneously suggest the end of a formal process and beginning of a new one, yet the cadential 6/4 chord that follows (m. 19) may retrospectively lead us to hear the entire A-flat major passage as an extended upbeat to this cadential 6/4 chord (m. 19).

Despite the success with which the phrase and cadential deviations in Schubert's countersignature appear to sever the passacaglia text and unravel the theme's purported sentential design, we may nonetheless still decipher the passacaglia text's components: by eliding measures 7–19, we can conjoin the two scions from the passacaglia text (mm. 1–6 and mm. 20–21) and obtain a complete iteration (ex. 6.13). In measure 6, the G5 supported by the tonic harmony would proceed to a falling scale that would lead to a perfect authentic cadence in the same register. The phrase elision of this authentic cadence with the beginning of the varied restatement of the theme in measure 21 (which marks the beginning of the transition in the sonata form) might then recall the passacaglia's continuous variation procedure, which Schubert's composition appears to preserve.[34]

Notwithstanding these differences among Beethoven's and Schubert's countersignatures, both composers position the descending, chromatic bass line in C

Example 6.13. Schubert, Sonata in C Minor, D. 958, i, mm. 1–21. Graft of passacaglia.

minor—a key that had become associated with stormy, dramatic works by the late eighteenth century[35]—as opposed to D minor, "the most eminent of keys in Baroque keyboard music" (Lindley 2001).[36] Such a tonal reframing can alter the emotional register of a musical pattern that had, by then, become tied to the lament (Rosand 1979; Williams 1997).

An Additional Countersignature: Mozart's Piano Concerto in C Minor, K. 491, mm. 1–34

The notion that Beethoven's and Schubert's themes each engage with a version of the passacaglia can encourage us to reinscribe their themes within a broader

Beyond Homage and Critique 179

Table 6.2.

The C minor theme (annotated in ex. 6.3) that serves as the basis for the thirty-two variations features a chromatic descending bass line paired with thick chords in the lower register and an ascending chromatic line in the melody. The expectation of an eight-bar sentence may arise after the basic idea (mm. 1–2) is followed by a varied repetition (mm. 3–4). During the continuation phrase (mm. 5–8), Beethoven first elides the basic idea's thirty-second-note run (here, from C to F) with the descending octave leap (from F-sharp to F-sharp) (cf. mm. 2.3–4.1). He then foreshortens the basic idea again (m. 6); the right-hand's thirty-second-note run that leads to the G on the next downbeat (m. 6.1) is not followed by the octave descent that we might expect at this point (see ex. 6.4, "Beethoven, theme recomposed," m. 6). Instead, the G surprisingly ascends to A-flat, a melodic goal that is emphasized by the thick F minor chords in each hand and the *sforzando* dynamic. While the metric placement of the F minor chord comports with the theme's recurring accent on beat 2, the denial of the G melodic octave leap (see ex. 6.4, m. 6) nonetheless creates the effect of a double accent: the A-flat appears to have entered too soon. This second foreshortening of the basic idea extends the bass's descending chromatic tetrachord by one step, from	The C minor theme (annotated in ex. 6.5) functions as the main theme of a sonata form movement and features a chromatic ascending melody that is paired with thick chords and a c-pedal in the bass. The varied repetition of the basic idea (mm. 3–4) may initially suggest that an eight-bar sentence is underway. The sweeping scale (m. 3) that breaks up the blocked chords in the presentation phrase (mm. 1–4) and that facilitates a register transfer to the higher octave introduces the fantasia topic to this sonata allegro movement—one that becomes increasingly prominent as the sentence's eight-bar, tight-knit structure begins to unravel. Here the potential for cadential closure (mm. 7–8) is undermined by two phrase extensions that lead to a striking, climactic point of arrival on bare A-flats, which are emphasized by their extreme registral placement in the upper and lower registers and by the *fortissimo* dynamic (m. 12). In leading up to this climax, Schubert composes a varied repetition of the two-bar segment (compare mm. 9–10 with mm. 7–8), suggesting that the second repetition (mm. 11–12) will continue the reaching-over pattern in the upper voice	The C minor theme (annotated in ex. 6.14) features a concealed, chromatic descending line from ^6 to ^2 (mm. 3–8) that is threaded within the contours of a disjunct, melodic line that is played in unison by the orchestra. During the unfolding of this embedded, chromatic descent, the last two bars of the opening four-bar group (or compound basic idea) are sequenced twice (mm. 5–6 and 7–8), leading us to ^3 (E-flat) in the bass (m. 9). If the first eight bars suggested a melody, this melody appears to transform into a bass line when the oboes begin to retrace the bass line's chromatic descent from ^6 to ^2 (mm. 8–12). The cadential progression initially suggested by ^3 in the bass (m. 9) is abandoned at first (mm. 10–11) and then reapproached just before the melody completes its descent to ^1 (mm. 12–13). Altogether, this main theme contains the remnants of an eight-bar sentence theme type, yet its phrase extensions and abandoned cadence unravel its initial tight-knit construction. The arrival of the perfect authentic cadence at the end of this theme elides

C–G to C–F: the suggested cadential 6/4 becomes a passing chord, and the contrapuntal focus retrospectively shifts to the unfolding of the subdominant harmony (F minor, mm. 4–7) (cf. 6.4). The F minor harmony lingers in the following measure amid the registral and textural shift (m. 7), threatening to disrupt the 3/4 meter by denying a change of harmony across the bar line. The right hand's registral shift down an octave to A-flat and then G (now accompanied by a lone A-flat and G in the bass) recovers the denied octave leaps suggested in the second and third fragmentations (see the dotted arrows in ex. 6.3, mm. 6–7). Although the theme attains melodic, motivic, and harmonic closure, it does not achieve the kind of registral, textural, or dynamic closure that the opening measures may warrant. The variations that follow might be heard, then, as a response to the open-ended musical "questions" posed by the theme.

([A-flat]–G, C–B-natural, E-flat–D) and the hypermetric trochaic pattern of strong and weak beats (ex. 6.6). Both patterns are usurped by the A-flats (m. 12), which interrupt the completion of the last pair in the reaching-over pattern (E-flat–D) and transform a hypermetric weak beat into a strong beat, causing two consecutive, hypermetric strong beats. Accompanying this climatic point is a reversal between consonance and dissonance with respect to G and A-flat. Whereas A-flat first sounds as a dissonant upper neighbor to a consonant G in both the melody and the bass during the tonic prolongation (ex. 6.7, mm. 7–16), this dissonant-consonant relationship is reversed during the tonicization of A-flat major (mm. 12–16), where G temporarily functions as the leading tone. The D-natural (ex. 6.5, m. 17; cf. mm. 15–16) embedded within the broken octave ascending scale begins to undo the tonicization of A-flat major, and the cadential 6/4 chord (m. 19) restores the initial consonance-dissonance relationship between G and A-flat. Motion toward a perfect authentic cadence is then confirmed in m. 21, with the cadential arrival eliding with the beginning of the transition.

with a varied repetition of the main theme, where the opening melodic line is now heard above a tonic pedal that gives way to a descending, chromatic bass line. The onset of ^5 in the bass (m. 21) suggests that we are nearing the end of a formal process, yet this cadential 6/4 chord does not resolve as we might expect. The bass surprisingly descends to ^4 and then repeatedly traverses the same melodic third (F–G–A-flat and A-flat–G–F). During the repetitions of this melodic third, the cadential 6/4 chord transforms into a passing chord as the hypermeasure groups change from two to three, and the contrary motion between the outer voices attempt to override the similar motion that had previously prevailed. The decisive turn out of this whirling passage occurs when the second oboes and violas play an F-sharp (m. 27), signaling the onset of an augmented sixth chord that ushers in the dominant arrival (m. 28).[1] The standing-on-the-dominant passage that follows (mm. 29–34) maintains the dramatic intensity of the dominant 5/3 resolution that had been deferred up to this point, while the contrary motion continues to linger in the counterpoint amid a dominant pedal point.

---

[1] In this opening ritornello, both the loose-knit construction near the cadential 6/4 chord (m. 21) and the half-cadence arrival (m. 28) can suggest that the varied repetition of the main theme becomes the nonmodulating transition.

Example 6.14. Mozart, Piano Concerto in C Minor, K. 491, i, mm. 1–36. Orchestral reduction.

Example 6.14. (Continued)

network of musical works that similarly attempt to combine this older musical practice with the formal rhetoric of the classical style. As one example, let us briefly turn to the first thirty-four measures of the opening ritornello from Mozart's Piano Concerto in C Minor, K. 491 (1786) (see table 6.2).

When listening to and reading the analysis of Mozart's theme within the context of the Schubert-Beethoven/Beethoven-Schubert graft, we may readily observe how its shared key and time signature, descending chromatic line, melodic leaps, fragmentation, and cadential aversion are both foreign and familiar. Like Beethoven's theme, Mozart's theme can draw our attention to the friction between the passacaglia's descending tetrachord and the ascending motion to ^5 that is typical of bass lines in the classical style. The extent to which the theme appears to suppress this tension can be especially observed in the varied repetition (mm. 13–28), which, in following the passacaglia, elides with the first authentic cadence that closes the initial statement of the main theme (m. 13). The compound basic idea that begins the varied repetition is set to a tonic pedal (mm. 13–16), which helps convey that a new formal process has begun. The last two chords within this pedal point, 6/3 and 4/3 (mm. 15–16), launch the beginning of a sequential progression, suggesting a temporal overlap between being in the beginning (via the tonic pedal) and being in the middle (via the model of the sequential progression, 6/3–4/3) of the formal process (see also mm. 3–4 in the same example, where the contrasting idea within the compound basic idea appears to retrospectively become the model for the proceeding sequential progression).

Compared to Beethoven's theme, the descending bass progression in Mozart's theme unfolds within a medial formal context, the continuation phrase, as opposed to an initiating phrase. Yet similar to Beethoven's and Schubert's themes, cadential closure in Mozart's theme is deferred. Such treatment of closure in all three themes may be attributed to the import of the passacaglia bass within a classical rhetoric, as previously discussed, and to the ways in which all three respective opening themes appear to both anticipate and retrospectively balance the proportions and dramatic trajectory of the remaining music.

Beyond Homage and Critique

The discussion thus far has attempted to demonstrate how the notion of grafting may help dismantle the potential hierarchies between Schubert's and Beethoven's themes, not only by showing how the potentiality of one theme may be realized in the other theme and how both themes may be conceived as rhetorical reversals of one another, but also by exploring how the two themes engage with a musical practice that precedes them. Positioning the passacaglia in the center of the Schubert-Beethoven/Beethoven-Schubert graft brings to the fore how the two themes are only but two instances within a larger corpus of compositions from the late eighteenth and nineteenth centuries that appear to reinscribe this older compositional practice within a classical formal rhetoric that renders it as both foreign (as a new beginning) and familiar (as a prolongation of a prior musical discourse). Affixing the opening ritornello from Mozart's Piano Concerto in C Minor to the Schubert-Beethoven/Beethoven-Schubert graft attempts to illuminate this broader engagement with the passacaglia, exposing among all three themes the tension between the passacaglia's descending bass pattern and the harmonic progressions and formal rhetoric of the sentence theme type.[37] This graft within a graft within a graft, and so on, simultaneously lays bare the incongruities between the two musical styles while also bringing to the fore a small sample of how these stylistic components might be combined or joined together.

A more extensive analysis of Schubert's main theme from his Sonata in C Minor would not only identify other grafts besides the ones suggested here;[38] it would also take into account the iterability of these repetitions—how a shift in context can generate a proliferation of meanings for each musical repetition. Whether such an analysis of this kind could ever be completed, however, remains to be seen. First, our ability to identify the source of an iteration ultimately depends on what we count as a musical repetition, an ontological conundrum that can bear significant consequences for the interpretive process in terms of deciding which musical texts should be grafted together and, ostensibly, what constitutes a part and a whole.

Second, each musical text that we identify as a source will likely contain more repetitions of other texts, precluding our attempt to find an original. As suggested in the third section of this chapter, pursuing the source for the passacaglia in Beethoven's C minor theme suggests that its bass line is only one of many possible variants of passacaglia ground basses, each existing in a play of difference that denies the possibility of an original and each serving as a possible beginning in and of itself.

What appears to emerge from this search for an origin for Schubert's main theme, then, is a bottomless text, or the repetition of a graft within a graft, wherein the context for understanding the meaning of Schubert's apparent reference to Beethoven's theme becomes boundless. That Schubert's Sonata in C Minor presents us with several possible texts that are spliced together subverts the very idea that Beethoven's theme can function as an origin or beginning. On this illusory nature of beginnings, Derrida ([1972] 1981) writes in *Dissemination*:

> Clip out an example, since you cannot and should not undertake the infinite commentary that at every moment seems necessarily to engage and immediately to annul itself, letting itself be read in turn by the apparatus itself. . . . It is of course a beginning that is forever fictional, and the scission, far from being an inaugural act, is dictated by the absence . . . of any de-cisive beginning, any pure event that would not divide and repeat itself and already refer back to some other 'beginning,' some other 'event,' the singularity of the event being more mythical than ever in the order of discourse. (300)

For Derrida, the possibility that a scission can function as a point of origin conflicts with the very idea of the scission. Any attempt to trace the scission's origin only leads to another division, or another scission. With respect to Schubert's Sonata in C Minor, the ability to name the Beethoven excerpt as a possible beginning only points toward another beginning: the Beethoven excerpt divides itself in a moment of difference, yielding another potential beginning—Mozart's Piano Concerto in C Minor or, further yet, a passacaglia bass and all of its potential rewritings, which can divide themselves again. What results from this process is the emergence of a heterogeneous musical text that contains multiple discourses that both join together and recede into one another through the act of cutting and transplanting. To quote Derrida ([1972] 1981) once again from *Dissemination*, "The tree is ultimately rootless. And at the same time, in this tree of numbers and square roots, everything is a root, too, since the grafted shoots themselves compose the whole of the body proper, of the tree that is called present" (356). Or to use a different metaphor, the "work itself" begins to resemble a palimpsest—a (musical) surface that contains the traces of previous erasures.

If, as Derrida ([1972] 1981, 356) suggests, "the heterogeneity of different writings is writing itself," then what repercussions arise when we remove the frames that allow for the formation of a stable text and context for understanding Schubert's reference to Beethoven? Although Derrida's notion of grafting cannot provide the final answer to some of the most challenging issues that surround musical influence, it can encourage us to rethink the conditions that enable homage and critique to emerge as stable constructs. As Culler (2007, 140) suggests, the interpretive process depends on one's ability to distinguish between what is central and what is marginal to one or more texts. Although Schubert's Sonata in C Minor contains several different grafts, prior analyses of this work have tended to position Beethoven's C minor variations at the center of its discourse and the passacaglia (as well as other potential musical texts) in the margin. The potential to name the passacaglia (or possibly Mozart's Piano Concerto in C Minor) as the center of an analysis, as opposed to Beethoven's theme, does not necessarily invert the implicit hierarchy between center and margin in this analysis as compared to Cone's and Hinrichsen's respective readings; rather, the act of displacing both center and margin calls into question the ontological status of such a binary. To graft another question of Culler's (2007, 140) into my own text: "What is a center if the marginal can become central?" The possibility of decentering the Beethoven reference can also undermine other binarisms—original and copy, and metaphorical representations of self and Other, for example—that often structure the ways in which musical influence is conceptualized. If Schubert's theme contains a graft of the Beethoven theme, which itself contains a graft of the passacaglia (and possibly Mozart's Piano Concerto in C Minor, and so on), the distinctions between these binaries may thus become subverted: What is a *paragon* if it can become a *parergon*?

Grafting can thus invite us to read Schubert's sonata as a heterogeneous text that contains multiple discourses, breaking the oft-construed binaries that frame the ways in which musical influence is conceived. Like homage and critique, it can still provide us with the thread to sew musical texts together, yet also encourage us to reinscribe these texts within the fabric of our discipline in ways that promote new relationships between musical texts that move "beyond privileged contexts," through the act of decentering an apparent origin.[39]

Grafting can also invite us to explore other ways to conceive the historical field. Friedrich Nietzsche's notion of *the unhistorical* and *the suprahistorical* in his essay "On the Uses and Disadvantages of History for Life" ([1874] 1997), for instance, offers us one such alternative, because it complements the idea of the perpetually rewritten or countersigned that underlies grafting. Nietzsche's essay begins by suggesting that, rather than allow the burden of history to stifle life as lived in the present, history can instead be used in the service of life in three ways, each of which corresponds to one of his three "species of history": the monumental, the antiquarian, and the critical (67). The monumental mode reassures one "that the greatness that once existed was in any event *possible* and may thus be possible again" (69, italics original); the antiquarian mode reveres the past and seeks to preserve for others in the present the circumstances that enabled one to "come into existence" (72–73); and the critical mode helps allay the anxieties that can accompany monumental and antiquarian histories, such as the fear of subordination or lack of ambition to cultivate the present (White 1973, 350), by encouraging one to "employ the strength to break up and dissolve a part of the past" by moralizing or judging this past (Nietzsche [1874] 1997, 75). As Nietzsche cautions, however, each of these three modes of remembering and forgetting has the capacity to distort our memory of the past (and thereby affect one's motivation for living in the present) when one mode overpowers the other two. Monumental history runs the risk of reducing differences to sameness, thus emphasizing the effects while minimalizing the causes (70). This form of history can persuade one into believing that the potential for greatness has already been achieved and exhausted by one's predecessors (White 1973, 350). An antiquarian history also tends to jeopardize the present, in this case by indiscriminately revering the past over the present. Anything that is perceived as new is viewed with an air of suspicion and ultimately cast aside (350). And finally, the attempt to free oneself from the chain of hereditary roots by way of a critical history can lead one to unmercifully and ruthlessly condemn the entire past (Nietzsche [1874] 1997, 76), making the present vulnerable to a similar fate when it becomes the past. With respect to Schubert's apparent reference to Beethoven's Theme and Variations in C Minor, the overtones of a monumental, antiquarian, and critical form of history may be heard in the divergent analytical interpretations of homage and critique, respectively: whereas homage tends to either reduce Schubert's Sonata in C Minor to Beethovenian models or position Beethoven's music in the center of a privileged aesthetic, critique renders Beethoven's past achievements as somehow flawed. While each of these historical perspectives offer us a way to connect apparent repetitions between musical texts into meaningful constellations, the question remains as to whether the perspectives inadvertently limit the size of our aperture by presuming that an entire musical tradition can be represented univocally within a single musical work.

For latecomers who wrestle with the burden or "malady of history," Nietzsche ([1874] 1997) proposes that the unhistorical and the suprahistorical, combined, can offer a potential antidote: "With the word 'the unhistorical' I designate the art and power of *forgetting* and of enclosing oneself within a bounded *horizon*; I call the 'suprahistorical' the powers which lead the eye away from becoming towards that which bestows upon existence the character of the eternal and stable, towards *art* and *religion*" (120). For Nietzsche, forgetting permits one to live freely in the present, counteracting history's potential threat to annihilate one from the past or present, and the suprahistorical moves away from viewing history as a process of becoming, which either positions one as a servant to history or leads one to believe that one's present is the goal for which all of history's efforts are directed (White 1973, 354).[40] The suprahistorical instead conceives the past and present as identical, whereby "the world is complete and reaches its finality at each and every moment" (Nietzsche [1874] 1997, 66). Both the unhistorical and suprahistorical, when put together, speak to the potential within which one can arrest history's sovereignty by (re)ordering the chaos of select historical phenomena in ways that speak to the needs of one's present. In viewing history as presented to us as an arrangement of historical phenomena that is informed by the requisites of a given present, history begins to shed its ontological status as a world process removed from human action, standing instead as an art or form of invention where "human action and the process of the world" are one and the same (White 1973, 353). Through augmentation and invention at each and every present, phenomena that were once familiar can thus become strange in a chain of repetitions that differ and defer: "[History's] value will be seen to consist in its taking a familiar, perhaps commonplace theme, an everyday melody, and composing inspired variations on it, enhancing it, elevating it to a comprehensive symbol, and thus disclosing in the original theme a whole world of profundity, power and beauty" (Nietzsche [1874] 1997, 93). With respect to Schubert, Beethoven, Mozart, and other composers who similarly appear to engage with the passacaglia in all of its potential manifestations, the musical chaos of their respective historical pasts can be ordered and reordered, and hence, augmented in a way that speaks to the needs of their respective presents, granting every composer the chance to be both the heirs of the past and initiators of the future (123). They become "both the historian[s] and the agent[s] of [their] own language[s]" (Korsyn 1993a, 90; de Man 1983; 152) as we become creators in the present.

Notes

1. This chapter is loosely based on the article "Beyond Homage and Critique? Schubert's Sonata in C Minor, D. 958, and Beethoven's Thirty-Two Variations in C minor, WoO 80," which was published in *Music Theory Online* 19, no. 1. I would sincerely like to thank William Caplin and Kevin Korsyn for their support and for sharing their insights on the topic of musical influence and on the lament bass in eighteenth- and early nineteenth-century music. I would also like to thank Sten Thomson for his assistance with the German translations.

2. See also Gibbs 2003.

3. Scott Messing (2006, 61) further remarks that "the conceptual framework, if not the specific language" can be traced to Robert Schumann.

4. On Hüttenbrenner's remark, Otto Erich Deutsch (1947) warns that "[he] is not to be trusted about details" (232). Maynard Solomon (1979) seems to find Hüttenbrenner's testimony more credible, though still cautions: "It is evident that he was

repeating to Peters what he took to be the truth; the risks of inventing such a story outweighed any possible advantage. That it actually *was* the truth is somewhat less evident. In view of Beethoven's zealous belief in the uniqueness of his own genius, it is doubtful that he would have made this prediction about any composer. More likely, his expression of appreciation or even enthusiasm for some work of Schubert's was exaggerated in the retelling" (116).

5. See, however, Spaun's 1829 obituary of Schubert, which conveys a more tentative view on the matter: "Whether Schubert's larger compositions excel equally the future will show.... Much of that which came before the public in conformity with these exigencies entitles us to the fairest hope in respect of such works as well, which the death of their creator will now doubtless release from the fetters that have so far kept them in obscurity" (Deutsch 1947, 875). On this paragraph in the obituary, Deutsch offers the following clarification: "For all his veneration of Schubert Spaun very much doubted whether he would ever make his way as an instrumental composer" (882).

6. For a slightly different translation of the first part of this paragraph and the previously quoted passage of Spaun's letter to Bauernfeld, see Gingerich 2014, 48–49.

7. John Gingerich (2014) similarly suggests that "only much later, after the gradual discovery of other previously hidden large instrumental works including the last three piano sonatas, the C-major Quintet, and above all the 'Great' C-major Symphony, did he [Spaun] change his opinion" (49).

8. On the correspondence related to Schumann's discovery and assessment of this symphony, Mendelssohn's performance, and preparations for Breitkopf & Härtel's publication, see Deutsch 1952. For more on the history surrounding the performance, discovery, and reception of this work, see especially Gingerich 2014, 198–235.

9. Deutsch (1947, 64) affirms that "'one of our greatest German artists' is clearly Beethoven" and that Schubert's reference to the eccentric (*bizaar*) "was Amadäus Wendt's word for 'Beethoven's manner' in the Leipzig 'Allgemeine musikalische Zeitung' (1815, cols. 387–9)."

10. See also Solomon 1979, 114, where Solomon concludes that "Schubert's early repudiation of Beethoven" comports with Beethoven's waning reputation in Vienna during the time at which Schubert wrote this diary entry.

11. As Kevin Korsyn has pointed out in a private correspondence in 2012, the dynamic between active and passive is especially relevant to the gendering of the two composers in Schubert's reception history.

12. See also Fisk 2001, 180–81, which, in addition to discussing some of the same readings, offers additional remarks on the reception surrounding this comparison.

13. On the dialectic between remembering and forgetting, see Nietzsche (1874) 1997. I return to this essay in the final section of this chapter.

14. For a general summary of theories of intertextuality from structuralism to Marxism, see Allen 2011.

15. See, for instance, Snarrenberg 1987; L. Kramer 1990; Scherzinger 1995; Littlefield 1996; Subotnik 1996; Krims 1998a. Adam Krims's (1998a, 305) critique of music theory's appropriations of Derrida's work points out the tension between the discipline's tendency to essentialize analytical models and poststructuralism's tendency

to resist "methodological closure," a dissonance that seems to arise from the unique conditions that have led music theory and poststructuralism to come to fruition as distinct areas of study. The incongruities between music theory's and poststructuralism's (anti-)metaphysical claims, however, need not prevent us from contributing to this interdisciplinary dialogue.

16. See also Korsyn 2003, 91–123, which explores the ontology of compositional identity in relation to repetition and music analysis.

17. Music scholarship has explored the advantages of other intertextual models for understanding musical influence and history. See, for instance, Korsyn 1991 and Straus 1990, both of which engage with Harold Bloom's theory of poetic influence. For a critical stance on Korsyn's and Straus's work in this area, see Taruskin 1993. Korsyn (1996) also uses Bloom's theory in conjunction with Mikhail Bakhtin's concept of dialogism to "capture the tensions of Brahms's stratified discourse" (46). Drawing from several structural and poststructural writers, including Lévi-Strauss, Barthes, and Derrida, Michael Klein (2005) also explores intertextual relationships in works by Bach, Chopin, Liszt, Lutosławski, and others.

18. In *Dissemination*, Derrida ([1972] 1981, 357) writes, "Never will any citation have so aptly meant both 'setting in motion' (the frequentative form of 'to move'—*ciere*) and, also since it is a matter of shaking up a whole culture and history in its fundamental text, solicitation, i.e., the shakeup of a whole."

19. Example 6.1 might be similarly viewed as a graft from prior discourse, a portion of which appears in Fisk 2001, 182; Rosen 2010, 25; and other texts. Whereas Charles Fisk (2001) places Schubert's theme above Beethoven's, Charles Rosen (2010) reverses this orientation. See also Fisk 2000b.

20. This observation has also been noted by Fisk (2001, 181).

21. This is not to suggest that each composer does not in one way or another deviate from these formal patterns; rather, the discussion aims to highlight the expectations that can arise from the formal context within which each theme appears.

22. For further discussion of the connections between Schubert's Sonata in C Minor, D. 958, and Beethoven's Sonata in C Minor, op. 13, see Temperley 1981, Dürr 1991, and Fisk 2000b, 2001. See also Kinderman 2016, which proposes that Schubert's "Der Atlas" "is motivically connected to the main movement of the C minor Sonata, D 958" (49).

23. See also measures 58–61 and 117–120 at the end of the first two couplets from the same sonata rondo movement. My thanks go to Joseph Kraus for suggesting this hearing to me after my presentation of an early version of this paper at the Annual Meeting of the Society for Music Theory in Minneapolis, Minnesota, 2011.

24. Edward Cone (1970, 780) proposes a similar connection between Beethoven's bass and the chaconne, and Fisk (2000b, 636; 2001, 182), between Beethoven's bass and the chaconne and passacaglia.

25. For an in-depth discussion of the passacaglia as it relates to the ciaconna, see Hudson 1981. Peter Williams (1997) views the passacaglia descending bass as only one of several ways in which the chromatic fourth has been used by composers, a practice that goes as far back as the mid-sixteenth century.

26. On countersignatures, see Caputo 1997, 189–98.

27. The variations that follow appear to leave unresolved which pattern may have served as the basis for Beethoven's theme, as they contemplate both possible placements of the structural dominant. In Variations 1–5, 12–17, 22–23, 25, and 29–30, the structural dominant occurs one bar from the end of each variation (m. 7), whereas in Variations 6–11, 18–21, 24, and 26–28, this dominant occurs two bars from the end (m. 6). In Variation 31 and in the beginning of 32, the tonic pedal negates either possibility. The second statement of the variations in Variation 32 (measures 19–33) recovers the structural dominant, placing it in the "seventh" measure (measure 25 in the score). Beethoven then promotes a rhetorical sense of closure to the entire variations by prolonging this dominant in measures 26–27 (withholding motion to the perfect authentic cadence in m. 28), approaching the cadence "one more time" (mm. 29–33) and appending a coda (mm. 33–end). My sincere thanks go to Frank Samarotto for suggesting this point.

28. Notably, the bass pattern in the lower left-hand corner may function as a subset of another pattern, such as the natural minor scale.

29. Here Caplin (2014) remarks on the tension between the descending chromatic tetrachord and form functionality, suggesting that the bass (conceived within the context of the lament) "becomes a touchstone for highlighting stylistic differences among earlier and later works within the eighteenth century" (415). Korsyn makes a similar point in a private correspondence in 2012.

30. See also Caplin 2005.

31. For further discussion of the harmonic progressions that support the formal functions within the sentence theme type, see Caplin 1998, 35–48, and relatedly, Caplin 2013, 33–72.

32. An alternative harmonization for measure 3 would be a minor V^6 chord. For a summary of "standard harmonizations associated with lament bass," see Caplin 2014, 416–21.

33. The penultimate variation of Beethoven's Theme and Variations also features a tonic pedal throughout its entirety, and the last variation, a tonic pedal in the first eight measures.

34. On Schubert's variation procedures in the first movements of his last three piano sonatas, see Martinkus 2017, especially pp. 135–52, which offers an excellent synopsis of Schubert's variation techniques in the Sonata in C Minor. As Caitlin Martinkus proposes more generally, "the last sonatas employ variation as a compositional technique *and* as a means of structuring large-scale formal units, thus creating relationships between restatements of thematic material through the course of the piece beyond their meaning in sonata form" (134). See also Dahlhaus 1986, which reads the first movement of the String Quartet in G Major, D. 887, as a "variation cycle" (4).

35. On the dramatic tenor of C minor in Beethoven's music and others, see especially Kerman 1979; Tusa 1993; Taruskin 2005, 2:691–739 ("C Minor Moods: The Struggle and Victory Narrative and Its Relationship to Four C-minor Works of Beethoven"); Rosen 2010, 72–86 ("The C Minor Style"). As Joseph Kerman (1979) contends, Beethoven's "affection for this tonality in the early years amounted to a mania,

one that was not really played out until the Sonata in C minor, Op. 111, in 1822. Back of all these pieces lay an expressive vision of Mozart's, in such compositions as the great C-minor Concerto, the C-minor Quintet, and especially the Fantasy and Sonata for Piano in C minor" (70, quoted in Tusa 1993, 5–6). Michael Tusa (1993, 6) similarly proposes that "many of the technical-structural assumptions behind Beethoven's early image of C minor were already present in specific Mozartean models," including the first movement of Mozart's Piano Concerto in C Minor, K. 491.

36. The link between D minor and the descending tetrachord may be partly a consequence of tuning and temperament of string and keyboard instruments (Williams 1997; see also Lindley 2001).

37. Although Mozart's theme appears to open with a four-bar compound basic idea instead of a four-bar presentation, the theme—here construed as a hybrid, c.b.i. + continuation—may nonetheless be heard as an "offshoot" of the sentence theme type. On the "relation of the hybrids to the sentence and the period," see Caplin 1998, 63; 2013, 110–14.

38. Rosen (2010), for instance, suggests that "Schubert may have been thinking here of the rhythm of the Beethoven Variations, but the motif was enough of a cliché that he could have found it elsewhere" (25). Rosen also discusses the potential connections between Beethoven's C minor variations, Schubert's Sonata in C Minor, and Bach's Chaconne in D Minor for Solo Violin, BWV 1004. Here he states that the descending chromatic fourth was "a useful formula for writing serious music with an *ostinato* and survived for a long time" (24). On Handel's Chaconne in G Major, HWV 442, as a possible source for Beethoven's C minor variations, see Staehelin 2001.

39. Korsyn identifies these privileged contexts as the monologic subject, the autonomous work of art, and continuous history, which together form "The Bermuda Triangle of Aesthetic Ideology" (2001, 67; 2003, 42–46).

40. As Hayden White (1973, 354) explains, Nietzsche's rejection of the notion of history as a process of becoming arises, in part, as a response to his critique of Hartmannian, Hegelian, and Darwinian historical philosophies.

Closing Remarks

Just as the posthumous performances and publications of Schubert's instrumental music have helped prevent these works from becoming obsolete, emendations to his biography, revisions to our interpretive practices, and reassessments of our values have invited us to come to know these works anew. As proposed earlier, the most recent shift in the reception of Schubert's instrumental music appears to have been mainly motivated by efforts to reconsider his musical aesthetic, primarily by reexamining his approach to harmony and form. Rather than continue to view Schubert's harmonic progressions and forms as arbitrary, strange, and excessive, contemporary music scholarship has instead proposed new or revised contexts for interpreting his distinct approach to composition, thereby reenergizing the discourse on his music while also ushering in a marked shift in the reception history of his instrumental works. By aiming to show how musical phenomena may be conceived as coherent through novel demonstrations of unity, contemporary readings of Schubert's instrumental works have demonstrated how his harmonic progressions and forms need not be viewed as redundant, aimless, or deficient. When paired with revisions to Schubert's biography, scholarship has also proposed that deviations from some of the apparent conventions of the high classical style invite us to further contemplate how his approach to composition may be informed by certain events in his life and sociocultural milieu. As suggested in the opening chapter, while these changes in perspective have had a positive impact on Schubert's musical reception, they can raise new questions about the ways in which we currently theorize and analyze his music, not least with respect to aesthetic engagement: How might the assimilation of strange, musical events into a larger whole, or the re-presentation of such events as conventional affect our aesthetic engagements with his music? That demonstrations of certain kinds of musical coherence and unity in Schubert's music have become a feature of contemporary writings on his instrumental works shortly after the formation of our modern music theory discipline may suggest that such approaches and subsequent conclusions carry a historical index, one that bears traces of the aesthetic values that have helped sustain music theory as a research discipline.

In proposing an alternative poetics for Schubert's instrumental works, my aim throughout this book has not been to revise our contemporary music theories but rather to ask whether there might be other ways to engage with musical moments that seem peculiar and idiosyncratic—to take as the basis of inquiry whether that which seems foreign need always be assimilated or resolved (How else might we engage with the tensions created by those phenomena that we perceive to be strange?) and, more fundamentally, ask whether the musical attributes that we seek to understand are amenable to complete explanations. In exploring this alternative poetics of interpretation, the preceding chapters have consequently introduced alternative subject positions, ones that do not aim to construct or define a unified and harmonious order among different kinds of part-whole relationships. Such subject positions instead have attempted to revel in contradictory meanings of the same musical moment as well as contradictory hearings of the same music when it repeats or returns; trace the ways in which a provisional understanding of a relational system may change, and consider how such changes may give rise to multiple, irreconcilable musical structures; explore how frames, or contexts for listening, may intersect, and contemplate how one frame may call into question the stability of another frame as a musical process unfolds; and engage with the iterability of a musical repetition that differs and defers. All of these suggested positions aim to offer alternatives to conceiving part-whole relationships as the expression of an always already given, where the reconciliation of the strange or unusual is prefigured before the music-theoretical or analytical act begins.

Just as I have attempted to historicize our contemporary modes of reading by showing how they may carry a historical index, readers may similarly locate a historical index in the alternative poetics suggested here, one that resonates with a postmodernist reluctance to accept a single or objective reality and engage with master narratives. In reflecting on the constellation of alternative subject positions introduced—here within the realm of selected Schubert instrumental works, the majority of which have been piano pieces (a likely consequence of my musical training as a pianist)—I acknowledge that such positions are conditioned by the sociocultural milieus that have shaped my own lived experiences, experiences that have prompted me to continuously question what might be gained and lost from assimilation. The alternative poetics and subject positions presented here might be seen as one way to re-present these lived experiences.

Returning to Hanslick's question once more—"If Schubert's contemporaries justly gazed in astonishment at his creative power, what indeed must we, who come after him, say, as we incessantly discover new works of his?" (Deutsch 1951a, 202–3; 1958, 383)—we might conversely ask: "How would Schubert respond to all that has been said about his music and life since the time of his death? Would he similarly gaze in astonishment at our creative powers?" If our collective writings have the potential to uncover the rationale for Schubert's compositional decisions and musical aesthetic, perhaps they also have the capacity to reveal certain aspects of our sociocultural histories and lived experiences in our continuous efforts to come to know his music and its wondrous sounds.

Works Cited

Aarts, Bas. 2014. "Hypotaxis" and "Parataxis." In *The Oxford Dictionary of English Grammar*, 200–201 and 288–89. 2nd edition. New York: Oxford University Press.
Abbate, Carolyn. 1989. "What the Sorcerer Said." *19th-Century Music* 12 (3): 221–30.
———. 1991. *Unsung Voices: Opera and Musical Narrative in Nineteenth Century*. Princeton, NJ: Princeton University Press.
Abrams, M. H. 1953. *The Mirror and the Lamp: Romantic Theory and the Critical Tradition*. New York: Oxford University Press.
Adler, Guido, and Theodore Baker. 1928. "Schubert and the Viennese Classical School." *Musical Quarterly* 14 (4): 473–85.
Agawu, Kofi. 1991. *Playing with Signs: A Semiotic Interpretation of Classic Music*. Princeton, NJ: Princeton University Press.
———. 1993. "Schubert's Sexuality: A Prescription for Analysis?" In "Schubert: Music, Sexuality, Culture," edited by Lawrence Kramer, special issue. *19th-Century Music* 17 (1): 79–82.
Agmon, Eytan. 1987. "Music and Text in Schubert Songs: The Role of Enharmonic Equivalence." *Israel Studies in Musicology* 4:49–58.
Allen, Graham. 2011. *Intertextuality*. 2nd ed. London: Routledge.
Almén, Byron. 2003. "Narrative Archetypes: A Critique, Theory, and Method of Narrative Analysis." *Journal of Music Theory* 47 (1): 1–39.
———. 2008. *A Theory of Musical Narrative*. Bloomington: Indiana University Press.
Austin, J. L. 1975. *How to Do Things with Words*. 2nd ed. Cambridge, MA: Harvard University Press.
Bailey, Robert. 1985. "An Analytical Study of the Sketches and Drafts." In *Richard Wagner: Prelude and Transfiguration from Tristan und Isolde*, edited by Robert Bailey, 113–46. New York: W. W. Norton and Company.
Barthes, Roland. (1970) 1974. *S/Z: An Essay*. Translated by Richard Miller. New York: Hill and Wang. Originally published as *S/Z*. Paris: Seuil.
———. 1971. "A Conversation with Roland Barthes." In *Signs of the Times: Introductory Reading in Textual Semiotics*, edited by Stephen Heath, Colin MacCabe, and Christopher Prendergas, 44–55. Cambridge, UK: Granta.

Beach, David. 1998. "Modal Mixture and Schubert's Harmonic Practice." *Journal of Music Theory* 42 (1): 73–100.
Benjamin, Walter. 1996. "The Concept of Criticism in German Romanticism." In *Walter Benjamin: Selected Writings, Volume 1: 1913–1926*, edited by Marcus Bullock and Michael W. Jennings, 116–200. Cambridge, MA: Harvard University Press.
Benton, Michael. 2009. *Literary Biography: An Introduction*. Chichester, UK: Blackwell.
Bergé, Pieter, William Cample, and Joroen D'hoe, eds. 2009. *Beethoven's Tempest Sonata: Perspectives of Analysis and Performance*. Leuven, Belgium: Peeters.
Bergé, Pieter, and Markus Neuwirth, eds. 2015. *What Is a Cadence? Theoretical and Analytical Perspectives on Cadences in the Classical Repertoire*. Leuven, Belgium: Leuven University Press.
Bharucha, J. J. 1984. "Event Hierarchies, Tonal Hierarchies, and Assimilation: A Reply to Deutsch and Dowling." *Journal of Experimental Psychology: General* 113 (3): 421–25.
Black, Brian. 2015. "Schubert's 'Deflected-Cadence' Transitions and the Classical Style." In *Formal Functions in Perspective: Essays on Musical Form from Haydn to Adorno*, edited by Steven Vande Moortele, Julie Pedneault-Deslauriers, and Nathan Martin, 165–97. Rochester, NY: University of Rochester Press.
Byrne Bodley, Lorraine, and Julian Horton, eds. 2016a. *Rethinking Schubert*. New York: Oxford University Press.
———, eds. 2016b. *Schubert's Late Music: History, Theory, Style*. New York: Oxford University Press.
Bowie, Andrew. 2002. "Music and the Rise of Aesthetics." In *The Cambridge History of Nineteenth-Century Music*, edited by Jim Samson, 29–54. New York: Cambridge University Press.
———. 2003. *Aesthetics and Subjectivity: From Kant to Nietzsche*. Manchester, UK: Manchester University Press.
Brauner, Charles. 1981. "Irony in the Heine Lieder of Schubert and Schumann." *Musical Quarterly* 67 (2): 261–81.
Brendel, Alfred. 2015. *Music, Sense, and Nonsense: Collected Essays and Lectures*. London: Robson.
Brett, Philip. 1997. "Piano Four-Hands: Schubert and the Performance of Gay Male Desire." In "Franz Schubert: Bicentenary Essays," edited by James Hepokoski and Lawrence Kramer, special issue. *19th-Century Music* 21 (2): 149–76.
Bribitzer-Stull, Matthew. 2006. "The A♭–C–E Complex: The Origin and Function of Chromatic Major Third Collections in Nineteenth-Century Music." *Music Theory Spectrum* 28 (2): 167–90.
Brown, Maurice J. E. 1958. *Schubert: A Critical Biography*. London: St. Martin's Press.
———. 1965. Review of *Schubert: Die Dokumente Seines Lebens* by Otto Erich Deutsch. *Music & Letters* 46 (2): 166–68.

Brown, Maurice J. E., Eric Sams, and Robert Winter. 2001. "Schubert, Franz." *Grove Music Online*. https://doi.org/10.1093/gmo/9781561592630.article.25109.
Burnham, Scott. 1995. *Beethoven Hero*. Princeton, NJ: Princeton University Press.
———. 1999. "The 'Heavenly Length' of Schubert's Music." *Ideas* 6 (1). National Humanities Centre. http://nationalhumanitiescenter.org//ideasv61/burnham.htm.
———. 2013. *Mozart's Grace*. Princeton, NJ: Princeton University Press.
Burstein, L. Poundie. 2002. "Devil's Castles and Schubert's Strange Tonic Allusions." *Theory and Practice* 27:69–84.
———. 2014. "The Half Cadence and Other Such Slippery Events." *Music Theory Spectrum* 36 (2): 203–27.
Butler, Judith. 1990. *Gender Trouble: Feminism and the Subversion of Identity*. New York: Routledge.
Cadwallader, Allen, and David Gagné. 1998. *Analysis of Tonal Music: A Schenkerian Approach*. New York: Oxford University Press.
Caplin, William. 1998. *Classical Form: A Theory of Formal Functions for the Instrumental Music of Haydn, Mozart, and Beethoven*. New York: Oxford University Press.
———. 2004. "The Classical Cadence: Conceptions and Misconceptions." *Journal of the American Musicological Society* 57 (1): 51–117.
———. 2005. "On the Relation of Musical *Topoi* to Formal Function." *Eighteenth-Century Music* 2 (2): 113–24.
———. 2010. "What Are Formal Functions?" In *Musical Form, Forms, and Formenlehre*, edited by Pieter Bergé, 21–40. Leuven, Netherlands: Leuven University Press.
———. 2013. *Analyzing Classical Form: An Approach for the Classroom*. New York: Oxford University Press.
———. 2014. "Topics and Formal Functions: The Case of the Lament." In *The Oxford Handbook of Topic Theory*, edited by Danuta Mirka, 415–52. New York: Oxford University Press.
———. 2018. "Beyond the Classical Cadence: Thematic Closure in Early Romantic Music." *Music Theory Spectrum* 40 (1): 1–26.
Caputo, John D. 1997, ed. *Deconstruction in a Nutshell: A Conversation with Jacques Derrida*. New York: Fordham University Press.
Cho, Hyunree. 2015. "Music as Poetry." *Perspectives of New Music* 53 (1): 143–87.
Christensen, Thomas. 2001. "Musicology: Theoretical and Analytical Method." In vol. 17 of *The New Grove Dictionary of Music and Musicians*, edited by Stanley Sadie and John Tyrrell, 488–533. New York: Oxford University Press.
Chua, Daniel K. L. 2004. "Rethinking Unity." *Music Analysis* 23 (2–3): 353–59.
Chusid, Martin. 1968. *Franz Schubert: Symphony in B minor ("Unfinished"): An Authoritative Score*. A Norton Critical Score. New York: W. W. Norton.
Clark, Suzannah. 2002. "Schubert, Theory and Analysis." *Music Analysis* 21 (2): 209–43.

———. 2011a. *Analyzing Schubert*. New York: Cambridge University Press.
———. 2011b. "On the Imagination of Tone in Schubert's *Liedesend* (D473), *Trost* (D523), and *Gretchens Bitte* (D564)." In *The Oxford Handbook of Neo-Riemannian Theories*, edited by Edward Gollin and Alexander Rehding, 294–321. New York: Oxford University Press.
Clive, Peter. 1997. "Breitkopf & Härtel." In *Schubert and His World: A Biographical Dictionary*. New York: Oxford University Press, 20–21.
Cohn, Richard. 1996. "Maximally Smooth Cycles, Hexatonic Systems, and the Analysis of Late-Romantic Triadic Progressions." *Music Analysis* 15 (1): 9–40.
———. 1998. "Introduction to Neo-Riemannian Theory: A Survey and a Historical Perspective." *Journal of Music Theory* 42 (2): 167–80.
———. 1999. "As Wonderful as Star Clusters: Instruments for Gazing at Tonality in Schubert." *19th-Century Music* 22 (3): 213–32.
———. 2004. "Uncanny Resemblances: Tonal Signification in the Freudian Age." *Journal of American Musicological Society* 57 (2): 285–324.
———. 2011. "Tonal Pitch Space and the (Neo-)Riemannian *Tonnetz*." In *The Oxford Handbook of Neo-Riemannian Music Theories*, edited by Edward Gollin and Alexander Rehding, 322–48. New York: Oxford University Press.
———. 2012. *Audacious Euphony: Chromaticism and the Triad's Second Nature*. New York: Oxford University Press.
Coker, Wilson. 1972. *Music and Meaning: A Theoretical Introduction to Musical Aesthetics*. New York: Free Press.
Cone, Edward T. 1970. "Schubert's Beethoven." *Musical Quarterly* 56 (4): 779–93.
———. 1977. "Three Ways of Reading a Detective Story or a Brahms Intermezzo." *Georgia Review* 31 (3): 554–74.
———. 1982. "Schubert's Promissory Note: An Exercise in Musical Hermeneutics." *19th-Century Music* 5 (3): 233–41.
Cook, Nicholas, and Mark Everist, eds. 2001. *Rethinking Music*. New York: Oxford University Press.
Copley, R. Evan. 1991. *Harmony: Baroque to Contemporary*. Vol. 1. 2nd ed. Champaign, IL: Stipes.
Cuddon, J. A. 1991. *A Dictionary of Literary Terms and Literary Theory*. 3rd ed. Oxford: Blackwell.
Culler, Jonathan. 1973. "Structure of Ideology and Ideology of Structure." In *New Literary History* 4 (3): 471–82.
———. 1975. *Structural Poetics: Structuralism, Linguistics and the Study of Literature*. London: Routledge.
———. 1981. *The Pursuit of Signs: Semiotics, Literature, Deconstruction*. Ithaca: Cornell University Press.
———. 1983. *Barthes*. Glasgow: Fontana 1983. Revised version published in the series A Very Short Introduction. New York: Oxford University Press, 2002.

———. 1997. *Literary Theory. A Very Short Introduction*. New York: Oxford University Press.

———. 2007. *On Deconstruction: Theory and Criticism after Structuralism*. 25th anniversary ed. Ithaca, NY: Cornell University Press.

Curtis, Robert Lee. 1979. *Ludwig Bischoff: A Mid-Nineteenth-Century Music Critic*. Cologne, Germany: Arno Volk.

Cusick, Suzanne. 1994. "Feminist Theory, Music Theory, and the Mind/Body Problem." *Perspectives of New Music* 32 (1): 8–27.

Czerny, Carl. (1829) 1983. *A Systematic Introduction to Improvisation on the Pianoforte*. Translated by Alice L. Mitchell. New York: Longman. Originally published as *Systematische Anleitung zum Fantasieren auf dem Pianoforte*, op. 200. Vienna: A. Diabelli und Comp.

Dahlhaus, Carl. 1978. *The Idea of Absolute Music*. Translated by Roger Lustig. Chicago: University of Chicago Press.

———. 1986. "Sonata Form in Schubert: The First Movement of the G-major String Quartet, Op. 161 (D. 887)." In *Schubert: Critical and Analytical Studies*, edited by Walter Frisch, 1–12. Translated by Thilo Reinhard. Lincoln: University of Nebraska Press. Originally published as "Die Sonatenform bei Schubert," *Musica* 32, no. 2 (1978): 125–30.

———. 1991. *Ludwig van Beethoven: Approaches to His Music*. Translated by Mary Whittall. Oxford: Clarendon.

Dahms, Walter. 1912. *Schubert*. Berlin: Schuster und Loeffler.

Damschroder, David. 2010. *Harmony in Schubert*. New York: Cambridge University Press.

Daverio, John. 1993. *Nineteenth-Century Music and the German Romantic Ideology*. New York: Schirmer.

———. 2000. "'One More Beautiful Memory of Schubert': Schumann's Critique of the Impromptus, D. 935." *The Musical Quarterly* 84 (4): 604–18.

———. 2002. *Crossing Paths: Schubert, Schumann, & Brahms*. New York: Oxford University Press.

Dell'Antonio, Andrew, ed. 2004. *Beyond Structural Listening? Postmodern Modes of Hearing*. Berkeley: University of California Press.

de Man, Paul. 1983. "Literary History and Literary Modernity." Reprinted in *Blindness and Insight: Essays in the Rhetoric of Contemporary Criticism*, 142–65. 2nd ed. Minneapolis: University of Minnesota Press.

———. 1996. "The Concept of Irony." In *Aesthetic Ideology*, edited by Andrzej Warminski, 163–84. Minneapolis: University of Minnesota Press.

Derrida, Jacques. (1972) 1981. *Dissemination*. Translated by Barbara Johnson. Chicago: University of Chicago Press. Originally published as *La Dissémination*. Paris: Seuil.

———. (1974) 1986. *Glas*. Translated by John P. Leavey Jr. and Richard Rand. Lincoln: University of Nebraska Press. Originally published as *Glas*, Paris: Galilée.

Deutsch, Otto Erich. 1907. "Schuberts Herzeleid." *Bühne und Welt: Zeitschrift für Theaterwesen, Litteratur und Musik* 9 (18): 227–31.

———, ed. 1947. *The Schubert Reader: A Life of Franz Schubert in Letters and Documents*. Translated by Eric Blom. New York: W. W. Norton & Company.

———. 1951a. "The Reception of Schubert's Works in England." *Monthly Musical Record* 81: 200–203.

———. 1951b. "Schubert: The Collected Works." *Music & Letters* 32 (3): 226–34.

———. (1951) 1995. *Schubert: Thematic Catalog of All His Works in Chronological Order*. Unabridged, corrected republication. New York: Dover.

———. 1952. "The Discovery of Schubert's Great C-Major Symphony: A Story in Fifteen Letters." *Musical Quarterly* 38 (4): 528–32.

———, ed. 1958. *Schubert: Memoirs by His Friends*. Translated by Rosamond Ley and John Nowell. London: Adam & Charles Black.

Dilthey, Wilhelm. (1883) 1989. *Introduction to the Human Sciences*. Vol. 1 of *Selected Works*. Edited and with an introduction by Rudolf A. Makkreel and Frithjof Rodi. Princeton, NJ: Princeton University Press.

———. (1910) 2002. *The Formation of the Historical World in the Human Sciences*. Vol. 3 of *Selected Works*. Edited and with an introduction by Rudolf A. Makkreel and Frithjof Rodi. Princeton, NJ: Princeton University Press.

———. 1959. "The Understanding of Other Persons and Their Life-Expressions." Translated by J. J. Kuehl. In *Theories of History: Readings in Classical and Contemporary Sources*, edited by Patrick Gardiner, 213–25. New York: Free Press. From *Gesammelte Schriften*, 7:205–20.

Dubiel, Joseph. 2004. "What We Really Disagree About: A Reply to Robert P. Morgan." *Music Analysis* 23 (2–3): 373–85.

Dürr, Walther. 1991. "Klaviermusik." In *Franz Schubert*, edited by Walther Dürr, Arnold Feil, and Walburga Litschauer, 266–305. Stuttgart, Ger.: Philipp Reclam.

Eagleton, Terry. 1990. *The Ideology of the Aesthetic*. Oxford: Blackwell.

Elkins, James. 1999. *Why Are Our Pictures Puzzles? On the Modern Origins of Pictorial Complexity*. New York: Routledge.

Feldman, Hali. 2002. "Schubert's *Quartettsatz* and Sonata Form's New Way." *Journal of Musicological Research* 21 (1–2): 99–146.

———. 2007. "Schubert's Sonata Form: The Case of the C-minor *Quartettsatz*." In *Le Style Instrumental de Schubert: Sources, Analyse, Évolution*, edited by Xavier Hascher, 83–92. Paris: Sorbonne.

Feurzeig, Lisa. 1997. "Idea in Song: Schubert's Settings of Friedrich Schlegel." PhD diss., University of Chicago.

———. 2014. *Schubert's Lieder and the Philosophy of Early German Romanticism*. London: Ashgate.

Fichte, Johann Gottlieb. 1982. *Science of Knowledge (Wissenschaftslehre): With the First and Second Introductions*. Edited by Peter Heath and John Lachs. New York: Cambridge University Press.

Field, Christopher D. S., E. Eugene Helm, and William Drabkin. 2001. "Fantasia." *Grove Music Online.* https://doi.org/10.1093/gmo/9781561592630.article.40048.
Fisk, Charles. 1990. "Rehearing the Moment and Hearing In-the-Moment: Schubert's First Two *Moments Musicaux*." *College Music Symposium* 30 (2): 1–18.
———. 1997. "What Schubert's Last Sonata Might Hold." In *Music and Meaning*, edited by Jenefer Robinson, 179–200. Ithaca, NY: Cornell University Press.
———. 2000a. "Schubertian Confidences." *GLSG Newsletter* 10 (2): 4–7.
———. 2000b. "Schubert Recollects Himself: The Piano Sonata in C minor, D. 958." In "Memory and Schubert's Instrumental Music," edited by Leon Botstein, special issue, *Musical Quarterly* 48 (4): 635–53.
———. 2001. *Returning Cycles: Contexts for the Interpretation of Schubert's Impromptus and Last Sonatas.* Berkeley: University of California Press.
Fisk, Charles, and Richard Cohn. 2000. "Comment and Chronicle." *19th-Century Music* 23 (3): 301–4.
Frisch, Walter. 1989. "'Schubert's Last Sonatas': An Exchange." *New York Review of Books.* March 16, 1989.
Frye, Northrop. (1957) 2000. *Anatomy of Criticism*. With a new foreword by Harold Bloom. Princeton, NJ: Princeton University Press.
Furst, Lilian. 1984. "The Metamorphosis of Irony." In *Fictions of Romantic Irony*, 23–48. Cambridge, MA: Harvard University Press.
Gann, Kyle. 2009. "So I'm Neo-Riemannian: Who Knew?" *PostClassic: An Arts Journal Blog.* March 6. https://www.kylegann.com/PC090306-SoImNeoRiemannian.html.
———. 2019. *The Arithmetic of Listening: Tuning Theory & History for the Impractical Musician.* Urbana: University of Illinois Press.
Gibbs, Christopher H. 1997a. "German Reception: Schubert's 'Journey to Immortality.'" In *The Cambridge Companion to Schubert*, edited by Christopher Gibbs, 241–53. New York: Cambridge University Press.
———. 1997b. "Poor Schubert." In *The Cambridge Companion to Schubert*, edited by Christopher Gibbs, 36–55. New York: Cambridge University Press.
———. 2000. *The Life of Schubert.* New York: Cambridge University Press.
———. 2003. "Writing under the Influence?: Salieri and Schubert's Early Opinion of Beethoven." *Current Musicology* 75:117–44.
Gingerich, John. 2014. *Schubert's Beethoven Project.* New York: Cambridge University Press.
———. 2016. "'Classical' Music and Viennese Resistance to Schubert's Beethoven Project." In *Schubert's Late Music: History, Theory, Style*, edited by Lorraine Byrne Bodley and Julian Horton, 19–34. New York: Cambridge University Press.
Godel, Arthur. 1985. *Schuberts Letzte Drei Klaviersonaten: Entstehungsgeschichte, Entwurf, und Reinschrift Werkanalyse.* Baden-Baden, Ger.: Koerner.

Goldenberg, Yosef. 2007. "Schenkerian Voice-Leading and Neo-Riemannian Operations: Analytical Integration without Theoretical Reconciliation." *Journal of Schenkerian Studies* 2:65–84.

Gollin, Edward. 2011. "From Matrix to Map: *Tonbestimmung*, the *Tonnetz*, and Riemann's Combinatorial Conception of Interval." In *The Oxford Handbook of Neo-Riemannian Music Theories*, edited by Edward Gollin and Alexander Rehding, 271–93. New York: Oxford University Press.

Gooley, Dana. 2018. *Fantasies of Improvisation*. New York: Oxford University Press.

Gramit, David. "Constructing a Victorian Schubert: Music, Biography, and Cultural Values." In "Schubert: Music, Sexuality, Culture," edited by Lawrence Kramer, special issue. *19th-Century Music* 17 (1): 65–78.

Grant, Aaron. 2022. "Structure and Variable Formal Function in Schubert's Three-Key Expositions." *Music Theory Spectrum* 44 (1): 63–98.

Graves, Charles L. 1903. *The Life and Letters of Sir George Grove*. London: Macmillan.

Gray, Cecil. 1928. *The History of Music*. London: Kegan Paul, Trench, Trubner, 1928.

Gray, Walter. 1928. "Schubert the Instrumental Composer." *Musical Quarterly* 64 (4): 483–94.

Griffel, L. Michael. 1997. "Schubert's Orchestral Music: 'Strivings after the Highest in Art.'" In *The Cambridge Companion to Schubert*, edited by Christopher Gibbs, 193–206. New York: Cambridge University Press.

Grove, Sir George. 1883. "Schubert, Franz Peter." In *A Dictionary of Music and Musicians*, edited by Sir George Grove, 319–82. Vol. 3. New York: Macmillan. Reprinted in Sir George Grove, *Beethoven, Schubert, Mendelssohn*. London: Macmillan, 1951.

Guck, Marion. 1994. "Analytical Fictions." *Music Theory Spectrum* 16 (2): 217–30.

———. 2006. "Analysis as Interpretation: Interaction, Intentionality, Invention." *Music Theory Spectrum* 28 (2): 191–209.

Handwerk, Gary. 2000. "Romantic Irony." In *The Cambridge History of Literary Criticism*. Vol. 5. New York: Cambridge University Press.

Hanslick, Eduard. (1870) 1968. "On the First Performance." In *Franz Schubert: Symphony in B minor ("Unfinished"): An Authoritative Score*. A Norton Critical Score. Translated by Martin Chusid, 113–15. New York: W. W. Norton. Originally published in *Geschichte des Concertwesens in Wien, Aus dem Concertsaal*. Zweiter Theil. Vienna: Wilhelm Braumüller, 350–51.

Harrison, Daniel. 2002. "Nonconformist Notions of Nineteenth-Century Enharmonicism," *Music Analysis* 221 (2): 115–60.

Hartman, Geoffrey. 2007. "Criticism, Indeterminacy, Irony." In *Criticism in the Wilderness: The Study of Literature Today*, 265–83. 2nd ed. New Haven, CT: Yale University Press.

Hascher, Xavier. 1997. "Schubert's Reception in France: A Chronology (1828–1928)." In *The Cambridge Companion to Schubert*, edited by Christopher Gibbs, 263–69. New York: Cambridge University Press.

Hatten, Robert. 1994. *Musical Meaning in Beethoven: Markedness, Correlation, and Interpretation*. Bloomington: Indiana University Press.
———. 2004. *Interpreting Musical Gestures, Topics, and Tropes: Mozart, Beethoven, Schubert*. Bloomington: Indiana University Press.
———. 2016. "Schubert's Alchemy: Transformative Surfaces, Transfiguring Depths." In *Schubert's Late Music: History, Theory, Style*, edited by Lorraine Byrne Bodley and Julian Horton, 91–110. New York: Cambridge University Press.
Henahan, Donal. 1989. "The Dark Side of Schubert." *New York Times*, August 27, 1989. https://www.nytimes.com/1989/08/27/arts/music-view-the-dark-side-of-schubert.html.
Hepokoski, James, and Warren Darcy. 2006. *Elements of Sonata Theory: Norms, Types, and Deformations in the Late-Eighteenth-Century Sonata*. New York: Oxford University Press.
Hinrichsen, Hans-Joachim. 1994. *Untersuchungen zur Entwicklung der Sonatenform in der Instrumentalmusik Franz Schuberts*. Tutzing, Ger.: Hans Schneider.
Hitschmann, Edward. 1915. "Franz Schuberts Schmerz und Liebe." *Internationale Zeitschrift für ärztliche Psychoanalyse* 3:287–92. Translated by Edna Spector as "Franz Schubert's Grief and Love." *American Imago* 7 (1950): 67–76.
Horton, Julian. 2005. "Bruckner's Symphonies and Sonata Deformation Theory." *Journal of the Society for Musicology in Ireland* 1:5–17.
———. 2017. "Criteria for a Theory of Nineteenth-Century Sonata Form." *Music Theory and Analysis* 4 (2): 147–91.
Hudson, Richard. 1981. *Passacaglio and Ciaccona: From Italian Guitar Music to Keyboard Variations in the 17th Century*. Ann Arbor: UMI Research Press.
Hunt, Graham. 2009. "The Three-Key Trimodular Block and Its Classical Precedents: Sonata Expositions of Schubert and Brahms." *Intégral* 23:65–119.
———. 2014. "When Structure and Design Collide: The Three-Key Exposition Revisited." *Music Theory Spectrum* 36 (2): 247–69.
Hutching, Arthur. 1945. *Schubert*. London: J. M. Dent.
Hyland, Anne. 2014. "The Tightened Bow: Analysing the Juxtaposition of Drama and Lyricism in Schubert's Paratactic Sonata-Form Movements." In *Irish Musical Analysis: Irish Musical Studies*, vol. 11, edited by Gareth Cox and Julian Horton, 17–40. Dublin: Four Courts Press.
———. 2016a. "In Search of Liberated Time, or Schubert's Quartet in G Major, D. 887: Once More between Sonata and Variation." *Music Theory Spectrum* 38 (1): 85–108.
———. 2016b. "*[Un]Himmlische Länge*: Editorial Intervention as Reception History." In *Schubert's Late Music: History, Theory, Style*, edited by Lorraine Byrne Bodley and Julian Horton, 52–76. New York: Cambridge University Press.
Johnson, Jeannine. 2014. "New Criticism." In vol. 4 of *Encyclopedia of Aesthetics*, 2nd ed., edited by Michael Kelly, 492–96. New York: Oxford University Press.
Kerman, Joseph. 1979. *The Beethoven Quartets*. New York: W. W. Norton.

———. 1980. "How We Got into Analysis and How to Get Out." *Critical Inquiry* 7 (2): 311–31.

Kessler, Deborah. 2006. "Motive and Motivation in Schubert's Three-Key Expositions." In *Structure and Meaning in Tonal Music: Festschrift in Honor of Carl Schachter*, edited by David Gagné and L. Poundie Burstein, 269–75. New York: Pendragon.

Kierkegaard, Søren. 1989. *The Concept of Irony with Continual Reference to Socrates*. Edited and translated by Howard V. Hong and Edna H. Hong. Princeton, NJ: Princeton University Press.

Kinderman, William. 2016. "Franz Schubert's 'New Style' and the Legacy of Beethoven." In *Rethinking Schubert*, edited by Lorraine Byrne Bodley and Julian Horton, 41–60. New York: Oxford University Press.

Kinderman, William, and Harald Krebs, eds. 1996. *The Second Practice of Nineteenth-Century Tonality*. New York: Oxford University Press.

Klein, Michael. 2004. "Chopin's Fourth Ballade as Musical Narrative." *Music Theory Spectrum* 26 (1): 23–56.

———. 2005. *Intertextuality in Western Art Music*. Bloomington: Indiana University Press.

Kopp, David. 2002. *Chromatic Transformations in Nineteenth-Century Music*. New York: Cambridge University Press.

Korsyn, Kevin. 1991. "Towards a New Poetics of Musical Influence." *Music Analysis* 10 (1/2): 3–72.

———. 1993a. "Brahms Research and Aesthetic Ideology." *Music Analysis* 12 (1): 89–103.

———. 1993b. "J.W.N. Sullivan and the *Heiliger Dankgesang*: Questions of Meaning in Late Beethoven." In *Beethoven Forum*, vol. 2, edited by Christopher Reynolds, Lewis Lockwood, and James Webster, 133–76. Lincoln: University of Nebraska Press.

———. 1996. "Directional Tonality and Intertextuality: Brahms's Quintet op. 88 and Chopin's Ballade op. 38." In *The Second Practice of Nineteenth-Century Tonality*, edited by William Kinderman and Harald Krebs, 45–83. Lincoln: University of Nebraska Press.

———. 2001. "Beyond Privileged Contexts: Intertextuality, Influence, and Dialogue." In *Rethinking Music*, edited by Nicholas Cook and Mark Everist, 55–72. Oxford: Oxford University Press.

———. 2003. *Decentering Music*. New York: Oxford University Press.

———. 2004. "The Death of Musical Analysis? The Concept of Unity Revisited." *Music Analysis* 23 (2–3): 337–51.

Koslovsky, John Charles. 2009. "From *Sinn und Wesen* to *Structural Hearing*: The Development of Felix Salzer's Ideas in Interwar Vienna and Their Transmission in Postwar United States." PhD diss., Eastman School of Music, University of Rochester.

Kramer, Jonathan. 2004. "The Concept of Disunity and Musical Analysis." *Music Analysis* 23 (2–3): 361–72.

Kramer, Lawrence. 1990. *Music as Cultural Practice, 1800–1900*. Berkeley: University of California Press.

———, ed. 1993. "Schubert: Music, Sexuality, Culture." Special issue, *19th-Century Music* 17 (1).

Kramer, Richard. 1994. *Distant Cycles*. Chicago: University of Chicago Press.

———. 2016. "Against the Grain: The Sonata in G (D. 894) and a Hermeneutics of Late Style." In *Schubert's Late Music: History, Theory, Style*, edited by Lorraine Byrne Bodley and Julian Horton, 111–33. New York: Cambridge University Press.

Kreissle, Heinrich von Hellborn. 1869. *The Life of Franz Schubert*. 2 vols. London: Longmans, Green.

Krims, Adam. 1998a. "Disciplining Deconstruction (for Music Analysis)." *19th-Century Music* 21 (3): 297–324.

———, ed. 1998b. "Introduction: Postmodern Musical Poetics and the Problem of 'Close Reading.'" In *Music/Ideology: Resisting the Aesthetic*, 1–15. Amsterdam: G + B Arts International.

Kristeva, Julia. (1969) 1980. *Desire in Language: A Semiotic Approach to Literature and Art*. Translated by Thomas Gora, Alice Jardine, and Leon S. Roudiez. Edited by Leon S. Roudiez. New York: Columbia University Press. Originally published as *Séméiôtiké: Recherches pour une Sémanalyse*. Paris: Edition du Seuil.

Kurth, Richard. 1997. "Music and Poetry, a Wilderness of Doubles: Heine—Nietzsche—Schubert—Derrida." *19th-Century Music* 21 (i): 3–37.

Lerdahl, Fred. 1988. "Tonal Pitch Space." *Music Perception* 5 (3): 315–49.

———. 2011. *Tonal Pitch Space*. New York: Oxford University Press.

Lewin, David. 1986. "Music Theory, Phenomenology, and Modes of Perception." *Music Perception: An Interdisciplinary Journal* 3 (4): 327–92.

Lindley, Mark. 2001. "Temperaments." *Grove Music Online*. https://doi.org/10.1093/gmo/9781561592630.article.27643.

Lindmayr-Brandl, Andrea. 2016. "The Myth of the 'Unfinished' and the Film *Das Dreimäderlhaus* (1958)." In *Rethinking Schubert*, edited by Lorraine Byrne Bodley and Julian Horton, 111–27. New York: Oxford University Press.

Littlefield, Richard. 1996. "The Silence of the Frames." *Music Theory Online* 2 (1). https://www.mtosmt.org/issues/mto.96.2.1/mto.96.2.1.littlefield.html.

Lochhead, Judith. 2016. *Reconceiving Structure in Contemporary Music: New Tools in Music Theory and Analysis*. New York: Routledge.

———. 2020. "Music's Vibratory Enchantments and Epistemic Injustices: Reflecting on Thirty Years of Feminist Thought in Music Theory." *Zeitschrift der Gesellschaft für Musiktheorie* 17 (1): 15–29.

Longyear, Rey M., and Kate R. Covington. 1988. "Sources of the Three-Key Exposition." *Journal of Musicology* 6 (4): 448–70.

MacDonald, Hugh. 1984–85. "To Repeat or Not to Repeat?" *Proceedings of the Royal Musical Association* 111:121–38.

Mak, Su Yin. 2004. "Structure, Design, and Rhetoric: Schubert's Lyricism Reconsidered." PhD diss., University of Rochester.

———. 2006. "Schubert's Sonata Forms and the Poetics of the Lyric." *Journal of Musicology* 23 (2): 263–306.

———. 2010. *Schubert's Lyricism Reconsidered: Structure, Design and Rhetoric*. London: Lambert Academic Publishing.

———. 2015. "'Sonata Form in Franz Schubert' (1928): An English Translation and Edition with Critical Commentary." Translated by Su Yin Mak. *Theory and Practice* 40:1–21.

———. 2016. "Formal Ambiguity and Generic Reinterpretation in the Late Music." In *Schubert's Late Music: History, Theory, Style*, edited by Lorraine Byrne Bodley and Julian Horton, 282–306. New York: Cambridge University Press.

Makkreel, Rudolf A. 1975. *Dilthey: Philosopher of the Human Studies*. New Jersey, NJ: Princeton University Press.

———. 2021. "Dilthey, Wilhelm (1833–1911)." *Routledge Encyclopedia of Philosophy Online*. https://www.rep.routledge.com/articles/biographical/dilthey-wilhelm-1833-1911/v-2.

Martin, Nathan, and Steven Vande Moortele. 2014. "Formal Functions and Retrospective Reinterpretation in the First Movement of Schubert's String Quintet." *Music Analysis* 33 (2): 130–55.

Martinkus, Caitlin G. 2017. "The Urge to Vary: Schubert's Variation Practice from Schubertiades to Sonata Forms." PhD diss., University of Toronto.

———. 2018. "Thematic Expansion and Elements of Variation in Schubert's C Major Symphony, D. 944/i." *Music Theory & Analysis* 5 (11): 190–202.

———. 2021. "Schubert's Large-Scale Sentences: Exploring the Function of Repetition in Schubert's First-Movement Sonata Forms." *Music Theory Online* 27 (3).

Marston, Nicholas. 2000. "Schubert's Homecoming." *Journal of the Royal Musical Association* 125 (2): 248–70.

Mason, Daniel Gregory. 1906. *The Romantic Composers*. New York: Macmillan.

Maus, Fred. 1988. "Music as Drama." *Music Theory Spectrum*, 10th anniversary issue, 10:56–73.

———. 1993. "Masculine Discourse in Music Theory." *Perspectives of New Music* 31 (2): 264–93.

———. 2004. "The Disciplined Subject of Music Analysis." In *Beyond Structural Listening? Postmodern Modes of Hearing*, edited by Andrew Dell'Antonio, 13–43. Berkeley: University of California Press.

McClary, Susan. 1993a. "Narrative Agendas in 'Absolute' Music: Identity and Difference in Brahms's Third Symphony." In *Musicology and Difference: Gender and Sexuality in Music Scholarship*, edited by Ruth Solie, 326–44. Berkeley: University of California Press.

———. 1993b. "Music and Sexuality: On the Steblin/Solomon Debate." In "Schubert: Music, Sexuality, Culture," edited by Lawrence Kramer, special issue. *19th-Century Music* 17 (1): 83–88.

———. 1994. "Constructions of Subjectivity in Schubert's Music." In *Queering the Pitch: The New Gay and Lesbian Musicology*, edited by Philip Brett, Elizabeth Wood, and Gary C. Thomas, 205–34. New York: Routledge.

McCreless, Patrick. 1991. "Syntagmatics and Paradigmatics: Some Implications for the Analysis of Chromaticism in Tonal Music." *Music Theory Spectrum* 13 (2): 147–78.

———. 1996a. "Contemporary Music Theory and the New Musicology: An Introduction." *Music Theory Online* 2, no. 2.

———. 1996b. "An Evolutionary Perspective on Nineteenth-Century Semitonal Relations." In *The Second Practice of Nineteenth-Century Tonality*, edited by William Kinderman and Harald Krebs, 87–113. New York: Oxford University Press.

———. 1997. "Rethinking Contemporary Music Theory." In *Keeping Score: Music, Disciplinarity, Culture*, edited by David Schwarz, Anahid Kassabian, and Lawrence Siegel, 13–53. Charlottesville: University Press of Virginia.

———. 2000. "Music Theory and Historical Awareness." *Music Theory Online* 6 (3). https://www.mtosmt.org/issues/mto.00.6.3/mto.00.6.3.mccreless.html.

McKay, Elizabeth Norman. 1996. *Franz Schubert: A Biography*. New York: Oxford University Press.

Médicis, François de. 2015. "'Heavenly Length' in Schubert's Instrumental Music." In *Formal Functions in Perspective*, edited by Steven Vande Moortele, Julie Pedneault-Deslauriers, and Nathan Martin, 198–222. Rochester: University of Rochester Press.

Messing, Scott. 2006. *Schubert in the European Imagination*. Vol. 1, *The Romantic and Victorian Eras*. Eastman Studies in Music. Rochester, NY: University of Rochester Press.

———. 2007. *Schubert in the European Imagination*. Vol. 2, *Fin-de-Siècle Vienna*. Eastman Studies in Music. Rochester, NY: University of Rochester Press.

Meyer, Leonard. 1956. *Emotion and Meaning in Music*. Chicago: University of Chicago Press.

Mirka, Danuta, ed. 2014. *The Oxford Handbook of Topic Theory*. New York: Oxford University Press.

Monelle, Raymond. 2000. *The Sense of Music: Semiotic Essays*. Princeton, NJ: Princeton University Press.

———. 2006. *The Musical Topic: Hunt, Military and Pastoral*. Bloomington: Indiana University Press.
Moreno, Jairo. 2003. "Subjectivity, Interpretation, and Irony in Gottfried Weber's Analysis of Mozart's 'Dissonance" Quartet.'" *Music Theory Spectrum* 25 (i): 99–120.
Morgan, Robert P. 2003. "The Concept of Unity and Music Analysis." *Music Analysis* 22 (1–2): 7–50.
Muxfeldt, Kristina. "Political Crimes and Liberty, or Why Would Schubert Eat a Peacock?" In "Schubert: Music, Sexuality, Culture," edited by Lawrence Kramer, special issue. *19th-Century Music* 17 (1): 47–64.
Narmour, Eugene. 1992. *The Analysis and Cognition of Emotional Complexity: The Implication-Realization Model*. Chicago: University of Chicago Press.
Nattiez, Jean-Jacques. 1990. "Can One Speak of Narrativity in Music?" Translated by Katharine Ellis. *Journal of the Royal Musical Association* 115 (2): 240–57.
Newbould, Brian. 1997. *The Music and the Man*. Berkeley: University of California Press.
Nietzsche, Friedrich. (1874) 1997. "On the Uses and Disadvantages of History for Life." In *Untimely Meditations*, edited by Daniel Breazeale, 57–124. Translated by R. J. Hollingdale. New York: Cambridge University Press. Originally published as "Vom Nutzen und Nachteil der Historie für das Leben," in *Zweites Stück: Unzeitgemäße Betrachtungen*. Leipzig: Fritzsch.
Noack, Friedrich. 1953. "Eine Briefsammlung aus der ersten Hälfte des 19. Jahrhunderts." *Archiv für Musikwissenschaft* 10 (4): 323–37.
Parker, Jesse. 1974. "The Clavier Fantasy from Mozart to Liszt." PhD diss., Stanford University.
Perrey, Beate. 2002. *Schumann's 'Dichterliebe' and Early Romantic Poetics: Fragmentation of Desire*. New York: Cambridge University Press.
Pesic, Peter. 1999. "Schubert's Dream." *19th-Century Music* 23 (2): 136–44.
Petty, Wayne. 1999. "Chopin and the Ghost of Beethoven." *19th-Century Music* 22 (3): 281–99.
Proctor, Gregory. 1978. "Technical Bases of Nineteenth-Century Chromatic Tonality: A Study in Chromaticism." PhD diss., Princeton University.
Ratner, Leonard. 1980. *Classic Music: Expression, Form, and Style*. New York: Schirmer.
Reed, John. 1997. "Schubert's Reception History in England." In *The Cambridge Companion to Schubert*, edited by Christopher Gibbs, 254–62. New York: Cambridge University Press.
Rehding, Alexander. 2009. *Music and Monumentality: Commemoration and Wonderment in Nineteenth-Century Germany*. New York: Oxford University Press.
Richards, Annette. 2001. *The Free Fantasia and the Musical Picturesque*. New York: Cambridge University Press.
Ricoeur, Paul. 1980. "Narrative Time." *Critical Inquiry* 7 (1): 169–90.

Rings, Steven. 2007. "Perspectives on Tonality and Transformation in Schubert's Impromptu in E flat, D. 899, no. 2." *Journal of Schenkerian Studies* 2:33–63.

———. 2011a. "Riemannian Analytical Values, Paleo- and Neo-." In *The Oxford Handbook of Neo-Riemannian Theories*, edited by Edward Gollin and Alexander Rehding, 487–511. New York: Oxford University Press.

———. 2011b. *Tonality and Transformation*. New York: Oxford University Press.

Rosand, Ellen. 1979. "The Descending Tetrachord: An Emblem of Lament." *Musical Quarterly* 65 (3): 346–59.

Rosen, Charles. 1972. *The Classical Style: Haydn, Mozart, Beethoven*. New York: W. W. Norton.

———. 1988. *Sonata Forms*. New York: W. W. Norton.

———. 1994a. "'Music à La Mode.'" *New York Review of Books*, June 23, 1994.

———. 1994b. Reply to Steblin's response to "'Music à La Mode.'" *New York Review of Books*, October 20, 1994.

———. 1995. *The Romantic Generation*. Cambridge, MA: Harvard University Press.

———. 2010. *Music and Sentiment*. New Haven, CT: Yale University Press.

Rusch, René. 2007. "Imagining Tonal Spaces: Conceptions of Hierarchy, Chromaticism, and Social Constructs in Schubert's Music." PhD diss., University of Michigan.

———. 2009. "Schubert's References to Beethoven: Musical Homage or Critique?" Paper presented at "Réflexions sur la monumentalité musicale en Europe." Université de Montréal, September 24.

———. 2011. "Rethinking Conceptions of Unity: Schubert's Moment Musical in A♭ Major, D. 780 (Op. 94), No. 2." *Music Analysis* 30 (1): 58–88.

———. 2013a. "Beyond Homage and Critique? Schubert's Sonata in C minor, D. 958, and Beethoven's Thirty-Two Variations in C minor, WoO 80." *Music Theory Online* 19 (1). https://mtosmt.org/issues/mto.13.19.1/mto.13.19.1.rusch.html.

———. 2013b. "Schenkerian Theory, Neo-Riemannian Theory and Late Schubert: A Lesson from Tovey." *Journal of the Society for Musicology in Ireland* 8:3–20.

———. 2016. "The Four-Key Exposition? Schubert's Sonata Forms, the Fantasia, and Questions of Formal Coherence." Paper presentation at the Annual Meeting of the Society for Music Theory, Vancouver, BC, November 2016. An earlier version was presented at MTSMA, Philadelphia, PA, April 2016.

Sams, Eric. 1980. "Schubert's Illness Re-Examined." *Musical Times* 121 (1643):15–19 and 21–22.

Salzer, Felix. 1926. *Die Sonatenform bei Schubert*. PhD diss., University of Vienna.

———. 1928. "Die Sonatenform bei Franz Schubert." *Studien zur Musikwissenschaft* 15:86–125.

Satyendra, Ramon, ed. 1998. "Special Issue: Neo-Riemannian Theory." *Journal of Music Theory* 42 (2): 167–341.

Saussure, Ferdinand de. 1973. *Cours de linguistique générale*. Edited by Tullio de Mauro. Paris: Payot. English translation by Wade Baskin. New York: McGraw Hill, 1976.

Scherzinger, Martin. 1995. "The Finale of Mahler's Seventh Symphony: A Deconstructive Reading." *Music Analysis* 14 (1): 69–88.

Schiff, András. 1998. "Schubert's Piano Sonatas: Thoughts about Interpretation and Performance." In *Schubert Studies*, edited by Brian Newbould, 191–208. New York: Ashgate.

Schlegel, Friedrich. 1963. *Philosophische Lehrjahre 1796–1806*. Edited by Ernst Behler. Paderborn, Ger.: Ferdinand Schöningh.

———. 1968. *Dialogue on Poetry and Literary Aphorisms*. Translated by Ernst Behler and Roman Struc. University Park: Pennsylvania State University Press.

———. 1971. "On Incomprehensibility." In *Lucinde and the Fragments*. Translated by Peter Firchow, 257–72. Minneapolis: University of Minnesota Press.

———. 1991. *Philosophical Fragments*. Translated by P. Firchow. Minneapolis: University of Minnesota Press.

Schleuning, Peter. 1971. *The Fantasia*. Vols. 1 and 2. Translated by A. C. Howie. Cologne, Germany: Arno Volk.

Schmalfeldt, Janet. 1995. "Form as the Process of Becoming: The Beethoven-Hegelian Tradition and the Tempest Sonata." *Beethoven Forum* 4:37–71

———. 2002. "On Performance, Analysis, and Schubert." *Per Musi* 5 (6): 38–54.

———. 2010. "One More Time on Beethoven's 'Tempest,' from Analytic and Performance Perspectives: A Response to William E. Caplin and James Hepokoski." *Music Theory Online* 16 (2). https://mtosmt.org/issues/mto.10.16.2/mto.10.16.2.schmalfeldt3.html.

———. 2011. *In the Process of Becoming: Analytic and Philosophical Perspectives on Form in Nineteenth-Century Music*. New York: Oxford University Press.

Schulte-Sasse, Jochen, Haynes Horne, Elizabeth Mittman, and Lisa C. Roetzel, eds. 1997. *Theory as Practice: A Critical Anthology of Early German Romantic Writings*. Minneapolis: University of Minnesota Press.

Schumann, Robert. 1838. "Franz Schubert, 4 Impromptus f. Pianoforte. Op. 142." *Neue Zeitschrift für Musik* 9:192–93.

———. (1838) 1965. "Schubert's Grand Duo and Three Last Sonatas (1838)." In *Schumann on Music: A Selection from the Writings*. Translated and edited by Henry Pleasants, 141–44. New York: Dover.

———. (1840) 1965. "Schubert's Symphony in C (1840)." In *Schumann on Music: A Selection from the Writings*. Translated and edited by Henry Pleasants, 163–68. New York: Dover. Originally published as "Die 7te Symphonie von Franz Schubert." *Neue Zeitschrift für Musik* 12 (21): 81–83.

Schweisheimer, Waldemar. 1921. "Der krank Schubert." *Zeitschrift für Musikwissenschaft* 3:552.

Seyhan, Azade. 1992. *Representation and Its Discontents: The Critical Legacy of German Romanticism*. Berkeley: University of California Press.

Snarrenberg, Robert. 1987. "The Play of Différance: Brahms's Intermezzo, Op. 118, No. 2." *In Theory Only* 10 (3): 1–25.

Solomon, Maynard. 1979. "Schubert and Beethoven." *19th-Century Music* 3 (2): 114–25.

———. 1981. "Franz Schubert's 'My Dream.'" *American Imago* 38 (2): 137–54.

———. 1989a. "Franz Schubert and the Peacocks of Benvenuto Cellini." *19th-Century Music* 12 (3): 193–206.

———. 1989b. "Schubert's Sexuality: The Findings Clarified." *New York Times*, September 17, 1989.

———. 1993. "Schubert: Some Consequences of Nostalgia." In "Schubert: Music, Sexuality, Culture," edited by Lawrence Kramer, special issue. *19th-Century Music* 17 (1): 34–46.

———. 1998. *Beethoven*. 2nd ed., rev. New York: Schirmer.

Spivak, Gayatri Chakravorty, trans. 1997. Translator's preface to *Of Grammatology*, ix–lxxxviii. Baltimore: Johns Hopkins University Press.

Staehelin, Martin. 2001. "Auf eine Wirklich Ganz 'Alte' Manier'? Händel-Anlehnung und Eigenständigkeit in Beethovens Klavier-Variationen c-Moll WoO 80." In *"Critica Musica": Studien zum 17. und 18. Jahrhundert; Festschrift Hans Joachim Marx zum 65 Geburtstag*, edited by Nicole Ristow, Wolfgang Sandberger, and Dorothea Schröder, 281–97. Stuttgart, Ger.: Metzler.

Steblin, Rita. 1993. "The Peacock's Tale: Schubert's Sexuality Reconsidered." In "Schubert: Music, Sexuality, Culture," edited by Lawrence Kramer, special issue. *19th-Century Music* 17 (1): 5–33.

———. 1994. "Schubert à la Mode." *New York Review of Books*, October 20, 1994.

Straus, Joseph N. 1987. "The Problem of Prolongation in Post-tonal Music." *Journal of Music Theory* 31 (1): 1–21.

———. 1990. *Remaking the Past: Musical Modernism and the Influence of the Tonal Tradition*. Cambridge, MA: Harvard University Press.

Strauss, Dietmar, ed. 2008. *Eduard Hanslick: Sämtliche Schriften*. Band 1/6, Aufsätze und Rezensionen 1862–1863. Vienna: Böhlau.

Street, Alan. 1989. "Superior Myths, Dogmatic Allegories: The Resistance to Musical Unity." *Music Analysis* 8 (1–2): 77–123.

Subotnik, Rose. 1996. "How Could Chopin's A-Major Prelude Be Deconstructed?" In *Deconstructive Variations: Music and Reason in Western Society*, 39–147. Minneapolis: University of Minnesota Press.

Szondi, Peter. 1978. "Introduction to Literary Hermeneutics." Translated by Timothy Bahti. *New Literary History* 10 (1): 17–29.

———. 1986. "Friedrich Schlegel and Romantic Irony, with Some Remarks on Tieck's Comedies." In *On Textual Understanding and Other Essays*, translated by Harvey Mendelsohn, 57–76. Minneapolis: University of Minnesota Press.

———. 1995. *Introduction to Literary Hermeneutics*. Translated by Martha Woodmansee. New York: Cambridge University Press.
Taruskin, Richard. 1993. "Revising Revision." *Journal of the American Musicological Society* 46 (1): 114–38.
———. 2005. *The Oxford History of Western Music*. 6 vols. New York: Oxford University Press.
Temperley, Nicholas. 1981. "Schubert and Beethoven's Eight-Six Chord." *19th-Century Music* 5 (2): 142–54.
Tovey, Donald Francis. (1927) 1949. "Franz Schubert." In *The Main Stream of Music and Other Essays*, 103–33. Cleveland: Meridian.
———. (1928) 1949. "Tonality." *Music and Letters* 9:341–63. Reprinted as "On Tonality in Schubert." In *Essays and Lectures on Music*, 134–59. London: Oxford University Press.
Tusa, Michael C. 1993. "Beethoven's 'C-minor Mood': Some Thoughts on Structural Implications of Key Choice." In *Beethoven Forum 2*. Edited by Christopher Reynolds, with Lewis Lockwood and James Webster, 1–27. Lincoln: University of Nebraska Press.
Vande Moortele. 2013. "In Search of Romantic Form." *Music Analysis* 32 (3): 404–31.
Webster, James. 1978. "Schubert's Sonata Form and Brahms's First Maturity." *19th-Century Music* 2 (1): 18–35.
———. 1979. "Schubert's Sonata Form and Brahms's First Maturity (II)." *19th-Century Music* 2 (1): 52–71.
———. 1993. "Music, Pathology, Sexuality: Beethoven, Schubert." In "Schubert: Music, Sexuality, Culture," edited by Lawrence Kramer, special issue. *19th-Century Music* 17 (1): 89–93.
Wellbery, David. 2000. "The Transformation of Rhetoric." In *The Cambridge History of Literary Criticism*, vol. 5, *Romanticism*, edited by Marshall Brown, 185–202. New York: Cambridge University Press.
White, Hayden. 1973. *Metahistory: The Historical Imagination in Nineteenth-Century Europe*. Baltimore: Johns Hopkins University Press.
———. 1987. "The Value of Narrativity in the Representation of Reality." In *The Content of the Form: Narrative Discourse and Historical Representation*, 1–25. Baltimore: Johns Hopkins University Press.
Williams, Peter. 1997. *The Chromatic Fourth during Four Centuries of Music*. Oxford: Clarendon.
Winter, Robert S. 1993. "Whose Schubert?" In "Schubert: Music, Sexuality, Culture," edited by Lawrence Kramer, special issue. *19th-Century Music* 17 (1): 94–101.
Wollenberg, Susan. 2011. *Schubert's Fingerprints: Studies in the Instrumental Works*. New York: Ashgate.
Zaslaw, Neal. 1989. "Repeat Performance." *New York Review of Books*, April 27, 1989.

Index

Note: Italicized page numbers indicate illustrations. When followed by *t* these pages indicate tables.

Aarts, Bas, 122n25
Abrams, M. H., 23n22
Adler, Guido, 3, 11
aesthetics and aesthetic values:
and approaches to music theory and analysis, xi, 13, 192; and interpretations of Schubert's work, vii–x, 20; and shift in Schubert reception history, 5; and views of coherence, ix. *See also* musical hermeneutics; musical interpretation and analysis; musical unity and coherence; subjectivity
Almén, Byron, 158n33
alternative poetics: and indeterminacy, 16; and interpretations of Schubert's work, viii ix, x; and other subject positions, 16, 20, 194. *See also* German Romanticism; historiography; musical hermeneutics; musical unity and coherence; Romantic irony; subjectivity
antiquarian history, 186–87

Bailey, Robert, 90n33
Baker, Theodore, 11
Barthes, Roland, 125n44, 166; *S/Z*, 23n21

Beach, David, 51n24, 134–39
Beethoven, Ludwig van: and C minor, 191n35; fantasias and, 94; as model for Schubert, 145–46, 158n36, 161–65; Schumann's comparison of Schubert to, 141. *See also* musical homage and critique; Schubert, Franz: on Beethoven
Beethoven, Ludwig van, works by: Cello Sonata in D Major, op. 102, no. 2, 51n27; Piano Sonata in A-flat Major, op. 26, 30, *31*; Piano Sonata in C Minor, op. 13 ("Pathétique"), 165, 173–74, 190n22; Piano Sonata in C Minor, op. 111, 192n35; Piano Sonata in D Minor, op. 31, no. 2 ("Tempest"), 125n43; Piano Sonata in G Major, op. 31, no. 1, 145; String Quartet in A Minor, op. 132, 156n19; Symphony no. 2 in D Major, op. 36, 144; Symphony No. 3 in E-flat Major, op. 55 *(Eroica)*, 51n27, 120n11; Symphony No. 9 in D Minor, op. 125, 51n27. See also Thirty-Two Variations in C Minor, WoO 80 (Beethoven)
Benjamin, Walter, 50n19
Bischoff, Ludwig, 7
Black, Brian, 89n19, 119n3

Bodley, Lorraine Byrne, 154n2
Bowie, Andrew, 2, 17
Brahms, Johannes, 5, 22n13, 51nn31, 52n32
Brauner, Charles, 49n9
Breitkopf and Härtel, 21n1, 22n12
Brendel, Alfred, 165
Bribitzer-Stull, Matthew, 57
Brown, Maurice, 154n1, 155n3
Burnham, Scott, 77

Cadwallader, Allen, 27, 40, 42, 49nn5–6; *Analysis of Tonal Music* (with Gagné), 26
Caplin, William: analysis of *Moment musical*, no. 2 by, 50n23; on antecedent as a mini-sentence, 121n22; bass lines and stylistic differences, 191n29; on cadences, 89n18, 121n17, 121n20; on closing sections, 121n21, 124n36; on formal functions and musical topics, 122n28, 177; on sonata form, 125n42; on temporality in musical form, 95–96, 120n12, 122n28; and theory of formal functions, 8, 95–96; on three-key expositions, 93, 118n1; on tight-knit and loose-knit phenomena, 121n16; *Classical Form*, 121n17, 121n21; "Topics and Formal Functions," 177
Cho, Hyunree, "Music as Poetry," 15
Christensen, Thomas, 155n9
chromaticism and chromatic phenomena: chromaticizing the tonic, 82; and classical tonality, 53; Schubert's approach to, 5–6; tonal coherence and, 18–19. *See also* diatonic indeterminacy and aesthetic experience; enharmonicism; neo-Riemannian theory
Chusid, Martin, "Beethoven and the Unfinished," 144
Clark, Suzannah, 3, 76, 82, 157n28; *Analyzing Schubert*, ix–x, 58

Clive, Peter, 21n1
closure: avoidance of in music analysis, 82, 118, 190n15; deflected cadences, 89n19, 119n3; enharmonic group closures, 86, 87; musical unity and, 16; narrative and, 15, 133, 140, 147; and stability, 12; through liquation, 101. *See also specific works*
Cohn, Richard: equal divisions of the octave, 89n16; exchange with Fisk, 58; on harmonic relationships in the Piano Sonata in B-flat Major, 53, 55–57, 65, 77, 78, 89n23, 90nn24–25, 90nn28–30; on *Tonnetze*, 87n2; *Audacious Euphony*, 53, 55–57, 87n1
Coker, Wilson, 126
Cone, Edward T.: Beach on Cone's article, 134–36; on Beethoven's Thirty-Two Variations and the chaconne, 190n24; Guck on Cone's analysis of Schubert, 130; hermeneutic model of, 126–27, 129–30, 155nn7–8, 155n11; and moral meaning of the *Moment musical* no. 6, 140; on Schubert's Piano Sonata in C minor as a musical homage, 163; "Schubert's Promissory Note," 10, 126–29, 128t, 132, 133, 138–39, 158n34, 186; and second readings, 86. *See also Moment musical* in A-flat Major, D. 780, no. 6 critical history, 186–87
C. S. Richault, 21n3
Culler, Jonathan: on contexts and understanding, 147, 158n37; on deconstruction and Derrida, 166–67, 174; on hermeneutics and poetics, 23nn20–21; on the interpretive process, 23n21, 186; on poststructuralism, 18, 24n26; on structure, 90n34; on texts and grafting, 166–67, 174

Czerny, Carl, 122n26; *A Systematic Introduction to Improvisation*, 103–4, 106, 108, 122n26, 125n42. *See also* fantasia

Dahlhaus, Carl, 96, 120n14, 123n29, 191n34
Darcy, Warren, 8
Daverio, John, 51n31, 120n8
Dell'Antonio, Andrew, ed., *Beyond Structural Listening*, 14
de Man, Paul, 28, 36, 44, 48, 50nn16–19
Derrida, Jacques: concept of grafting, 20, 166–67; and music theory scholarship, 189n15; and scissions, 185; subversion of binary oppositions, 166–67; *Dissemination*, 166, 185, 190n18. *See also* grafting
Deutsch, Otto Erich: on Beethoven, 189n9; on the G Major piano sonata, 120n9; on Josef Hüttenbrenner, 188n4; on Schubert's approach to harmony, 49n4; on Schubert's cuts to the Piano Trio, 22n11; on Schubert's disapproval of Beethoven, 161; on Schubert's illness, 150, 154n1; on Schubert's Schnorr-Schlegel connection, 49n10; on Spaun, 189n5; on works published during Schubert's lifetime, 21n1; *Schubert* (three-volume set), 9–10, 23n19
Diabelli (publisher), 21n3
diatonic indeterminacy and aesthetic experience, 59–60, 87. *See also* chromaticism and chromatic phenomena; enharmonicism; Piano Sonata in B-flat Major, D. 960, first movement; Piano Sonata in G Major, D. 894, last movement
Dilthey, Wilhelm, 19, 130, 131–32, 156nn13–16; *The Formation of the Historical World in the Human Sciences*, 131; *Introduction to the Human Sciences*, 131. *See also* lived experience
Drabkin, William, 124n34

Eagleton, Terry, 45
Elkins, James, 14–15; *Why Are Our Pictures Puzzles?*, 14–15, 24n24
enharmonicism, 57, 61, 88n5, 89n16. *See also* chromaticism and chromatic phenomena; diatonic indeterminacy and aesthetic experience; neo-Riemannian theory; Piano Sonata in B-flat Major, D. 960, first movement; Piano Sonata in G Major, D. 894, last movement

fantasia: freedom and restraint in, 111–15, 124n35; free fantasias, 103, 112, 119n7, 124n35; improvisational types in, 103–4, 108, 122n26; as a musical aesthetic, 119n6; as a musical genre, 19, 94–95, 103, 119n7; in the nineteenth century, 124n34; potpourri and salon fantasias, 108–9; and rondo, 94, 125n45; Schubert's named fantasias, 103–4, *104*; and sonata form, 19, 94, 125n45. *See also* Piano Sonata in B-flat Major, D. 960, first movement; Piano Sonata in B Major, D. 575, first movement; Schubert, Franz, works by; themes and thematic variations
Feurzeig, Lisa, 49n10
Fichte, Johann Gottlieb, 28, 31, 35, 50n17, 50n19; *Wissenschaftslehre*, 29
Fink, G. W., 94, 125n43
Fisk, Charles: on Beethoven's Thirty-Two Variations and the chaconne, 190n24; exchange with Cohn, 58; interpretation of *Moment musical* no. 2, 26–27, 42, 50n12, 51n28; on the Piano Sonata in A Major, 146; on the Piano Sonata in B-flat Major, 89n17; on the Piano Sonata in C Minor, 190n19, 190n24; *Returning Cycles*, 145

form: codependence with tonality, 78; comparative restraint and freedom from formal structure, 111–15; and perception of harmonic relationships, 19; Schubert's approach to, 17; tight-knit and loose-knit constructions in, 96, 121n16; variation form, 108, 134–35. *See also* Caplin, William; fantasia; passacaglia; sonata form; themes and thematic variations

Furst, Lilian, 49n8

Gagné, David, 27, 40, 42, 49nn5–6; *Analysis of Tonal Music* (with Cadwallader), 26
Gerber, Ernst Ludwig, 94
German Romanticism: concerns about unity, 29; and interpretive viewpoints, ix, 17; rapport between subjectivity and nature in, 34; rapport between subjectivity and objectivity, 34, 50n14; and subjectivity, 17–18, 50n14; view of language, 45. *See also* Romantic irony
Gibbs, Christopher, xiii n.1, 10, 154n2, 157n28, 158n39, 159, 161
Gingerich, John, 22n9, 155n3, 160, 189n7
Godel, Arthur, *Schuberts Letzte Drei Klaviersonaten*, 163, 165
Gollin, Edward, and Alexander Rehding, eds, *Oxford Handbook of Neo-Riemannian Music Theories*, 58
Gollin, Edward, 87n2
Gooley, Dana, 119n7
Gotthard, Johann Peter (J. P.), 94, 103, 104
grafting, See; Derrida's concept of, 20, 166; further use in understanding Schubert's C Minor sonata, 184–85; in musical analysis, 166–67, 184; and new relationships between musical texts, 186. *See also* Piano Sonata in C Minor, D. 958; Thirty-Two Variations in C Minor, WoO 80
Grant, Aaron, 125n37
Grove, George, 8–9, 22n13, 23n19, 157n28
Guck, Marion, "Analysis as Interpretation," 130

Hanslick, Eduard, 1, 144, 194–95
Hardenberg, Friedrich von (Novalis), 28
harmony: criticism of Schubert's harmonic practices, 3–6, 25–26; shift in interpretation of, 11, 25, 191. *See also* chromaticism and chromatic phenomena; diatonic indeterminacy and aesthetic experience; enharmonicism; neo-Riemannian theory; Schenkerian theory; tonality
Hartman, Geoffrey, 88n13
Haslinger, Tobias, 94
Hatten, Robert, 151, 156n24
Heine, Heinrich, 28, 29
Henahan, Donal, 157n31; "The Dark Side of Schubert," 142–43
Hepokoski, James, 8
hermeneutics, 2, 21n5, 23n20, 130, 131. *See also* musical hermeneutics; musical interpretation and analysis
Hinrichsen, Hans-Joachim: *Untersuchungen zur Entwicklung der Sonatenform in der Instrumentalmusik Franz Schuberts*, 165
historiography, ix–x, 17–18. *See also* musical homage and critique; narrative; Schubert reception history and shift in
Horton, Julian, 7, 23n17, 154n2
Hunt, Graham, 119n2, 125n37, 125n39
Hüttenbrenner, Josef, 159–60, 188n4
Hyland, Anne, 3

Impromptu in A-flat Major, D. 935, no. 2: compared to the *Moment musical*

no. 2, 38–40, *38–39,* 43; opening measures, 30, *32,* 51n24
intertextuality, ix, 16, 166, 190n17

Kerman, Joseph, 191n35; "How We Got into Analysis, and How to Get Out," 12, 13
Kessler, Deborah, 89n17
Kierkegaard, Søren, 28
Kinderman, William, 11, 158n36, 190n22
Kopp, David, 88n6, 88n10
Korsyn, Kevin: on coherence and unity, 45, 87; on gendering in Schubert reception history, 189n11; on influence, 190n17; on interpretation, 11; on irony, 49n9, 52n32; on repetition, 190n16; "Bermuda Triangle of Aesthetic Ideology," 192n39; "Beyond Privileged Contexts," 167; "J.W.N. Sullivan and the *Heiliger Dankgesang,*" 133, 156n19
Kramer, Richard, 120n9
Krims, Adam, 189n15; *Music/Ideology* (ed.), 13
Kristeva, Julia, 166

language: early German Romantic views of, 28, 31, 37, 45; role of, 17. *See also* narrative; Romantic irony
Liszt, Franz, 5
lived experience: art as expressions of, 19–20, 131; classes of expressions for, 131, 156nn15–16; and Dilthey's *Erlebnis, Erlebnisausdruck,* and *Nacherleben,* 131–33; music analysis and, 20, 138–39, 146, 148, 151, 154, 194–95; and the sciences, 131. *See also* narrative; subjectivity
Lochhead, Judith, "Music's Vibratory Enchantments and Epistemic Injustices," 13–14

Mak, Su Yin, 3
Makkreel, Rudolph A., 131, 132, 156nn14–16
Marston, Nicholas, 82; "Schubert's Homecoming," 81–82
Martinkus, Caitlin, 191n34
McClary, Susan, 143–45, 146, 158n33; "Constructions of Subjectivity in Schubert's Music," 142, 143
McKay, Elizabeth Norman, 10, 154n2
Messing, Scott, 157n27, 159, 188n3
Moment musical in A-flat Major, D. 780, no. 2: analysis of, 29–43, *33–34,* 50n12, 51n23; Cadwallader and Gagné's analysis of, 26–27, 40, 42, 49nn5–6; and dialectical view of history, 47; and Fichte's system of judgments, 35, 36; Fisk's analysis of, 26–27, 42, 50n12, 51n28; irony in, 43–46, 51n28; juxtaposition of A-flat major and F-sharp minor in, 26, 29–30, 41, 47; parabasis in, 36–37, 38, 41, 43; pitch collections in, 43, *44;* score of, *46–48;* tropological narratives in, 36, 37, 41. *See also* Romantic irony
Moment musical in A-flat Major, D. 780, no. 6: annotated score examples, *127, 136–37;* Beach's analysis of, 134–36; Cone's analysis of, 10, 126–29, *128t,* 130, 138, 140; emplotment of, 137–40, 143; promissory note and chord in, 127–29, *127,* 134–39, *136–37,* 138–39, *139*
monumental history, 141, 157n26, 161, 186–87
Morgan, Robert, "The Concept of Unity and Musical Analysis," 14
Mozart, Wolfgang Amadeus, Piano Concerto in C Minor, K. 491, 20, 179–84, *180–81t, 182–83,* 184–86, 192n35, 192n37
musical genres: mixing of, 22n9; and the relationship to topics and styles, 124n33

Index 219

musical hermeneutics, 10, 11, 58, 126–27, 129–30. *See also* hermeneutics; musical interpretation and analysis

musical homage and critique: grafting and, 186; homage *versus* critique, vii, 166, 187; musical appropriation and repetition in, 20, 161, 163; varying interpretations regarding, 159–60, 163, 165, 187. *See also* Piano Sonata in C Minor, D. 958; Thirty-Two Variations in C Minor, WoO 80 (Beethoven)

musical interpretation and analysis: and changing sociocultural contexts, 140, 147; contextual assimilation in, viii, 193; narrativity's value in, 133–34, 146–54; poetics in, vii–ix, 23n20; using grafting for, 167. *See also* aesthetics and aesthetic values; alternative poetics; closure; historiography; lived experience; musical hermeneutics; musical homage and critique; musical unity and coherence; narrative; poststructuralism; Romantic irony

musical unity and coherence: and contemporary Schubert scholarship, vii, viii, ix, 12, 191–92; narrative relationships leading to understanding of, 20, 134; novel demonstrations in Schubert's work of, 5, 58, 193–94; puzzle metaphor in understanding, 14–15; rationalizing Schubert's modulations in terms of, 25, 26–27; varying conceptions of, 27. *See also* aesthetics and aesthetic values; closure; musical interpretation and analysis; part-whole relationships; subjectivity

narrative: ambivalence on whether music can tell stories, 133–34,
138–39; and archetypes, 148, 149, 158n33; and emplotment, 157n25; *in Moment musical* in A-flat Major, D. 780, no. 6, 137–39; and moral meanings, 139–44; and music as an unfolding continuity, 132–33; value in music analysis, 146–54; as vehicle between biography and music, 133, 143, 147. *See also* closure; historiography; musical interpretation and analysis; musical unity and coherence; temporality

neo-Riemannian theory, 5, 6, 53, 57, 58–59, 60, 86, 87, 87n1

Newbould, Brian, 10, 29, 125n40

New Criticism, 129, 155n9

New Musicology, 10, 12, 13–14, 129–30

Nietzsche, Friedrich, 192n40; "On the Uses and Disadvantages of History for Life," 186–88

parabasis, 36–37

paragons and parergons, 167, 186

part-whole relationships, 93, 111, 118, 134. *See also* musical unity and coherence

passacaglia: characteristics of, 174–75, 178, 190n25; later works' engagement with, 184, 188; ostinato patterns for, *175–76*; in relation to the ciaccona (chaconne), 190n24. *See also* Mozart, Wolfgang Amadeus, Piano Concerto in C Minor, K. 491; Piano Sonata in C Minor, D. 958; Thirty-Two Variations in C Minor, WoO 80 (Beethoven)

Pesic, Peter, 90n30

Petty, Wayne, 52n32

Piano Sonata in A Minor, D. 784: as an annal and chronicle, 148, *149t*; moral meanings in, 148, 150, 151, 154; publication of, 160; score examples, *150–53*; transcendence and tragedy in, 150–51

Piano Sonata in B-flat Major, D. 960, first movement: diatonic indeterminacy in, 56, 56–57, 60, 65, 85–86; elements of fantasia in, 125n38; exposition, 66, 66–79, 68–74, 76–77, 81, 83, 86, 89nn18–19, 89n23, 90nn25–27; four-key exposition in, 113; recapitulation, 54–55, 55–56, 66, 79–82, 80, 88n6, 90nn28–31; retransition to the recapitulation, 83–84, 85; tonicizations in, 74–76

Piano Sonata in B Major, D. 575, first movement: as a fantasia, 103–11, 109; as a four-key exposition, 95–102, 97–100, 102, 112, 113; as a hybrid form, 95, 111–15, 118; interpretive frames for, 91–93; score examples, 92, 97–100, 105–8, 110; topics and styles in, 105–9, 123n28, 124n33

Piano Sonata in C Minor, D. 958: chromatic counterpoint in, 172; compared to Beethoven's C Minor sonata, 172–74, 173; compared to Beethoven's Thirty-Two Variations, 162, 163–66, 164; as a countersignatures to the passacaglia, 174–79, 179; form in, 22n16; grafting opening measures with Beethoven's Thirty-Two Variations, 167–72, 168–69t, 169–71, 174, 180–81t; grafting opening measures with Mozart's Piano Concerto in C minor, 185, 186; harmonic relationships in, 9; modulations in, 6, 7–8; and musical appropriation, 20; publication of, 160; theme recomposed, 171, 179; use of variation in, 191n34

Piano Sonata in G Major, D. 894, last movement: analysis of measures, 124–70, 60–66; codependence of form and tonality in, 61–65, 62, 63; fantasia in title for, 94; modulations and enharmonic thirds, 64; publication of, 1; scholars' attention to, 147

poststructuralism, ix, 13–14, 17, 18, 24n26, 166–67, 189n15, 190n15

Probst, Heinrich Albert, 4, 22nn11–12

Proctor, Gregory, 88n8; "Technical Bases of Nineteenth-Century Chromatic Tonality," 57

Ratner, Leonard, 104
Richards, Annette, 119n6, 124n35
Ricoeur, Paul, 156n23
Rings, Steven, 57; "Riemannian Analytical Values, Paleo- and Neo-," 58–59
Romantic irony: as an alternative to the aesthetic of unity, 18, 28; in other composers' work, 49n9, 52n32; parabasis in, 36–37; philosophical concept of, 28; in Schubert's songs and instrumental works, 29; in Schumann's work, 49n9; self-reflexivity and, 29, 48; and theories of narrative, 44; transition from rhetorical irony to, 49n8. See also *Moment musical* in A-flat Major, D. 780, no. 2

Rosen, Charles, 119n5, 145–46, 192n38

Salieri, Antonio, 161
Salzer, Felix, "Die Sonatenform bei Franz Schubert," 3
Sams, Eric, 10, 133, 154n1, 155n3; "Schubert's Illness Re-examined," 126, 128t, 129, 141–42
Schenkerian theory, 5, 26, 27, 57, 88n10
Schlegel, Friedrich, 28, 36, 45, 46, 49n10, 50n19; *Athenaeum*, 29
Schleuning, Peter, 103, 104, 109
Schmalfeldt, Janet, 96, 120n13, 125n43

Schubert, Franz: on Beethoven, 160–61, 189n10; biography and relationship to his music, 9–11, 15, 17, 20, 133, 143, 147; drive toward high art, vii, xiii n.1; illness and death of, 10, 126, 141–42, 150, 154nn1–2, 155n3; image as song writer, 160; legacy of, 1, 11; "Mein Traum," 27, 145, 157n30; obituary for, 189n5; posthumous discovery of instrumental works, 1; publication of instrumental works by, 3–4, 22n12; rapport with Schnorr-Schlegel circles, 49n10; sexual orientation of, 141–43

Schubert, Franz, works by: 8 Variations on a Theme from Herold's 'Marie,' D. 908, 25; *Gesamtausgabe* (Breitkopf and Härtel), 21n1; Impromptu in E-flat Major, D. 899, no. 2, 57; Impromptus, D. 935, 119n8, 147; named fantasias, 103–4, *104*; Octet in F Major, D. 803, 22n9; Piano Four-Hand Fantasia in C Minor, D. 48 ("Grosse Sonate"), 94, 103, 104; Piano Quintet in A Major, D. 667 ("Trout"), 91, *92*, 122n24, 124n32, 160; Piano Sonata in A Major, D. 664, 160; Piano Sonata in A Major, D. 959, 119n7, 145–46, 147, 158n36, 160; Piano Sonata in A Minor, D. 537, 113–14, *114–15*, 115, 125nn39–41, 160; Piano Sonata in A Minor, D. 845, 1, 25, 94, 114, 115, *116*, 125n43, 147; Piano Sonata in B-flat Major, D. 960, 1, 59–60, 160 (*see also* Piano Sonata in B-flat Major, D. 960, first movement); Piano Sonata in B Major, D. 575, 160 (*see also* Piano Sonata in B Major, D. 575, first movement); Piano Sonata in D Major, D. 850, 1; Piano Trio in B-flat Major, D. 898, 22n9, 160; Piano Trio in E-flat Major, D. 929, 1, 4, 22n9, 22n11, 148; String Quartet in A Minor, D. 804 ("Rosamunde"), 1, 22n9, 147; String Quartet in D Minor, D. 810 ("Der Tod und das Mädchen"), 4, 147, 160; String Quartet in G Major, D. 887, 1, 22n9, 123n29, 147, 160; Symphony in B-flat Major, D. 125, 91–93, *92*, 119n2, 121nn23–24; Symphony in B Minor, D. 759 ("Unfinished"), 1, 143–45, 146, 148, 158n34; Symphony in C Major, D. 944 ("The Great"), 4, 7–8, 120n15, 148, 160; Symphony No. 2 in B-flat Major, D. 125, 123n32; *Wanderer Fantasy*, D. 760, 145. *See also* Impromptu in A-flat Major, D. 935, no. 2; *Moment musical* in A-flat Major, D. 780, no. 2; *Moment musical* in A-flat Major, D. 780, no. 6; Piano Sonata in A Minor, D. 784; Piano Sonata in C Minor, D. 958; Piano Sonata in G Major, D. 894, last movement; Schubert's instrumental music; String Quintet in C Major, D. 956

Schubert reception history and shift in: and concepts of knowing, 2; and discovery of instrumental compositions, 1; gender and sexuality in, 141, 142–44, 157nn27–28; motivation for, 193; and new understandings of harmony and form, 5–9; objections to his work, vii, 3–5, 22nn11–12, 49n4; poetics and, vii–viii, ix–x, 11–16; recursive tension in, 11; and revisions to Schubert's biography, 9–11; Schubert's image and, 158n39; sociocultural contexts and, 140; Spaun's change of opinion, 160. *See also* aesthetics and aesthetic values; form; harmony; historiography; musical interpretation and analysis; musical unity and coherence; Schubert, Franz, biography; Society for Music Theory; subjectivity

Schubert scholarship: attention to particular Schubert works, 147–48; Deutsch's influence on, 10; evolution of thought in, vii–viii; gender and sexual orientation in, 141–43, 157nn27–28, 157nn30–31, 189n11; recursive tension in, 2–3; research themes in, viii, 17; selected publications in, *142t*. *See also* lived experience; musical interpretation and analysis; Schubert reception history and shift in

Schubert's instrumental music: as cultural artifacts, 146–47; knowing the oeuvre anew, 1–2, 193; and sociocultural milieu, 10–11; unfixed intelligibility in, 17. *See also* form; harmony; musical homage and critique; musical interpretation and analysis; musical unity and coherence; narrative; Romantic irony; Schubert, Franz, works by; Schubert reception history and shift in; sonata form; themes and thematic variations

Schumann, Robert: on the C Major symphony, 120n15; Daverio on, 51n31; gendered depiction of Schubert, 157nn27–28; Messing's comment on Schubert and, 188n3; "Schubert's Grand Duo and the Three Last Sonatas," 140–41; on Schubert's impromptus, 119n8

Schuppanzigh, Ignaz, 4, 22n9

Society for Music Theory (SMT), ix, 5, 13, 129

Solomon, Maynard, 10, 157nn30–31, 161, 188n4, 189n10; "Franz Schubert and the Peacocks of Benvenuto Cellini," 142

sonata form: assessments of Schubert's approach to, 3, 95; and compositional freedom, 112; expanded conception of, 6–9, 11; experience of, compared to fantasia, 111–15; four-key expositions in, 91–93, 95, 113, 119n1; intersection with fantasia form, 19, 115, 118; key markers in form archetypes, 65; normative type, 7, 119n5; Schubert's extended length in, 3, 4, 78–79, 96, 120n15; in Schubert's impromptus, 119n8; three-key expositions in, 93, 102, 113, 118n1, 119n4, 125n37; transitions in, 89n19. *See also* fantasia; themes and thematic variations

Spaun, Joseph von, 189n5; "Notes on my association with Franz Schubert," 160

Spivak, Gayatri Chakravorty, 166

Street, Alan, "Superior Myths, Dogmatic Allegories," 13

String Quintet in C Major, D. 956: elements of fantasia in, 114, *117–18*; opening measures of, 115, 123n31; premiere of, 22n9; publication of, 160; Tovey on, 22n13

subjectivity: musical experience of being a stranger, 87; and musical interpretation, 2; self-reflection, 35. *See also* aesthetics and aesthetic values; alternative poetics; German Romanticism; musical interpretation and analysis; musical unity and coherence; Romantic irony

Sullivan, J. W. N., 156n19

Szondi, Peter, 21n5, 29, 46

temporality: Caplin on, 95–96, 120n12, 122n28; in musical form, 96, 113; and musical narrative, 134, 138, 139; Ricoeur on, 156n23

Index 223

themes and thematic variations: in Beethoven's Thirty-Two Variations, *168–69t, 180–81t,* 191n27; fantasias and, 19, 103, 109, 111–12; inter- and intrathemic functions, 65–66, 68; in Mozart's Piano Concerto in C Minor, *180–81t*; in Schubert's C Minor sonata, *168–69t, 170, 180–81t*; in theme and variations form and sonata allegro form, 122n28, 123n29, 172, 191n34; variation form, 108, 172. *See also* passacaglia

Thirty-Two Variations in C Minor, WoO 80 (Beethoven): as a countersignature to the passacaglia, 174–79, *178,* 185, 191nn28–29; grafting opening measures with Mozart's Piano Concerto in C minor, 185, 186; grafting opening measures with Schubert's Sonata in C Minor, 167–72, 174; and musical appropriation, 20, 163–66; penultimate variation, 191n33; placement of structural dominant, 191n27; score example with Schubert's Sonata in C Minor, *162, 164*; theme recomposed, *169, 178*

Tieck, Ludwig, 28

tonality: character of C minor, 178–79; character of D minor, 179, 192n36; circle of fifths in, 61, *79*; codependence with form, 61–66, 78, 85; fantasia and modulations, 111–12; Schubert's approach to, 17, 18, 89n21. *See also* chromaticism and chromatic phenomena; harmony

Tonnetze: and chromatic phenomena, 53; equal tempered, 6, 15, 53, 57, 64, 87n2; nodes in, 87n2; and Piano Sonata in C Minor, *9, 15. See also* Piano Sonata in B-flat Major, D. 960

Tovey, Donald Francis: codependence of tonality and formal structure, 78, 79; "Franz Schubert," 4; and hearing changes of tonality, 90n31; progressive view of compositional practices, 51n31; "purple patches," 77; on Schubert's C Major string quintet, 123n31; on Schubert's Piano Sonata in G major, 60–66; "Tonality," 4, 19, 22n13, 59, 60, *60,* 61–65, 66; voice leading and key relations, 88n10, 89n15

truth: in German Romanticism and poststructuralism, 17–18; subjectivity and, 2

voice-leading: harmonic understanding as a result of, 134–35; in the Impromptu in A-flat Major, no. 2, *38*; in the *Moment musical,* no. 2, 30, *33–34, 41–42*; in the Piano Sonata in C Minor, *171*; and strange harmonic progressions, 88n10; and Tovey's key relations, 89n15. *See also* neo-Riemannian theory; Schenkerian theory; specific works

Webster, James, 119n2; "Schubert's Sonata Form and Brahms's First Maturity," 93

White, Hayden, 140, 192n40; "The Value of Narrativity in the Representation of Reality," 148. *See also* historiography; narrative

René Rusch is Associate Professor of Music Theory at the University of Michigan School of Music, Theatre & Dance.

For Indiana University Press

Brian Carroll, Rights Manager
Allison Chaplin, Acquisitions Editor
Sophia Hebert, Assistant Acquisitions Editor
Brenna Hosman, Production Coordinator
Katie Huggins, Production Manager
Darja Malcolm-Clarke, Project Manager and Editor
Dan Pyle, Online Publishing Manager
Rachel Rosolina, Marketing and Publicity Manager
Pamela Rude, Senior Artist and Book Designer

www.ingramcontent.com/pod-product-compliance
Lightning Source LLC
Chambersburg PA
CBHW020650230426
43665CB00008B/378